ROUTLEDGE LIBRARY EDITIONS: THE BRITISH EMPIRE

Volume 2

THE BRITISH EMPIRE AT ITS ZENITH

THE BRITISH EMPIRE
AT ITS ZENITH

A. J. CHRISTOPHER

Routledge
Taylor & Francis Group

LONDON AND NEW YORK

First published in 1988 by Croom Helm

This edition first published in 2018
by Routledge
4 Park Square, Milton Park, Abingdon, Oxon OX14 4RN

and by Routledge
605 Third Avenue, New York, NY 10017

Routledge is an imprint of the Taylor & Francis Group, an informa business

British Library Cataloguing in Publication Data
A catalogue record for this book is available from the British Library

ISBN: 978-0-8153-5278-5 (Set)
ISBN: 978-1-351-02850-9 (Set) (ebk)
ISBN: 978-0-8153-9955-1 (Volume 2) (hbk)
ISBN: 978-0-8153-9960-5 (Volume 2) (pbk)
ISBN: 978-1-351-17152-6 (Volume 2) (ebk)

Publisher's Note
The publisher has gone to great lengths to ensure the quality of this reprint but points out that some imperfections in the original copies may be apparent.

Disclaimer
The publisher has made every effort to trace copyright holders and would welcome correspondence from those they have been unable to trace.

THE BRITISH EMPIRE AT ITS ZENITH

*Frontispiece: Victoria, Queen-Empress, Port Elizabeth, Cape of Good
Hope. In common with many towns and cities throughout the British
Empire, the citizens of Port Elizabeth erected a statue in honour of
Queen Victoria. It stands outside the new Municipal Library opened in
the year of her death, while to the right is the Collegiate Church of St
Mary the Virgin, founded in 1825, when she was six years of age. The
influence of Church and state, symbolised by the Crown, impressed itself
upon colonial towns and farms, whose main lineaments were drawn in
the course of her lifetime.*

The
British Empire
at its Zenith

A.J. CHRISTOPHER

CROOM HELM
London • New York • Sydney

© 1988 A.J. Christopher
Croom Helm Ltd, Provident House,
Burrell Row, Beckenham, Kent BR3 1AT

Croom Helm Australia, 44–50 Waterloo Road,
North Ryde, 2113, New South Wales

Published in the USA by
Croom Helm
in association with Methuen, Inc.
29 West 35th Street,
New York, NY 10001

British Library Cataloguing in Publication Data

Christopher, A.J.
   The British Empire at its zenith.
   1. Great Britain — Colonies — History
   — 19th century 2. Great Britain —
   Colonies — History — 20th century
   I. Title
   325'.32'0941   JV1011
   ISBN 0-7099-3418-1

Library of Congress Cataloging-in-Publication Data

Christopher, A.J.
   The British empire at its zenith.

   Bibliography: p.
   Includes index.
   1. Great Britain — Colonies — History — 20th century.
2. Great Britain — Colonies — Administration — History —
20th century. 3. Great Britain — Politics and government —
1910–1936. I. Title.
DA16.C424   1988   325'.341'09   87-27620
ISBN 0-7099-3418-1

Filmset by Mayhew Typesetting, Bristol, England
Printed and bound in Great Britain by
Biddles Ltd, Guildford and King's Lynn

Contents

Figures

Tables

Preface

The year 1987 marked a number of important anniversaries. One hundred years ago Queen Victoria commemorated her golden jubilee, the first of a long line of royal pageants continuing to the present day. Ten years later the celebrations for her diamond jubilee presented the greatest spectacle Imperial Britain ever launched. The diamond jubilee did not however mark the height of British economic and political power. In territorial terms the Empire attained its maximum extent as a result of the First World War, which in many ways was a crippling factor. In terms of relative economic strength the zenith of British power had passed after the mid-nineteenth century, as other European powers and the United States underwent industrialisation. The year also marked the one hundred and tenth anniversary of the proclamation on 1 January 1877 of Queen Victoria as Empress of India. While in August 1947 the 'Jewel in the Crown' was removed with the Empire's demise.

Whatever the year which marks the Imperial zenith of economic, military or political power, the citizens and servants of the Empire continued to build and to develop the colonies and dominions. Indeed the monumental creation of New Delhi, inaugurated in 1931, may be regarded as the zenith of the Imperial impress upon the landscape. In Gavin Stamp's (1981: 372) terms 'New Delhi is one of the greatest things the British have ever done'. The creation of a new Indian capital no less than the new dominion capital at Canberra, inaugurated four years earlier, marked the height of an Imperial concept in town planning, only to be shattered by the Great Depression and the Second World War, which finally bankrupted Great Britain and led to Imperial disintegration. This may be in line with the observation that empires in decline often undergo a resurgence of cultural vigour before the end.

The physical impress of British planning upon other continents and countries is immediately noticeable as the inhabitant of, or visitor to, the ex-British possessions is aware. In a period ranging from a few decades to several centuries British administrators, settlers, traders, clerics and others built and organised other countries around the world in the image of England. Exact reproductions were rare owing to environmental and social differences between the British Isles and the colonies. Nevertheless, the impress is to be discerned to a greater or lesser extent and forms the theme of this volume.

The range of material available to the researcher is vast and what follows can be no more than an overview with specific examples. Other examples, other frameworks could have been employed, but the emphasis has been placed upon the overall unity of the Imperial experience and the influence which is brought to bear upon the landscapes of other continents. Thus colonies lightly touched by direct intervention appear infrequently, while India and the mid-latitude dominions dominate the volume, as they dominated Imperial planning prior to the 1930s.

Research was undertaken in part while a Sabbatical Visitor at Mansfield College, Oxford, and as Lady Davis Visiting Professorial Fellow at the Hebrew University of Jerusalem. Both institutions provided academic environments conducive to sustained research and writing. In addition the author consulted numerous archives, libraries, societies, companies and institutions, notably in London at the British Library, Public Record Office, Guildhall Library, Royal Geographical Society, Royal Commonwealth Society, India Office Library and United Africa Company. Additional fieldwork and research were undertaken in various parts of the late British Empire, more especially India, Canada, Kenya, South Africa and Malta. Financial assistance from the University of Port Elizabeth and the Human Sciences Research Council is gratefully acknowledged. Also at the University of Port Elizabeth, Mrs Anna Bouwer and Mrs Dulcy Dangers performed their typing tasks with their usual expertise. Finally I wish to express my appreciation of the constant support given by my wife Anne, in the fieldwork, research and editing involved in this work.

A.J. Christopher
Port Elizabeth

For my Parents
Who remained in the
Metropole

Introduction

'It is not as caretakers that we shall be judged in the eyes of posterity but as builders.'

Sir Philip Mitchell, Governor of Uganda, 1936 (Ehrlich, 1973)

Empires have left imprints in many forms, but most recognisably in erected structures and plans. The Roman Empire bequeathed an impressive heritage of law and language to its successors, but it is in its building and engineering feats that it is most often remembered. Similarly the British Empire has left behind a formidable heritage in tangible form, whose essential unity across the globe requires exploration in a post-colonial age.

The extension of European enterprise overseas to other continents in order to create a series of worldwide empires in the wake of the Age of Discovery initiated one of the major epochs in world history. The various European powers sought colonial empires for a variety of reasons, including most importantly, economic gain. In establishing the organisation to achieve private and state profits, significant numbers of Europeans migrated permanently and temporarily to other parts of the world. The migrants ranged from servants of the Crown to individual pioneers and convicts. They took with them a vast cultural baggage of preconceived ideas and mental approaches which were applied to the problems they encountered in the new environments of the colonies. As far as possible settlers sought to recreate their homeland both in physical construction and social organisation.

Theories of colonisation devised in Europe were often highly specific, ranging from the layout and planning of towns and farms to the social structure to be established in the 'New Lands'. New France in the seventeenth and eighteenth centuries was planned to recreate feudal France on the North American continent (Harris, 1966). Social planning in British colonies was more varied according to the perceptions of the colonial promoters, extending from theocratic New England to socially hierarchical New South Wales.

European theories of colonisation were implemented and impressed upon the landscapes of large parts of the world, as few regions remained independent of colonial control throughout the last

1

500 years. Clearly each colonial empire devised its own version of the colonial model, yet these differences are small compared with the overall similarities of introducing variants of European culture to other continents and peoples. However, even the best of plans could go astray. Planning undertaken in European capitals often took no account of the colonial physical environment. The disasters which befell the initial Jamestown settlement in Virginia in the early seventeenth century attest to a lack of understanding of environments which Europeans could not imagine and which they refused to appreciate (Earle, 1979). Similarly planning was often too elaborate, assuming a complete transfer of European institutions overseas. In differing social relationships within the colonies many of the theories were abandoned. A simplification of Europe overseas took place, reflecting changed relationships not only of man to man but of man to land (Harris, 1977).

Colonial systems were characterised by overall plans emanating from the European capital, but exhibiting often highly eccentric variations in response to new environments. Thus not all colonial cities look alike nor do farming regions reproduce European conditions. In order to appreciate the impact of the uniformity of the Imperial model and the regional variation in its implementation, the largest and most complex of the empires will be examined, namely the British Empire. This political entity impressed its image upon more than a quarter of the world's area at one time or another and represents the most geographically widespread experiment in landscape transformation under colonial conditions. It is not proposed to examine the 'informal' Empire — areas which were developed under the impetus of British capital but without the political control of formal Empire. In the words of Platt and di Tella (1985: 16–17) 'the mores of the British Empire in such matters as trade and public ownership are clearly distinct' and not shared by informal Empire, notably Latin American. Clearly the 'mores of the British Empire' are of importance in comprehending the imprint of British imperialism upon the landscape.

COLONIES

The British Empire has passed into history as decolonisation has fragmented one of the largest world empires in the course of the last half century. The Empire reached its outward apogee with the spectacular celebrations of the diamond jubilee of Queen Victoria in

1897, yet only 50 years later the 'Jewel in the Crown', India, gained its independence. Now, 40 years on from this event, it is possible to look back at the imprint of this Empire with some measure of detachment, and assess its impact upon the world's landscapes. The British overseas were great builders, and it is in the physical imprint left behind that the Empire is most frequently remembered. Monuments and edifices ranging from Imperial New Delhi to small settler cottages in Australia and Canada reflected a concerted construction drive which accompanied British imperialism. As an economic system imperialism rested upon communications and it is through the ports, roads and particularly the railways that the links between Great Britain and its colonial possessions were forged. The railway systems of Australia, Canada and India remain as permanent testimonies to the ingenuity of engineers as well as the new economic relationships established by the imposition of colonial control.

The British imperial system, if such a term may be applied, operated essentially for the benefit of the metropole in the classic terms of dependency theory. The British Empire acted as an agent to integrate parts of the globe into the world economy, of which the British Isles formed a portion of the core from the seventeenth century onwards (Wallerstein, 1974, 1980). Early British colonial enterprises, illuminated in an aptly entitled book, *Trade, plunder and settlement*, sought to invest for high financial rewards (Andrews, 1984). The initial primary windfalls were sought or seized, while the later less rewarding aspects of direct exploitations through settlement, and profit through trade and industry, became more significant only in the seventeenth century. The two basic forms of colonialism, namely European settlement and the exploitation of indigenous societies, dominated metropolitan planning. They resulted in the formation of two very different social and economic systems within the colonies, and hence distinctive landscapes. In this respect the grand theories of colonisation involving evangelism and civilising missions were usually only subsidiary to the main impetus, the creation of wealth both for the individual and the state.

Colonies of settlement were established mainly in mid-latitude regions for the colonisation and exploitation of the land and its resources by settlers of British or European origin. In this manner a 'Greater Britain' took form with a common language, heritage and outlook. Accordingly settlers from Europe, predominantly from the British Isles, populated lands with sparse indigenous populations effectively obliterating the imprint of those they displaced. New states were consciously established in the image of Great Britain, which through the exploitation of the agricultural and mineral wealth of the land were able to become profitable primary producers for the industrial markets of the metropole. In classic form primary products of the peripheral regions were exchanged for the manufactured goods and services of the core. Many overseas settlements were established with the express aim of avoiding industrialisation and recreating an agrarian society free from the perceived evils of urbanisation as it was manifested in the British Isles in the eighteenth and nineteenth centuries. Clearly such philosophies were compatible with, and in many ways complementary to, the industrial expansion within the United Kingdom during the same period. Industry and Empire were two aspects of the era, growing in symbiosis with one another (Hobsbawm, 1968).

Colonies of exploitation were established in tropical and closely settled regions where there were limited opportunities for the re-creation of a complete British society. In these regions it was European management which was the significant stamp of colonialism. Management took several forms, always including European control of the governmental, military and external trade functions. However, European management might include the operation of the internal communication system, wholesale and even retail trade, while production systems remained in indigenous hands. It was, however, the organisation of the plantation which introduced one of the most significant and distinctive colonial enterprises. Tropical crops were grown in the colonies under European management, often with imported labour. An intercontinental movement of plants, people, technology, products and profits profoundly affected large areas of the tropical as well as the temperate world. The distinctiveness of temperate and tropical colonies was often blurred as initial colonial schemes were modified and new forms of enterprise were adopted, reflecting changed economic, political and demographic realities. Countries such as South Africa or Jamaica defy easy classification and exhibit within their landscapes a variety of colonial models.

MOVEMENT AND MIGRATION

Movement and migration were significant characteristics of the Imperial system. Communication involved not only the exchange of products for consumption, but a far wider transfer. A two-way trade involves no inevitable change in either party. However, it was the movement of men and women, primarily from Europe, Africa, India, China and on a lesser scale other countries, to all parts of the British Empire which diversified the colonies socially. With the migrants went their ideas, both about economic goals, if free, and about the way that things should be done. Capitalists sought to produce profitable crops, exploit minerals or control trade. To do so required planning and financial and political backing. Others sought to escape from conditions at home, through economic improvement by the acquisition of independent farms or for no more than wage labour and survival. The push and pull factors in Imperial migration were extreme, ranging from the lure of instant wealth on the goldfields to the forced shipment of African slaves to the West Indies.

Whatever the motive behind intercontinental migration, preconceived ideas were transported to the colonies. Exported cultural baggage ranged from methods of building construction to planning and operating a railway, which with comparatively minor adjustments were capable of virtually universal application. Other ideas developed in a specific physical environment such as those related to agriculture and stock raising were less suitable for intercontinental transfer. Inevitably many preconceived ideas were inapplicable, but wherever possible, however inappropriate, they were retained and translated into the circumstances of the new settlements. Cultural complexity therefore increased as the complexity of the population composition increased. Nowhere is this more apparent than in the outward structural expression of religion, where English and Scottish churches, Indian mosques and temples and Chinese pagodas provide a rapid index to social history. This is not to suggest that each group acted completely independently of one another. Cultural contact led to borrowings as the inappropriateness of inherited methods were exposed to more suitable solutions to the problems which the migrants met. Inevitably many borrowings were made, and often transferred to other parts of the Empire encountering similar problems. The Indian link was particularly important in introducing large numbers of British people to a highly developed civilisation other than their own. Thus in architecture, the verandah was adopted as a solution for houses in hot climates, transferred around the world, and even incorporated into English housing in the early nineteenth century. Accordingly Victorian and Edwardian architecture owes much not only to its European heritage, but also to the Imperial heritage of India. In agricultural terms indigenous African and Indian farming methods in hot and dry lands contributed markedly to the European agriculture in regions where British settlers had few inherited landmarks.

Intercontinental movement also involved the transfer of plants, animals and diseases. Plants, especially the plantation crops, notably sugar, cinchona and rubber, were transferred from one part of the world to another. By the nineteenth century this was highly organised through the agency of Kew Gardens and the network of Royal Botanical Gardens around the world. Commercial crops for temperate lands such as wheat, potatoes and many vegetables were transplanted from one part of the Empire to another, while improved strains bred by agricultural research institutes were disseminated thereafter. European grasses were exported to refurbish pastures of low nutritional value. Australian trees were transferred to lands with poor yielding forests or lacking them altogether. Animals similarly were transported to new lands. The sheep and cattle of many temperate colonies were taken by the settlers concerned, and English as well as many European breeds were dispersed widely. Thus Hereford cattle or Romney sheep may be found grazing on English-derived species of grass in many regions of the world. Not all importations were beneficial. Rabbits introduced to Australia as a poor man's meat had no predators in that continent and wreaked havoc with the pastures. Exotic plants invaded indigenous ecosystems to the impoverishment of the latter. Diseases affecting humans, animals and plants came with the invaders. Smallpox and other afflictions wiped out entire indigenous communities which had had no exposure to European diseases. Hence some West Indian islands were uninhabited when British colonisation began. Other communities, notably the Australian Aborigines, Canadian Indians and to a lesser extent the Maoris of New Zealand, suffered substantial demographic declines in the early colonial periods, weakening resistance to European settlement. Asian and many African peoples were less affected demographically although Oliver Ransford (1983: 3) has justifiably stated that 'the vital years 1885–1930 were ones of epidemiological disaster for Africa', as earlier eras had been for the indigenous inhabitants of the West Indies and Atlantic seaboard of North America.

IMPERIAL SYSTEM

The changes wrought by the imposition of the colonial system were profound, leading to the creation of new landscapes. The degree of change depended upon the period of incorporation into the system and the type of regime imposed. Colonies under British control for the entire colonial period clearly exhibit the major impact of the colonial system. Bermuda and Barbados from the seventeenth century and Australia from the eighteenth century thus exhibit a purely British colonial imprint upon landscapes which owed little to previous cultures. In contrast Iraq, under British control for less than 15 years in the twentieth century, was little affected by the colonial regime in terms of its cultural landscape. Crown colonies were subject to British laws and in mid-latitudes to British settlement, while protectorates retained a degree of autonomy and often excluded permanent European settlers, thereby reducing the British impact markedly.

Colonial cities, the most conspicuous aspect of economic imperialism, reveal much of the style of the British Empire and the impress of the system. With ample space available in the colonies, the high-density European city was modified in favour of more sprawling entities. As trading and administrative centres, rather than industrial cities, it was southern rather than northern England which provided the inspirations, both in form and appearance. Eighteenth-century neo-classical designs as well as the more florid late Victorian and Edwardian styles were reproduced throughout the Empire in the wealth of public buildings and private houses. Domestic architecture though was generally more modest if more expansive in the colonies. The English country house and the multiple-storey urban terrace were often less evident than the Indian bungalow in colonial cities. By the 1930s Internationalism in architecture had resulted in the corporate adoption of styles indistinguishable from those in the United States. However, rising dominion nationalism had produced statements in brick and stone of a different trend, notably French-Canadian and Cape-Dutch. The most spectacular Imperial architectural statement of all was the Anglo-Indian New Delhi. Here the blending of styles from western Europe and the Hindu and especially Moghul traditions of India produced an Anglo-Saracenic style, whose offshoots appeared throughout the Islamic areas of the Empire from Nigeria to Malaya.

It would be a truism to say that the British built cities for themselves to live and work in. The colonies with a substantial indigenous population exhibited a dualism in city form between the European and 'Native' quarters. Often the two had little link in terms of plan, although operating as a single functional unit. Class-conscious English society became even more divided and separated from the ruled in the tropical colonies. Cities were organised on the basis of segregation and differentiation, attaining their ultimate fragmentation in India with separate indigenous, military, government, railway and commercial towns within towns. Social distances were translated wherever possible into physical distances.

The Imperial system thus permitted great diversity within the dominant unifying forces of a common dominant society, which had a profound influence upon the landscapes of the British Empire. The visual impact of British Imperialism was often long lasting (Morris, 1982). Few countries have attempted to obliterate the Imperial heritage, although minor changes such as the removal of statues of Imperial heroes have occurred. Pakistan has built a new capital more in line with its modern image as an Islamic republic, and in recognition that Karachi has a firmly impressed British image. For the most part changes have not been revolutionary. Queen Victoria, immortalised in stone and bronze, still looks out over the predominantly eighteenth and early nineteenth century classical style centre of Calcutta, and Imperial financier Cecil Rhodes still contemplates the view towards the centre of Africa from above the University of Cape Town. Indeed the Victoria Memorial in Calcutta is one of the largest and most important monuments to be erected anywhere in the present century. Conceived by the Viceroy, Lord Curzon, in 1905, it was completed in 1921 as the symbol of Empire, commemorating the Queen-Empress and those who helped to build British India. The Imperial heritage is still the dominant influence upon the landscape in many of the ex-colonies and a significant element in the remainder.

Although attention is usually directed towards the economic and administrative aspects of Empire, the religious input was often profound. Indeed the three aspects were usually mutually supportive. David Livingstone, the most illustrious of the nineteenth-century missionary explorers, regarded evangelism as a precursor to trade and Empire.

The attitudes of the evangelical church were significant for the general development of the Empire, as the Church sought to change indigenous societies into the image of England. The image of England was essentially hierarchical. Verses from two popular Victorian hymns, one now expurgated, summed up the attitudes which were impressed upon other lands and other peoples:

From Greenland's icy mountains,
From India's coral strand,
Where Afric's sunny fountains,
Roll down the golden sand,
From many an ancient river,
From many a palmy plain,
They call us to deliver,
Their land from error's chain.

Reginald Heber, Bishop of Calcutta (1783–1826),
English Hymnal no 547

The rich man in his castle,
The poor man at his gate,
God made them, high or lowly,
and order'd their estate.
Mrs Cecil Frances Alexander (1818–95), *English Hymnal* no 587

The British Empire operated as an agent for conversion to Christianity through its established Church and the host of missionary societies and other denominations which were attracted by endeavour in the colonies. As early as 1662 the revised Book of Common Prayer introduced a new service of adult baptism which 'may be always useful for the baptizing of Natives in our Plantations' (Church of England, 1662: ix). The missionary effort was directed towards indigenous peoples and often involved the establishment of mission stations in advance of administrative control. Nowhere was this more noticeable than in Africa in the nineteenth century where considerable missionary effort was expended (Johnson, 1967). The mission station thus became one of the components of Empire and a powerful agent in the process of breaking down indigenous society and acculturating the population to European standards and expectations. Success was uneven, just as the distribution of endeavour was uneven. Many of the Pacific islands' populations embraced Christianity in its entirety, creating an indigenous Church which rapidly became independent of colonial metropolitan control. In other areas the indigenous religious systems, notably Islam and Hinduism, proved to be too cohesive for penetration by the missionaries.

Conversion of the indigenous population was one arm of the Church's activities in the colonies, the other was the cure of the souls of the European and settler communities. In this respect the Church of England played a pre-eminent role as the state Church to which the majority of the European population at least nominally adhered until the twentieth century. As the state Church it was given prominence in town planning schemes and in the provision of Crown lands for its financial support. In order to care for the overseas population a series of bishoprics, latter autonomous provinces, were established, initiated with the creation of the diocese of Calcutta in 1814. The foundation of permanent episcopal sees was a significant element in the establishment of a permanent overseas population, no longer dependent directly upon the Church of England. The new bishops followed the examples of their English brethren and built, often on a grand scale. Cathedrals in the colonies were constructed in the image of England, often to designs based on specific cathedrals. Thus the twentieth-century tower of the metropolitan St Paul's cathedral in Calcutta was modelled on the medieval Bell Harry tower at Canterbury. Although churches and cathedrals were built in classical styles in the seventeenth and eighteenth centuries, the major boom in colonial church building took place in Queen Victoria's reign, when neo-gothic was supreme.

The Church hierarchy thus paralleled that of the state. Government House and the cathedral were two essential elements of all colonial capital plans, and the same dualism continued through the various levels of urban place. Church-inspired colonies such as Canterbury in New Zealand placed the cathedral in the centre of the design. Occasionally it was the Church of Scotland which played the major role as in Dunedin (Edinburgh), also in the south island of New Zealand, while other denominations including Roman Catholic, Methodist and non-conformist also ministered to the needs of settlers, erecting churches and contributing to colonial townscapes.

THE RECORD

One of the major heritages of the imprint of colonial rule was the imposition of a massive bureaucracy. The administration sought to order society and to change it. In order to do so it required information. Colonial governments undertook a vast accumulation of material on many aspects of colonial life and lands. The information collected ranged from the geological surveys directed towards prospecting for useful minerals to the determination of farmers' land rights, usually as a step in the taxation system. The random reports of the early colonial period gave way to the systematic annual reports of colonial administrations, notably the Blue Books and their successor Statistical Registers inaugurated in 1822. Similarly censuses were taken which by 1891 were intended to be regular and on an Empire-wide basis. Indeed the censuses provide vast accumulations of statistics on the colonial period, making certain aspects of society amenable to modern techniques of study. An examination of the development of Toronto illustrates the wealth of the census and the possibilities for its study (Goheen, 1970). However, censuses are by nature classificatory. Groups were devised, usually of British making, and imposed on societies:

> Individuals find themselves firmly fixed as members in various groups of a particular dimension and substance. Thus the census imposes order and order of a statistical nature. In time the creation of a new ordering of society by the census will act to reshape that which the census sought to merely describe. (Barrier, 1981: 75)

Certainly men used statistics to a greater extent than ever before and indeed relied upon them to show trends and 'development'. Growth trends, whether in population, production, trade or revenue, were followed in Statistical Registers and compared. Information was circulated within the Empire both at the individual report level and in the more general *Statistical Abstract* published annually. Intercolonial rivalry, particularly for the colonies of settlement, was often intense as boosterism in the plan to attract colonists led to greater attention to statistics. Economic growth rates, wage rates, agricultural produce prices were all significant elements in fostering an image of a colonial society as growing and prosperous. However, statistics were selective in their collection. The colonial administrations and post-Union statistical services of South Africa had little interest in the Black population, resulting in estimates and often 'Whites only' censuses. Similarly Gold Coast statistics and reports prior to 1914 devote considerable attention to European gold mining activities but are comparatively silent on the rise of the indigenous cocoa industry. In what follows, the colonial statistical and census services have provided an invaluable storehouse of material, much of it still awaiting the researcher.

The British government also maintained a wide ranging correspondence between the authorities in London and the colonial administrations. The correspondence, together with the fact-finding commissions of enquiry undertaken at the behest of the Imperial and colonial governments, provide a remarkable record of colonial enterprise. They are preserved in the substantial Colonial Office holdings of the Public Record Office in London, while the individual official colonial government documents are housed in the archives in the capitals of the successor states. A series of correspondences was also maintained between the colonial governments and their local officials. Often extensive and temporarily long runs of records were kept on all matters of administrative concern. The written record became progressively more voluminous until the early twentieth century when the telephone began to have an impact on the means of communication. Selections from these correspondences were published as British Parliamentary Papers and as Blue Books and Parliamentary Papers of the colonies concerned.

Commissions of Enquiry, both of the Imperial government and at local government level, undertook investigations into a wide variety of subjects and reported their findings with remarkable candour and often clarity. References to groups of people as 'lazy, dirty and independent' or 'white kaffirs' would be politically unacceptable in the modern age (Cape of Good Hope, 1893: 35; Transvaal, 1908: 63). Governments wished to be informed and launched enquiries to ensure that they possessed at least the main outlines if not the details of the problems they had to confront. Inevitably the questions asked were often not those researchers would ask today, leaving some surprising gaps in colonial knowledge, more especially concerning indigenous populations. However, as an assessment of contemporary knowledge and thinking the official reports are an invaluable source (Christopher, 1984a; Powell, 1974).

The level of colonial government record making was often impressive when compared with British metropolitan standards where official interference with private enterprise was minimal. Thus complete records of land ownership were maintained in most colonies of settlement before the Land Registry was established in London. Even in colonies of indigenous settlement land records for taxation purposes were highly developed with cadastral surveys or sketches to determine the size and location of plots and farms. It is not without significance that British officials in parts of India held the title of 'Collector' (of taxes). The records of taxation and expenditures were retained and scrutinised by the colonial authorities ensuring their survival. Owing to the greater government intervention in the economy of the colonies, government departments ran and reported on topics such as railway development, irrigation works, forests and conservation long before they became the concern of the metropolitan government.

Private and corporate records are more patchy in their survival. The Victorian era was one of considerable letter writing activity. Literacy was extended to all sections of the British population in the last quarter of the nineteenth century. Thus by the time of the South African War (1899–1902) the army ranks were also literate committing an even wider field of observation and viewpoints to paper (Emery, 1986). Collections of private letters provide some of the missing detail and help to fill out the colonial picture. The senior colonial officials were often prolific writers and educated within a system which valued fluent prose. It was they who through private correspondence and published writings often made the colonies known to a wide audience. Possibly one of the most illustrious viceroys, Lord Curzon, wrote voluminously, travelled extensively, and disseminated his findings as President of the Royal Geographical Society (Goudie, 1980). His graphic descriptions of India and its borderlands illustrate the power of the writer and the influence his opinion commanded. As an example of this genre, his description of Srinagar in Kashmir provided a word picture of the city which would be hard to dispel (Curzon, 1984: 153).

Srinagar . . . was as much like Venice, as a hansom cab is like a gondola.
Srinagar was essentially tumbledown, slatternly, ignoble, unregenerate. It had in it nothing of the grandiose, or even imposing. Its colour was a uniform and dirty drab; its picturesqueness was that of decrepitude; its romance, if any, was that of decay.

Corporate records, where they survive, parallel those of the United Kingdom, on whose company laws colonial companies were modelled. Owing to the intricate histories of many firms, correspondences are often interspersed in the London records of the multinational corporations. Finally oral history has given a boost to the recollections of the survivors. *Plain Tales from the Raj* as radio and literature supplemented the record and introduced a more personal touch to the colonial experience, together with the succeeding series on Africa (Allen, 1975; 1979).

The colonial era additionally gave rise to a vast wealth of maps, mapping, painting and photography to provide a visual record of the changes wrought by the age. Surveying was one of the basic elements of exploration and this was transferred to the more detailed topographic and cadastral surveys undertaken throughout the colonial era. The major surveys of the colonies, and noticeably of India, provide an impressive cover in the colonial period together with successive revisions in the cases of the major towns. The coverage was by no means uniform as each colony devoted what resources it thought necessary to the enterprise. Some had little to show by the 1930s.

The British also created considerable pictorial records of the lands they occupied. As Ramaswami (1979: 1) wrote 'it could be said that the British landed in India ledger book in one hand and painting implement in the other'. The record often reflected the English background of the artist who placed a softer hue upon a strange landscape and sought the likeness of England. However, others adapted to the harsher and sometimes more monotonous scenery of the colonies. Painters such as Thomas Baines captured the landscapes of Australia and Africa in the era before major changes occurred. In time the painted record became supplementary to another art form — photography. The development of photography has resulted in the recording of colonial scenes from the 1850s onwards. The often prolific taking of photographs provides one of the best records of the last century of colonisation. They have been preserved in many archives and public libraries, as well as the major collections in London accumulated or commissioned by organisations such as the India Office Library, the Royal Geographical Society and the Royal Commonwealth Society. Again there are significant gaps as the exotic attracted more attention than the ordinary. Nondescript buildings in colonial towns were neither painted nor photographed to any extent, yet the natural features and the indigenous peoples were copiously photographed possibly from a sense that they were about to be displaced by the new colonial era and its artefacts,

The colonial record is thus remarkably rich and varied but by no means comprehensive. Comparative work thus becomes difficult if not impossible when pursued to any depth. Nevertheless, the very richness of the record may act as a deterrent to many who might otherwise have found the imprint of the British overseas a significant topic for investigation.

COLONIAL GEOGRAPHY

Attempts to create a colonial geography as a cohesive field of study go back at least 100 years. In 1887, the year of Queen Victoria's golden jubilee, Charles Lucas published his *Introduction to a historical geography of the British Colonies*. Lucas was a strong proponent of an Imperial Federation, although he recognised the problems of such a scheme, particularly as the United States was outside the British Empire, yet was an integral part of the Anglo-Saxon world. His approach was highly historical, seeking to create a measure of continuity from classical times to the nineteenth century. His introductory work was followed by a series of regional volumes, which remained in print for several decades. Echoes of Imperial Federation and Britain's place in the world as a major power came from the pen of Sir Halford Mackinder (Parker, 1982). A revival of such interest is evident in the expansion of the Wallerstein world-economy framework (Taylor, 1985).

Albert Demangeon in the 1920s produced a volume entitled *The British Empire: a study in colonial geography* in which he suggested that 'no other subject yields richer or fuller material for the study of colonial geography, properly understood as an independent branch of knowledge' (1925: 11). He further suggested that it was culture contact between coloniser and colonised which provided the most fruitful line of investigation. However, within his scheme of writing a third of the work was devoted to 'weapons of British Colonization', including transport, irrigation, capital, and scientific investigation and research. In 1933 Charles Fawcett published his *Political Geography of the British Empire*, which sought to draw together the political geographic pattern of the Empire, noting that the British Empire was 'the greatest experiment in human organization that the world has yet seen' (1933: 1). Nevertheless, despite these comprehensive works no field of study arose equivalent to the French school of colonial geography. The plea by Ronald Harrison-Church (1948) after the Second World War for geographers to explore the possibilities offered by a concerted programme of colonial development similarly fell upon deaf ears. Possibly this paralleled the often general public indifference to Imperial affairs (MacKenzie, 1984).

The significance of the Imperial era has become apparent to a greater extent as syntheses of individual regional work upon White settlement, colonial cities or indigenous rural impoverishment have resulted in comparisons being drawn from the experience of various parts of the Empire. Models of Imperial development propounded for one part of the Empire have been found to be equally applicable in other regions sharing a similar administrative history. The mercantile model expounded by James Vance (1970) has been expanded and developed elsewhere (Christopher, 1982; Heathcote, 1975; Meinig, 1982). The present work attempts to indicate some of the general findings and trends distinguished in various parts of the British Empire, and to suggest the enormous influence of the British Imperial impress upon the present landscape and upon the evolution of landscapes in many parts of the world. The post-colonial concentration of research and writing upon individual countries or regional blocks has resulted in the broader universal Imperial heritage being obscured. This volume is intended to draw attention to the common heritage shared by a quarter of the world's population.

In any survey of the British Empire and its impact upon the landscape certain general points and restrictions need to be made. First, this book makes no attempt to be comprehensive, sheer length restrictions would make such a task impossible. It does, however, seek to deal with a number of themes which the author considers to be significant in landscape development. Illustrative material is drawn from the sources available. No systematic historical geographies of the colonial era have appeared for many of the ex-colonies, indicating the wealth of research which remains to be undertaken. Secondly, to provide a measure of coherence to the work a general theme of examining the Imperial imprint in 1931 has been adopted to provide a comparative statement. It is not proposed however to present a geography of the British Empire of that year. The year 1931 has been selected as marking the end of an era of expansion, settlement and economic incorporation. Also it marked a significant stage of decolonisation with the symbolic Statute of Westminster granting complete political independence to the dominions. It is perhaps not without significance that two of the major Imperial capitals, Canberra inaugurated in 1927 and New Delhi in 1931, stand as monuments to the two strands of Imperial development.

The work is organised with an overview of the British Empire at its maximum extent as a preliminary to the main body of the study. There follow chapters upon the metropole, the United Kingdom, and the linkages which bound the metropole and the overseas possessions together. These set the frame for Imperial development, which in its day was regarded as the extension of Great Britain overseas. Next, a chapter on the colonial bases of power, whereby Imperial control was exercised and within which much of the energy and conspicuous spending of Empire was concentrated. Thereafter, four chapters examine the urban and rural landscapes produced during the colonial era, distinguishing between the settler and dual character colonial cities and between the rural lands of European settlement and the lands where the European impact was indirect. Finally, an overall assessment of the Imperial heritage is attempted as a pointer to the unity which existed between the many diverse lands for a brief period of their history. Because of the highly visible nature of the imprint of British Imperialism, extensive use of maps and photographs has been made in the hope that an appreciation of the imprint of the impact of the colonial era will be identified in areas otherwise neglected.

1

Overview

The British Empire, which attained its maximum territorial extent after the First World War, was one of the largest political entities ever constituted in world history (Figure 1.1). The Empire had been extended by a variety of means, including direct conquest from indigenous powers as in the case of parts of India or Hong Kong, through the legal process of annexation of apparently uninhabited regions as in Australia or Barbados, and acquisition by the conclusion of protection treaties with indigenous rulers in New Zealand and Fiji. Lands had been traded between the European powers in the course of expansion and even acquired as dowries, most significantly Catherine of Braganza's inheritance of Bombay; or by purchase in the case of the Dutch and Danish West African possessions; or seized in the course of European wars in the case of Canada and Jamaica. The history of Empire had not been a story of steady territorial expansion. The revolt and independence of the 13 North American colonies was the greatest and most disastrous loss prior to 1947, but territories had been abandoned as uneconomic and indefensible (Tangier, 1661–81), or granted independence but subject to indirect military control (Egypt, 1922). Possessions had also been exchanged with other powers for diplomatic gain (Heligoland to Germany, 1890) or ceded to friendly countries, when considered of limited value or political liability (Ionian Islands to Greece, 1864; Bay Islands to Honduras, 1860).

The picture which emerges in one of flux and change in territorial extent as well as change in terms of internal structure. In the 1930s Iraq became an independent kingdom while the Dominions gained formal recognition of their constitutional independence under the Statute of Westminster. The process of fragmentation thus took a major step forward, although it was only in the 1940s that the

Figure 1.1: The British Empire, 1931

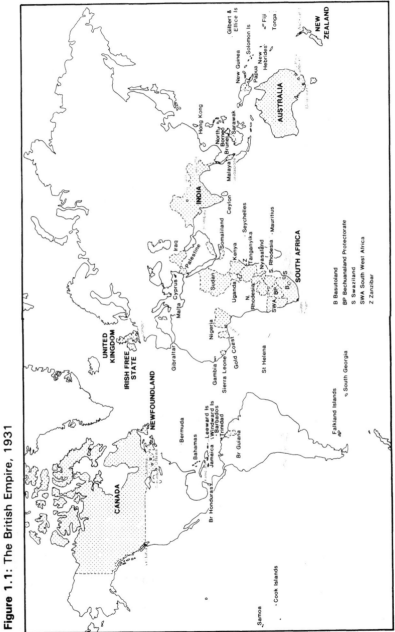

NEW ZEALAND

Gilbert & Ellice Is

Fiji

Tonga

Solomon Is

New Guinea

Papua

New Hebrides

AUSTRALIA

Hong Kong

North Borneo

Brunei

Sarawak

Malaya

INDIA

Ceylon

Seychelles

Mauritius

Iraq

Palestine

Malta

Cyprus

Somaliland

Kenya

Tanganyika

Sudan

Uganda

Z

N. Rhodesia

S. Rhodesia

Nyasaland

SWA

BP

B

S

SOUTH AFRICA

B Basutoland

BP Bechuanaland Protectorate

S Swaziland

SWA South West Africa

Z Zanzibar

UNITED KINGDOM

IRISH FREE STATE

NEWFOUNDLAND

Gibraltar

Nigeria

Gambia

Sierra Leone

Gold Coast

St Helena

South Georgia

Falkland Islands

Bermuda

Bahamas

Leeward Is

Windward Is

Barbados

Trinidad

Jamaica

Br Honduras

CANADA

Br Guiana

Samoa

Cook Islands

dissolution became more apparent after the strains of the Pyrrhic victory in the Second World War. The granting of independence to India, the key to the post-1784 British Empire, hastened decolonisation elsewhere. Thus to embrace the British Imperial imprint and the organisation behind it, no date later than the early 1930s can be entertained as the ensuing era of economic depression, war and independence blurs the semblance of a picture of an Imperial entity.

POLITICAL STRUCTURES

Political structures within the British Empire in the 1930s exhibited a remarkable diversity and lack of an overall philosophy of Imperial administration. Hyam (1976: 15) considered that 'there was no such thing as Greater Britain, still less a British empire, India perhaps apart. There was only a ragbag of territorial bits and pieces.' The concept of a single unit Empire or Imperial federation had died and the unique character of each of the component parts of the Empire was steadily enhanced in the twentieth century. If the special status of Northern Ireland and the Irish Free State are ignored, constitutional development in 1930 ranged from the virtually independent dominions of Canada, Australia, New Zealand, South Africa and Newfoundland, which maintained only tenuous links with Great Britain through a common sovereign, to directly administered colonies ruled by appointed governors and nominated councils subject to control from the Colonial Office in London.

In addition there were three ambiguous political statuses which further diversified the structure. In the first case the British government had entered into protection agreements with indigenous rulers who retained a measure of control over their own affairs. These ranged from the nebulous suzerainty agreement linking the Nizam of Hyderabad to the British Indian Empire, on the one hand, to the numerous small groups in Africa, on the other, whose chiefs retained no more than ceremonial functions under colonial control. Even the White Rajah, Charles Vyner Brooke, of Sarawak and the Chartered Company of British North Borneo were linked tenuously to the overall structure through protectorate agreements. The second anomaly was the various mandated territories acquired from Germany and Turkey after the First World War. Several of these territories were administered by the Dominion governments, not the Imperial government. These were subject to the supervisory power of the League of Nations and restrictions were placed upon the rights of the administrative power, with regard to guarantees of the rights of the indigenous peoples. The special international status of Palestine in this regard was particularly important and restrictive for the British administration. The third anomaly was the joint government maintained with other powers through condominium agreements. Thus the administration of the New Hebrides was shared with France and that of the Sudan with Egypt. In each of these anomalous cases British control was partial. Hence the impact of British ideas and organisation was far from uniform within the Empire. Extra-territorial extensions of Empire including the concessions of the Chinese treaty ports exhibited similar mixed traits (Western, 1985).

One of the major features of the structure of the British Empire was decentralisation with a strong element of self-government and indirect rule, both within colonies of European settlement and in protectorates with indigenous rulers. Self-government had been one of the distinguishing elements of the English colonial system from its inception, based on the precepts of English common law. In Virginia, when confronted with practical problems, the governor called a General Assembly in 1619 thereby establishing an institution which was to be emulated in numerous other colonies of English settlement (Robinson, 1957). Although subject to the control of a governor, usually appointed from London and at least nominally subject to the Crown, the colonial Councils and Assemblies were able to establish a high degree of local autonomy in matters of direct concern, such as land rights, dealings with indigenous peoples, regulation of internal trade and the raising and spending of local revenues. The solutions adopted to problems encountered in colonising a new land reflected the local environment, but also the cultural background of the immigrants themselves and the professional civil servants and soldiers of the Crown. The result was a wide variety upon a single theme, giving a degree of unity to the British Empire of settlement, but without any master plan.

The common theme is nowhere better illustrated than in the realm of the highly geographic trait of segregation. Official policies adopted in colonies where substantial numbers of the indigenous population survived the onslaught of British arms and the diseases attendant upon colonisation, reflected a general segregationist approach. The English and Scottish experience of subduing Wales and Ireland was carried overseas (Andrews *et al.*, 1979). Reservations, protected states and indirect rule resulted. Thus in many colonies two areas were defined reflecting differences in the degree of administrative control and the strength of European interests. Indigenous polities were incorporated within the Empire, often with depleted land areas and reduced powers, such as the Aboriginal reserves of Australia or the Indian reservations of Canada; while others including the sultanates of the Aden hinterland retained both their territory and their powers, beyond an undertaking not to deal directly with foreign powers. In both cases European settlers were excluded from the areas nominally within the reserve or protectorate.

The relative sizes of the European and indigenous areas were subject to a great range, as well as to redefinitions, as the political situation changed when the struggle between indigene and immigrant for land resources developed. In the West African colonies the European area was usually no more than a section of the towns, in other regions it included virtually the entire territory leaving only a small portion for the indigenous population. No overall philosophy was evident in official dealings with the indigenous population, although Lord Lugard's 'Dual Mandate' was a powerful influence in the twentieth century. Motives tending towards segregation ranged from the missionary movement, concerned with the saving of souls, to less rarely proclaimed economic motives for creating labour reserves for settler controlled agricultural and mining enterprises. In general British colonial policy sought to have as little as possible to do with indigenous populations. The British Empire was not an integrationist society. It was exclusive. Thus even the Hindu Maharajahs of Rajputana, whom the Moslem Moghuls had incorporated into their imperial administrative and power structure in the sixteenth and seventeenth centuries, achieved no secure place of power and influence within the British Indian Empire, let alone the British Empire as a whole. Even groups such as the Anglicised freed slaves of Sierra Leone or the Christian Anglo-Indians, who played a significant role in the rise of the Empire, were relegated to inferior positions once the structure was in place, and greater numbers of Europeans were available to fill the administrative and commercial posts involved.

THE EMPIRE IN 1931

For purposes of comparison the last attempted Empire-wide census of 1931 has been taken as a basic source of information. Owing to the depression the censuses for Australia and its dependencies were delayed until 1933 and those for South Africa and New Zealand until 1936. However, the estimates for 1931 have been used where possible.

In 1931 the British Empire covered some 35 million square kilometres, or over a quarter of the surface area of the globe, excluding Antarctica, most of which was in any case claimed for the Empire (Table 1.1). The British Empire was the home of some 496 million people, again approximately a quarter of the world's total. In terms of population the colonial states ranged in size from the Indian Empire, which with 352 million inhabitants constituted nearly three-quarters of the Imperial total, to the 3,000 inhabitants of the Falkland Islands. Even smaller island dependencies such as Tristan da Cunha or Pitcairn Island counted no more than 100 residents. In terms of area the Dominion of Canada with 9.5 million square kilometres and Australia with 7.8 million square kilometres dwarfed most other states, which at the other end of the scale included Gibraltar with only 5 square kilometres. Man-land relationships similarly differed from densely populated island and coastal colonies such as Hong Kong which had attained a density of 800 inhabitants per square kilometre, to the Falkland Islands, South West Africa and Bechuanaland Protectorate with one person for every 2 or 3 square kilometres.

In terms of economic power the United Kingdom clearly dwarfed the other members of the British Empire. In 1931 the revenue of the United Kingdom amounted to some £851.5 million. That of the rest of the British Empire only amounted to some £528.8 million, of which Australia (£162.2 million) and India (£153.6 million) were the major contributors.

British supremacy in Imperial trade was not so overwhelming. In 1930 the United Kingdom exported some £570.8 million worth of goods compared with the £683.7 million exported by the other members of the British Empire (Table 1.2). However, consideration of invisible exports would have reversed positions as the vast United Kingdom import bill illuminates (Table 1.3). It is significant that in both terms of imports and exports, Great Britain's trade with foreign countries exceeded that with its own dominions and colonies, although the colonial component had increased markedly since 1871. The other major trading countries of the Empire, the Dominions and India, exhibited diverse relationships. Canada received 64.8 per cent of its imports from, and sent 56.2 per cent of its exports to the United States; only in the sector of grain exports did the United Kingdom plays a dominant role. Indeed it was merely in specific primary

Table 1.1: Selected statistics for the British Empire, 1931

Country	Area $(000km^2)$	Population (000)	Railways (km)	Revenue (£ million)
United Kingdom	243.4	46,042	32,843	851.5
Canada	9,542.7	10,378	70,356	67.8
Australia	7,704.1	6,449	44,527	162.2
New Zealand	267.8	1,443	5,335	22.7
South Africa	1,222.3	8,133	19,761	32.1
Irish Free State	68.9	2,957	4,873	25.5
Newfoundland	971.6	282	1,460	2.0
India	4,675.6	351,400	68,901	153.6
Gibraltar	0.005	17	—	0.2
Malta	0.3	242	13	1.0
Cyprus	9.3	348	122	0.7
Gambia	10.4	200	—	0.2
Sierra Leone	80.3	1,672	501	0.9
Gold Coast	203.2	2,870	805	2.3
Nigeria	876.6	19,158	3,066	4.8
St Helena	0.2	4	—	0.01
S. Rhodesia	389.4	1,109	2,169	2.1
N. Rhodesia	745.8	1,345	985	0.9
Bechuanaland	712.2	180	642	0.1
Basutoland	30.3	650	1	0.3
Swaziland	17.4	125	—	0.1
Zanzibar	2.6	235	—	0.5
Kenya	572.4	3,041	2,601	3.0
Uganda	243.5	3,554	534	1.4
Nyasaland	124.2	1,603	280	0.4
Somaliland	176.1	345	—	0.1
Mauritius	2.1	404	219	0.9
Seychelles	0.4	27	—	0.1
Malaya	132.1	4,354	1,725	11.6
Brunei	6.5	39	—	0.04
Ceylon	65.6	5,307	1,530	7.6
North Borneo	82.1	270	209	0.3
Sarawak	108.8	600	160	0.5
Hong Kong	1.0	850	35	1.7
Papua	234.5	271	—	0.1
Fiji	19.3	183	483	0.6
Gilbert & Ellice Is.	0.5	34	—	0.1
British Solomon Is.	37.8	94	—	0.1
Tonga	1.0	29	—	0.1
Bermuda	0.5	28	—	0.5
Bahamas	11.4	60	—	0.4
Barbados	0.4	174	39	0.4
Jamaica	12.5	1,062	338	2.1
Leeward Is.	1.8	128	98	0.2
Windward Is.	1.3	236	—	0.3
Trinidad	5.1	412	190	1.6
British Honduras	22.3	51	40	0.2
British Guiana	231.8	311	127	0.9
Falklands	14.6	3	—	0.1

Table 1.1 *contd.*

Palestine	26.8	1,036	529	2.1
Iraq	302.0	3,500	1,209	3.5
Togo	34.3	294	–	0.03
Cameroons	88.3	770	–	0.1
South West Africa	835.0	241	2,165	0.5
Tanganyika	949.6	5,064	1,781	1.5
New Guinea	263.9	397	–	0.3
Nauru	0.02	3	–	0.01
W. Samoa	2.9	46	–	0.1
Sudan	2,611.0	5,606	3,214	5.3
New Hebrides	14.8	66	–	0.01
Total	35,045.2	495,732	273,866	1,380.30

Note: Figures for dependencies are included in those of colony, e.g.
Cayman Islands in Jamaica.
Source: Great Britain, 1933: Statistical Abstract for the British Empire
for each of the seven years 1925 to 1931, Cmd 4393.

Table 1.2: Imperial trade flows, 1930 — imports (£ millions)

Imports into	From United Kingdom	From British possessions	From foreign countries	Total
United Kingdom	–	304.0	739.9	1,044.0
Dominions	182.1	46.8	257.4	486.3
India	50.8	11.2	67.8	129.8
Colonies	51.0	45.2	95.6	191.8

Source: Great Britain, 1933: Statistical Abstract for the British Empire
1925-1931, Cmd 4393.

agricultural and mining products such as New Zealand meat and
dairy produce, Indian tea, Australian wool and South African gold
that British imports dominated the export trade of the dominions and
colonies. The colonies with the exception of Ceylon and Malaya
were comparatively minor trading entities, and exhibited a wide
range of trading partners.

The British Empire in 1930 was not a closed trading system. The
doctrine of free trade which had pervaded political thinking for
nearly a century had ensured the growth of British exports and
facilitated cheap imports. However, the changed circumstances of
depression and trade recession in 1929 were to have disastrous
effects upon the trade patterns of the Empire (Tomlinson, 1979).

Table 1.3: Imperial trade flows, 1930 — exports (£ millions)

Exports from	To United Kingdom	To British possessions	To foreign countries	Total
United Kingdom	—	248.3	322.4	570.8
Dominions	181.1	34.4	169.3	385.0
India	38.9	26.3	100.8	165.9
Colonies	39.8	18.6	73.8	132.8

Source: Great Britain, 1933: Statistical Abstract for the British Empire 1925–1931, Cmd 4393.

Reductions in demand affected the production of both primary producers and the manufacturing sectors. Protectionism in the form of either Imperial preferences or for a measure of individual dominion self-sufficiency eroded the basic system upon which the nineteenth century had been based, namely an industrial metropole and a non-industrial periphery. An appreciation of some of the salient features of the metropole as the first modern industrial power is necessary before a closer examination of the colonial periphery.

2

The Metropole

No attempt to analyse the impress of the British Empire upon its overseas territories and dominions would be possible without some consideration of the core — the United Kingdom. The British Isles by 1930 had been partitioned between the rump United Kingdom of Great Britain and Northern Ireland and the Irish Free State. The latter may be regarded as one of England's first experiments in overseas colonisation. The core state provided the impetus for the massive colonial expansion from the sixteenth century onwards, and provided men, money, expertise and organisation for many overseas enterprises. It also supplied in large measure the management cadre until the twentieth century. In return the United Kingdom secured profits from trade and through the exploitation of colonial resources the materials and markets for the development of the first industrial society. Industrialisation and colonisation were closely related as were industrial expansion and overseas trade. The degree to which the two were linked to political control of states peripheral to the world economy may be disputed. The United States after 1776 and the Latin American states after their independence from Spain and Portugal early in the following century, were significant trading partners of Great Britain and her individual colonies as well as recipients of British investment in the nineteenth and early twentieth centuries. This close economic relationship was achieved without British political involvement.

British trade and industry provided one link to Empire, another was emigration. In the period from the end of the Napoleonic Wars to the outbreak of the First World War some 22.6 million people emigrated from the British Isles. Approximately 40 per cent sailed to the constituent parts of the British overseas Empire. This flow of population and resultant settlement inevitably placed a British impress upon large parts of the world, notably among the successor states, the dominions of Canada, Australia and New Zealand. Colonists settled in most parts of the Empire and introduced British ideas and influences, more particularly British styles of building, planning and organisation. It is noticeable, however, that owing to the more spacious conditions encountered by the colonists in their new environments, the cultural landscapes which they produced in one colony, often have more in common with those in another colony than with those in the United Kingdom.

Administratively the whole edifice of Empire was held together by a bureaucracy whose headquarters were located in London. The Colonial Office and, after annexation in 1858, the India Office were two ministries of the British government. Until Joseph Chamberlain's assumption of the position of Colonial Secretary in 1895 neither was highly regarded. As a result ministers occupied the positions for only short periods of their careers, thereby leaving the permanent officials in control of great influence. Only with the dramatic expansion of Empire in the 1880s and 1890s was much popular notice taken in Great Britain through any major propaganda campaign. For the remainder of the time and for most British people the Empire was largely forgotten and its administration left to the bureaucrats based in London and responsible officials in the colonies.

Theories of colonial development were at best fragmentary and the notion of an Imperial policy of any cohesion was rarely enunciated. Chamberlain's concept of the Imperial 'estate' awaiting scientific development had had little impact by the outbreak of the Second World War. However, it was the possession of colonies which maintained Great Britain as a great power until 1947, and until then the whole acted as a unit in times of crisis, particularly in times of war. Nevertheless, there was little centralised planning in evidence and the problems of one colony tended to be dealt with in isolation.

The degree of control exercised by the Colonial Office, or indeed the British government as a whole, over the policies pursued by colonial and dominion governments varied. The blatant cutting of the telegraph wires at the time of the Jameson Raid on the Transvaal in 1895 might temporarily, if dramatically, free colonial subjects from Imperial supervision; but that supervision was present most of the time. Indeed control was tightened markedly as travel times both for people and messages were reduced in the course of the nineteenth century. Nevertheless, colonial policies formulated in London might

Figure 2.1: Colonial information flows (after Jeans, 1975)

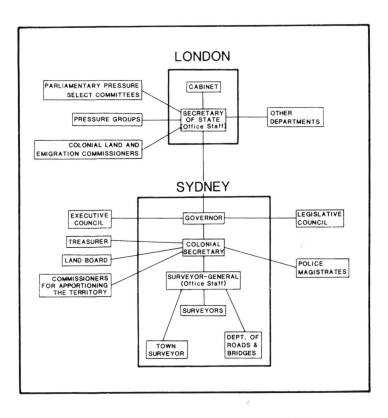

be ignored by officials in the colonies who sought to protect local interests. Hence grand colonisation policies laid down in London and applied to Australia were subject to considerable distortion as the colonial governments and Colonial Office officials reinterpreted each other's perceptions (Figure 2.1) (Jeans, 1975).

The flow of information and instructions which bound colonial regimes to Great Britain was not complete, although it improved in the nineteenth century. An appreciation of the distortions and partial nature of the flow of information, even the often deliberate withholding of information or rewriting of reports, is vital to an understanding of the manner in which colonisation took place. Official manipulation of information made available to settlers contemplating emigration to the Cape of Good Hope in 1820 and Western Australia in 1829 resulted in the implementation of schemes based on unsound foundations. The resultant disaster for many emigrants, who had no independent means of verifying official assessments of the agricultural potential of the colonies, was inevitable. Officials in London could not be expected to appreciate the environmental and social problems of lands which differed so markedly from England. The increased flow of information and increasingly people, helped to reduce the gap between perception and reality but the difference persisted until the end of the colonial era. The settler political sentiment that 'London' did not understand colonial problems promoted local separation and ultimately separate nationalisms.

Inevitably the colonial relationship was viewed differently depending upon where an individual was living. The relationships of ruler *vis-à-vis* ruled, exploiter *vis-à-vis* exploited and settler *vis-à-vis* bureaucrat were often uneasy. Clearly because ultimate control rested in London until 1931, colonial regimes could be coerced into adopting policies at variance with the colony's perceived interests. The old mercantile system which had led to rigid control of the trade system of the Empire through the Navigation Acts had been dismantled following the independence of the North American colonies. The Asian trade monopoly of the East India Company followed in the post-1815 era. However, more advanced systems of exploitation were devised to ensure that the colonies supplied raw materials for British industries and also posed no threat to English or Scottish industries through colonial industrialisation (McMichael, 1984). The degree of control differed in that Crown Colonies were more subject to direction than self-governing colonies. Thus the colony of Victoria was able to establish and protect existing industries from British competition. Exploitation through unfavourable conditions of trade applied to indigenous peoples and to settler communities producing primary products where the commodity markets, trade and finance organisations were based in London.

INDUSTRIAL BRITAIN

The British Isles underwent a major economic transformation from the early eighteenth century onwards. The pace of change accelerated in the nineteenth century with the result that an agrarian society gave way to an industrial urban based society. The progress of the Industrial Revolution was impressive. The annual output of coal and iron, the twin pillars of basic industry, increased from 57 million to 292 million tons and from 2.2 million to 11 million tons, respectively, between 1850 and the First World War. Heavy industry expanded and the British Isles became the major supplier of industrial goods to the world, a position undermined in the later nineteenth century as other countries underwent industrialisation.

Several significant points emerge from the well-known saga of industrialisation. The rapid demographic growth between 1801 and 1931 resulted in the population of Great Britain rising from 10.5 million to 44.5 million. Furthermore whereas in 1801 only one city, London, recorded a population in excess of 100,000 by 1931 there were 51 such cities and boroughs, which between them housed half the total population. The era witnessed a number of important modifications in the nature of the British city, although they are open to differing interpretations. Physical extent was one of the most noticeable changes. The compact walking size pre-industrial city was transformed into a sprawling built-up area in which distances were measured in kilometres. Within the city functional differentiation in the centre resulted by 1914 in the emergence of the distinctively zoned Central Business District with its separate financial, commercial, wholesale, industrial and administrative sectors. Beyond the core, differentiation of housing resulted in a high degree of class segregation ranging from terraced back-to-back houses to semi-rural villas.

The changes were made possible through the major technological innovations of the age. Public transportation in the form of buses, trams, particularly electric trams, and railways, including the electric tube underground railway, enabled large numbers of people to be transported from place of residence to place of work and back again each day at increased speeds and over longer distances. Further, rising standards of living in terms of real wage and salary rates enabled them to afford to do so. Innovations in public utilities, notably purified water, sewerage disposal, power supply (both gas and electricity), enabled the towns to function more efficiently and become healthier and generally more prosperous places than before.

New building techniques enabled steel frame and concrete buildings to achieve greater heights, while the invention of the lift enabled high-rise buildings to exceed the limitations imposed by walking access.

The new industrial economy was based on the results of the first Industrial Revolution whose foundations were coal and iron production. Dependent upon them were a series of major industries based on mechanisation. Steam power presented one of the most remarkable products of the early industrial age, and was applied to a wide variety of tasks before the advent of electric power. Nowhere was this more apparent than in the development of factories. Inanimate power was harnessed to replace human toil. The factory system centralised production, notably in textile and metal manufactures, and allowed larger quantities to be produced at lower costs. Increased volumes of production were disposed of through rising internal demand as wages and income rose, and through the development of export trades. Indeed many of the manufacturing industries were dependent on imports of raw materials for processing. The cotton industry is the most notable example. Trade on both an internal and international level was therefore essential for the propagation of the industrial system.

Intra-city and international transport was revolutionised through the application of new technologies, enabling increased volumes of commodities to be carried at reduced costs. The railway was possibly one of the most symbolic of the products of the Industrial Revolution and one which was most successfully exported as a measure of 'progress'. Some 33,000 kilometres of railway line had been opened in the United Kingdom by 1930 and some 241,000 kilometres elsewhere in the British Empire. Larger and more powerful engines were built and the costs of transportation for both men and goods steadily declined. Sea transport was similarly changed through the introduction of steam engines enabling vessels to sail independent of the wind and at speeds exceeding the general sailing ship. Regular sailings became possible resulting in the maintenance of regular flows of goods and more detailed planning of the trade system. Steel fabrication enabled larger vessels to be built and again costs of transport to be dramatically reduced. Mass production through the introduction of mechanisation resulted in the production of manufactures not only for British requirements but for its overseas Empire and foreign countries.

Urbanisation and industrialisation in Great Britain were achieved with comparatively little direct government intervention (Dennis,

1984). Free enterprise, *laissez-faire*, was the economic doctrine which dominated nineteenth- and early twentieth-century industrial activity. However, greater governmental supervision was apparent in social matters from the 1860s onwards. Minimum standards for new housing, health regulations, maximum working hours, safety regulations and even, just prior to the First World War, pensions characterised some degree of intervention with the free play of economic forces. The reform and increase in importance of local government led to major changes in the town as city, town and county councils spent on local services. The results were often highly regional in character prior to the First World War (Preston, 1985). The introduction of universal education in 1870 affected the whole population and led to the construction of 'Education Act' schools throughout the country. Additional services including public libraries, fire brigades, local police forces and a regulatory bureaucracy necessitated the construction of new official buildings and a greater governmental presence in towns than before. Civic pride was translated into a host of impressive town halls, while reformed county administrations erected county halls (Cunningham, 1981). The Victorian age was also one of increased religious activity and observance, reflected in a great over-supply of churches and chapels in the cities.

The other side of urban industrial development was the relative decline of the rural areas. The agricultural and resultant demographic disaster in Ireland in the 1840s was one of the earliest and most dramatic manifestations of neglect and ill-adjustment in agriculture. The Highland clearances represented another community disaster as lands were devoted to hunting, shooting and fishing. The middle decades of the nineteenth century represented a final flowering of rural profitability for landowners, who frequently converted their capital into conspicuous spending projects on estates and country mansions (Clemenson, 1982; Fuller, 1976).

However, the very success of the transport revolution in reducing costs which benefited industrial exports proved to be disastrous when applied to agricultural imports from low-cost production areas. The opening of the mid-latitude grasslands for extensive grain and beef and mutton production in the second half of the nineteenth century resulted in the emergence of low-cost production based on extensive use of land and low manpower. Only high transport costs and storage problems rendered these products uncompetitive on the British market. The rapid decline in ocean freight rates in the last third of the nineteenth century enabled foodstuffs to enter the country more cheaply than they could be produced locally. In the last quarter of the nineteenth century first grain prices and later meat prices fell to such an extent as to undermine the position of British farmers and farm workers. Agricultural depression ensued as official policy was committed to free trade from the abolition of the Corn Laws in 1846 until the Ottawa Conference of 1931, which resulted in low food prices in the towns and unfettered trade in manufactured goods. This benefited colonial food producers who obtained unrestricted access to the British market, but it also hindered attempts to create a colonial manufacturing industry. The colonies under the doctrine of free trade were not likely to emerge from being the suppliers of primary products and the importers of manufactured articles.

Industrial Britain thus had much to offer the dominions and colonies in the way of expertise. The supply of basic infrastructures for economic development in the form of communications systems and a market for primary goods enabled a symbiotic relationship to develop between the two. British industries and cities provided the models upon which the colonies built. Many colonial administrations sought to avoid the worst excesses of British industrial experience, through greater governmental intervention in the economic system and often direct ownership of the communications systems and even industries. At local level municipal by-laws and regulations again exceeded British experience as the systems were more flexible without the vested interests which were present in England. Industrial Britain thus offered a model but also a warning to colonial enterprise.

IMPORTS AND EXPORTS

Industrial development resulted in a substantial export trade in manufactured items and an import trade in raw materials and foodstuffs. This became ever more important as the scale of industrial activity increased and the opportunities for trade widened until the Depression beginning in 1929. In addition to the balance of trade was the invisible export of capital for colonial and foreign development projects and the provision of the services of shipping, insurance and expertise which resulted in a steady flow of invisible profits for the country.

Great Britain's trade included an ever increasing importation of foodstuffs and raw materials. Although no substantial Imperial preference was offered to the products of the British colonies, many colonial enterprises were designed to satisfy the needs of the British Isles. The demand for raw materials, notably minerals and fibres, was of considerable significance for the Empire and its development. The range of imports was substantial. Although the United Kingdom possessed within its own borders the key requirements for the first Industrial Revolution, coal and iron ore, together with a massive range of other minerals, there were significant weaknesses and certainly no possibility of self-sufficiency. Great Britain had been unable to produce sufficient to feed itself since the early nineteenth century. As standards of living rose so the trade deficits increased and the range of demands for exotic goods rose. In part the demands of the British economy were met from production in British colonial possessions. However, much British investment was directed towards non-British countries, particularly in Latin America, in order to satisfy such demands in the nineteenth and early twentieth centuries. During this period some 5 per cent of Gross National Product was invested overseas. This was a remarkable export partially designed to develop new sources of raw materials and foodstuffs for the British economy and facilitate their importation into the United Kingdom.

Although early British overseas enterprise derived much of its profit from plunder, it was directed by the mid-seventeenth century towards trade. The link between trade and Empire was legalised in the Navigation Acts which sought to develop colonial production and direct the sale of such production to Great Britain. The legacy of this position survived long after the repeal of the legislation with the generally close alignment of colonial trade with the United Kingdom; but British trade remained free of such political entanglements or Imperial preferences until the 1930s. Thus an examination of British trade figures reveals only a low Imperial component, but the colonies were more highly dependent upon the British market and sought their imports from the British Isles.

Early Imperial development was directed towards the acquisition of products not available in Great Britain. Thus the production of sugar in the West Indies and tobacco in North America fell within the realm of the direct exploitation of colonies through the British cultivation of crops required in the metropole. In Asia products such as tea and spices were obtained through trade with indigenous polities and only later to secure bases for that trade did a formal Empire come into being. In other cases natural resources, whether gold, silver or timber, were harvested as resources of formal and informal colonial possessions. The Industrial Revolution led to a widening of demands for raw materials such as cotton, wool and minerals, where supplies in the British Isles were depleted or inadequate to meet rising demands. In order to feed a rapidly growing population, foodstuffs played an ever increasing role in British trade in the nineteenth century as grains and later meat were imported to nourish an essentially urban, industrial society. Thus by the First World War, British imports sustained both population and industrial growth. Significantly only in a few sectors was the British colonial contribution dominant. The United Kingdom obtained its imports wherever it could, at the lowest possible price, frequently to the detriment of colonial exporters. In the twentieth century British industrial development was not so well catered for by Imperial production. The British Empire was noticeably deficient in petroleum reserves and certain strategic materials.

The pattern of British exports revealed an even less important place for the British Empire in terms of volume and value. However, the British colonies and dominions provided a relatively secure export market compared with some foreign countries and markets with few financial or political problems. Trade and investment elsewhere was liable to the problems associated with the political upheavals of many Latin American countries, or indeed the wholesale nationalisation associated with Russian investments after the October Revolution of 1917. Thus the British colonies imported British goods where possible and effectively provided an expanded home market for British manufacturers. Colonial trade barriers against British manufactured goods were usually minimal compared with the increasingly protective stances adopted by many other countries. Import substitution in the colonies was rarely a serious threat to British trade until the First World War interrupted accustomed patterns, and the rise of Indian nationalism sought to revive Indian textile industries. Through this export trade a certain uniformity in sales existed within the Empire, whether in railway rolling stock or cast iron ornamentation on buildings. Inevitably this tendency towards uniformity declined after 1914 as colonial industrialisation assumed greater importance.

EMIGRATION

The British Isles were a major source of manpower for the British Empire, both on the temporary administrative and commercial basis,

Table 2.1: Emigration from the United Kingdom, 1815–1924 (000s)

Period	Total	United States	British North America	Australia and New Zealand	South Africa	Others
1815-1819	98	43	53	–	–	2
1820-1824	110	26	67	3	6	8
1825-1829	129	56	60	5	1	7
1830-1834	386	143	224	13	1	5
1835-1839	292	149	97	40	1	5
1840-1844	497	222	171	63	2	9
1845-1849	1,029	691	257	65	6	10
1850-1854	1,639	1,158	197	260	7	16
1855-1859	801	472	72	228	10	18
1860-1864	774	490	69	184	9	31
1865-1869	1,065	826	101	113	4	30
1870-1874	1,356	1,010	163	125	11	47
1875-1879	797	461	75	179	30	51
1880-1884	1,839	1,316	208	207	49	58
1885-1889	1,733	1,253	185	200	38	77
1890-1894	1,506	1,093	171	80	67	83
1895-1899	1,173	765	129	57	135	86
1900-1904	1,891	1,160	352	73	201	84
1905-1909	2,513	1,440	649	132	126	166
1910-1914	3,051	1,353	981	353	151	213
1915-1919	473	158	142	45	36	92
1920-1924	1,894	726	622	269	136	141
Total	25,016	15,011	5,045	2,694	1,027	1,239

Source: Ferenczi, 1969; and British Parliamentary Papers. The figures before 1840 are incomplete and exclude involuntary emigration.

but more significantly as a source of permanent immigrants. In the period 1815–1924 approximately 25 million persons emigrated from the British Isles (Table 2.1). Some 15 million left for the United States, but virtually all the remainder migrated to British possessions around the world (Ferenczi, 1969). This migration was primarily directed towards the temperate colonies of settlement, more especially Canada (5 million), Australia and New Zealand (2.7 million) and Southern Africa (1 million). The figures exclude the 162,000 convicts who were transported to Australia between 1787 and 1868, mostly in the 1820s and 1830s.

This intercontinental migration was of the utmost importance in establishing a number of modified British societies in other continents and through the occupation of lands previously only lightly populated, impressing a British image. Accordingly the 'Doctrine of First Effective Occupation' propounded by Wilbur

Zelinsky (1973: 13–14) is of great significance:

> Whenever an empty territory undergoes settlement, or an earlier population is dislodged by invaders, the specific characteristics of the first group able to effect a viable, self-perpetuating society are of crucial significance for the later social and cultural geography of the area, no matter how tiny the initial band of settlers may have been . . . Thus in terms of lasting impact, the activities of a few hundred, or even a few score, initial colonizers can mean much more for the cultural geography of a place than the contribution of tens of thousands of new immigrants a few generations later.

The massive outmigration from the United Kingdom ensured that it was to be a British imprint which was dominant in large tracts of the world.

The pattern of migration varied through time. The push and pull factors changed their relative importance, while the ultimate in push factors, convict transportation, was an element in emigration until the 1860s. Although push factors might be dominant at times such as the Irish potato famine and during the various cyclical depressions which afflicted the British economy, the pull factors were more diverse. The dominant position of the United States in British emigration patterns meant that other countries were in competition with a highly efficient and effective immigration system which presented a number of major advantages in terms of the opportunities which the country had to offer settlers. British colonial administrations thus had to show rival attractions and often expend considerable effort to make people, who might already be decided upon emigration but undecided upon destination, choose to stay in the Empire. Elaborate recruiting campaigns were launched by most of the temperate colonies with incentives in the form of free passages and free land (Camm, 1985).

Emigration literature played a significant role in popularising individual colonies and spreading information about the colonies. Thus the war of words waged to attract settlers, the physical attributes of various colonies and their economic potential were stressed. This frequently meant the distortion of reality when official objectives were at stake. Hence in the promotion of the initial Western Australian settlement scheme, government officials deliberately rewrote passages of the exploratory mission's report to emphasise the advantages of the area (Cameron, 1974). In order to advise people and regulate emigration, the government in London established the Colonial Land and Emigration Commission in 1840. This body sought to disseminate information concerning the Empire, to guide potential settlers and also to use one of the major Imperial resources, the colonial Crown Lands, as a means of financing Imperial migration. The latter did not work well, but the former function was successful and in 1873 was taken over by the Emigrants Information Office. These two bodies provided the type of practical information and advice required by emigrants, including budgets and warnings on what to expect at the end of the voyage. Colonial emigration officers were attached to colonial and dominion offices in London and elsewhere in the British Isles to disseminate information. Commercial enterprises such as the Canadian Pacific Railway similarly maintained offices overseas one of whose functions was to attract settlers to the Company lands in the Prairie Provinces, through the offer of incentives including ready-made farms.

People were therefore one of the great exports which the British Isles had to offer and the colonies were variously successful in securing them. Prior to the First World War, Canada had been most successful in the early nineteenth century and in the immediate pre-war period. In the latter stage the opening of the Prairie lands and the economic opportunities offered elsewhere in the booming economy attracted 2.5 million immigrants in ten years (1904-13). However, under half (1 million) came from the British Isles and other countries such as Austria-Hungary (154,000) supplied a diverse group of persons. Australia experienced a boom in immigration from the gold strikes of the 1850s to the arousal of colonial protectionist sentiments in the 1880s. South Africa received few immigrants from the British Isles before the major gold strikes of the 1880s, but owing to the presence of a substantial indigenous population which occupied menial positions, there was no demand for British labourers in the nineteenth and twentieth centuries. In addition to the dominions, smaller entities such as the Falkland Islands, Bermuda and others offered opportunities for a limited number of permanent settlers.

The tropical colonies offered fewer permanent homes for settlers. India for example prohibited permanent European settlement until the 1830s. Others such as the Gold Coast and Nigeria had the unenviable reputation of being 'the White Man's Grave'. Indeed death rates in the tropics before the introduction of quinine severely limited the numbers of temporary European residents. Settlers who had migrated to the West Indies in the seventeenth and eighteenth centuries were not followed by a continuing stream in later years, as the economic opportunities of the older sugar-producing colonies were severely constrained after emancipation. Permanent settlers were only attracted to the tropics in Africa in the twentieth century where land could be farmed in the temperate climates of high altitudes in Kenya and Southern Rhodesia.

Significantly by 1900 emigration was predominantly urban orientated. The colonial promotion of schemes of land settlement had little bearing upon the course of British emigration (Newbury, 1984). Great Britain by the late nineteenth century was a predominantly urban society and consequently was exporting urban dwellers to other urban centres. Much therefore depended upon the opportunities offered for trade and industry in the dominions. Once again the United States in its massive industrialisation programme appeared to offer more than the British dominions and colonies. British migration was closely related to the investment booms in regions of recent European settlement where employment opportunities were created overseas rather than at home. Accordingly the pattern of British overseas investment materially influenced the course of British migration (Richardson, 1972).

Many British migrants were only temporary. The colonial civil services, the army and commercial firms all drafted men to the colonies for tours of duty with no intention of sending them permanently overseas. Many private individuals managing farms or firms similarly spent part or indeed all their working lives in the colonies, with the intention of retiring to the United Kingdom. Temporary migration to the British possessions was thus of some considerable importance in creating a British society in colonies which otherwise would have been little influenced by Europeans.

A two-fold division of such groups into the official and unofficial positions they occupied is possible. The official migrants were colonial government and military personnel from the Governor or, in India, the Viceroy, down to the privates in British regiments stationed for various periods of time at the military bases around the Empire, particularly in India. The colonial civil services, exemplified by the Indian Civil Service, were staffed at senior levels by British officials appointed to particular colonies and spending their entire careers in the colonies. Some senior officials were moved regularly from one colony to another. Hence many of the colonial governors of the nineteenth and early twentieth centuries had gained experience in their lives of a wide range of conditions and acquired deep understandings of colonial problems (Gann and Duignan, 1978). This often brought them into conflict with less sympathetic officials in the Colonial Office, who could however be overruled by prestigious governors. Hence, men such as Sir George Grey at the Cape of Good Hope and New Zealand laid the foundations of many institutions and practices of government still in operation today. The main body of civil servants, however, did not move and so established an understanding of the problems and prospects of particular parts of the world, often seeking to foster the interests of their colony in competition with others. The acrimonious exchanges between British officials in India and British officials in Natal over the conditions experienced by Indian indentured labourers in the latter colony is but one example.

The unofficial group was more diverse. The representatives of major British concerns at one end of the scale occupied positions of power and influence in colonial society. They were moved according to head office requirements as the London grip upon the commercial enterprises of the Empire tightened in the second half of the nineteenth century. In contrast individual planters employed by an agency business were often isolated and poorly remunerated, resulting in high turnovers of staff and a temporary character to the population. The commercial community was clearly vital to the functioning of the colonial trade system.

In the colonies of settlement the staff rapidly became locally based and permanent except for a few senior officials. However, in the tropical colonies the entire European staff was transient, although programmes of indigenisation were practised in a number of Asian concerns from the early stages of development. Also whereas the official community was exclusively British in origin, the commercial community was more cosmopolitan, reflecting the international nature of world trade. American, French, Dutch and German concerns were represented in most of the major centres of the Empire, often by their own nationals.

Intercontinental migration therefore was a significant element in maintaining the Imperial system and fostering a community of feeling and through this a uniform ethos and practice. Nowhere was this better illustrated than in the educational system, where British public and grammar schools and universities were 'exported' together with staff suitably qualified to maintain British standards and syllabuses. Although many educationalists were permanent migrants to the temperate colonies, those to the tropics were temporary; while the itinerant examiner despatched from institutions in the British Isles to conduct examinations in the colonies was an even more temporary but nonetheless influential part of the intercontinental migration.

IDEAS

The influence of migrant educationalists suggests a further influence of the British Isles in the development of the British colonies and dominions, namely in the realm of ideas and methodology. Not only were people, goods and money exported but also ideas, methods, ways of doing things, and most significantly the English language. As a lasting legacy of Empire these intangible aspects are the most important and binding. The English language united the British Empire as a single realm of communication, and linked it with the United States, the first possessions to leave the Empire. The free flow of information and ideas within the English-speaking world was undoubtedly of significance in achieving cohesion and in assisting people in various parts of the world, faced with similar problems, to learn from the experience of others. Educational, economic and social information in government papers, books, periodicals and newspapers circulated within the Empire and helped to maintain a degree of uniformity as colonists in temperate regions moved towards a new awareness of and identification with the new colonial lands. Australian and Canadian nationalism thus took on certain shared values with each other. This was expressed amongst other things in governmental structures recognisable from Victoria, British Columbia to Pietermaritzburg, Natal, as modified copies of the Westminster pattern. Information was dispensed through British newspapers, notably *The Times*, but also through the circulation of colonial and Indian papers such as the Melbourne *Age*, the *Asian* of Calcutta and the Toronto *Globe*, to all parts of the Empire.

The English language provided a colonial *lingua franca* for indigenous peoples educated within the English colonial system and thereby separated from those educated in other European languages. They too entered the English-speaking world's realm of ideas and communication. English in India provided the language of the independence movement as Fabian socialism provided some of its rhetoric. A uniform system of English language education assisted the building of state nationalisms, rather than incorporating the educated elite into the British colonial ruling classes. The system remained administratively British with no infusion of other groups. The result of this was an education system designed in England for colonial peoples. The buildings erected for the purpose reflected this concept, ranging from the Victorian gothic mid-nineteenth century structures at the universities of Bombay and Toronto to the modern style African universities established in the twentieth century. All taught English history and Classics as basic elements of a British education. At school level English educational principles were applied in the colonies with the establishment of grammar schools and noticeably the transplantation of the English public school. Accordingly Michaelhouse, Natal, and Bishop Cotton School, Simla, and many others were founded, built and run on English public school lines.

The educational and cultural dominance of the United Kingdom within the British Empire until the 1930s resulted in a general acceptance of British standards of taste and technology. Thus British architecture was emulated throughout the Empire as presenting the best and most desirable aesthetic values. This was as true of eighteenth-century classical Georgian reproduced in the West Indies and New South Wales as the High Victorian styles of Toronto and Melbourne a century later. Only when local circumstances proved to be particularly unsuitable were styles abandoned or radically transformed. Here borrowings from India such as bungalows, verandahs and balconies often supplied a want and even influenced taste in the metropole. Similarly in technology, British methods were followed, be it in railway systems or agricultural practice, but practical modifications were more readily adopted if shown to be necessary. Thus American agricultural experience in arid and semi-arid lands was of value to those in other arid lands in pioneering light metal windmills, barbed wire and labour-saving devices, such as harvesters and heavy ploughs. The practical experience gained in the United States was consequently freely borrowed, noticeably in the field of mechanisation required to farm large areas with minimal labour.

Scientific research institutions in Great Britain similarly sought to solve colonial problems. The collection and dispersion of plants at Kew Gardens for propagation and breeding has been mentioned. Other agricultural research stations also contributed to colonial endeavour. Rothampstead Research Station was founded in 1843 and the Cirencester Agricultural College two years later. Both contributed to the training of staff and solving of colonial agricultural and technical problems. More especially they provided the trained personnel to run the agricultural colleges and research services established in the colonies. In similar manner the School of Tropical Medicines, founded in 1897, and other medical faculties in Great Britain worked upon the health problems of colonial peoples, as well as providing trained personnel to serve in institutions within the colonies.

Theoretical practice, however, remained a metropolitan domain until the 1930s and often later. Research and training, whether in medicine, agriculture or town and country planning were centred within the United Kingdom and the principles then applied to the colonies. Metropolitan ideas on town and country planning are particularly relevant in this respect (King, 1980). Ebenezer Howard's garden cities concept was adopted far more readily in the colonies with extensive spaces available for such schemes, than in the closely organised landscapes of the British Isles. Garden City planning, however, might be intended for the British settlers only, as its application to the design of the new capital of Northern Rhodesia at Lusaka illustrates (Collins, 1980). Nevertheless, town planning principles as applied to street layouts and public utility provision were copied in the colonies, reflecting the greater government involvement in the details of town planning in colonial societies.

Thus the binding of the Empire through the influence of the metropole, and through the economic system developed in the British Isles and its trading system, was reinforced through the export of people and ideas. The tangible results of this influence are still present. The Indian Imperial capital of Calcutta illustrates this clearly. The most magnificent of memorials to Queen Victoria has been scrupulously maintained by a Marxist local administration acting through the medium of the English language. The structures and the ideas remain, although the system and the people who placed them there have departed. Calcutta thus continues as a recognisably 'British' city in outward appearance some 40 years after the Union Jack was lowered for the last time, and encompasses the inherited concepts of Empire most profoundly. Accordingly Nivad Chaudhuri (1959: 64) wrote of Calcutta and Bombay:

> It was only after seeing London that I discovered the true lineage (of these cities) . . . offspring of London, whereas the northern Indian cities were descended from the Islamic and pre-Islamic cities of the Middle East . . . London is the first and archetypical city of our age, created by modern government, bureaucracy, finance, world empire, international commerce and industrialism . . . It is the Mother Megapolis of our era.

3

Linkages

The British Empire was held together by a series of linkage systems which operated on a worldwide basis to facilitate the redistribution of men, money and goods. Foremost among them were the Royal Navy and the merchant marine, which acted on a global scale to protect the Empire and transport its trade. Secondly road and railway systems were constructed within the colonies to facilitate internal collection and redistribution. Thirdly there were the postal and telegraph systems designed to transfer information between the several parts of the Empire ensuring its smooth operation. Fourthly there was the organisation of the trade system through the wholesale, banking and insurance facilities offered for the transfer of goods and people through direct investment.

THE SEALANES

The Empire was formed in an era when naval power was the dominant consideration for Imperial expansion. Expansion within the British Isles had been completed with the incorporation of Ireland in the sixteenth and seventeenth centuries. Expansion beyond the British Isles depended upon the growth of trade based on secure trade routes maintained by a strong navy. The geopolitical concepts of Admiral Alfred Mahan of the United States and Sir Halford Mackinder enunciated in the decades before the First World War, emphasised the significance of sea power and the control of the major sealanes of the world based on the British Imperial experience of the previous two centuries. Control was achieved through the deployment of the Royal Navy and the establishment of shore stations for fleets to operate far from the British Isles and from where protection could be afforded British merchant shipping on the high seas or in foreign ports.

The sealanes, particularly the routes to India, were of prime concern to British naval and commercial planners. The route around the coast of Africa was reduced in importance with the opening of the Suez Canal in 1869. This feat was achieved largely by foreign interests, notably French, although financial control of the Suez Canal Company ultimately was acquired by the British government. British military control of the Canal and adjacent Canal Zone, attained in 1882, was to last for over 70 years. The Suez Canal was thus clearly a recognisable British sea route, even if it cut through a technically foreign country, as the bulk of the shipping passing through it flew British flags. Other sea routes were similarly recognisable by the flag on the vessels and by the forts guarding constrictions or strategic junctions in the routes, such as Aden and Penang, at the entrances to the Red Sea and Straits of Malacca, respectively. As a result the Indian Ocean was converted into a virtual 'British Lake'. Changing economic conditions led to the development of Singapore to largely displace Penang, as Penang had displaced Malacca before it. All three, however, were retained as British bases on the one sealane, administratively linked in the suitably styled colony of 'Straits Settlements'.

Plans to cut a canal through the Isthmus of Kra to link the Bay of Bengal and the South China Sea came to nought. Indeed few other canals were constructed for ocean-going vessels to link the various parts of the Empire. The central American schemes were eventually taken to fruition by American enterprise early in the present century. Indeed the British policy of avoiding conflict with the United States had led to the virtual demilitarisation of British colonies in the Americas in the course of the nineteenth century, with consequent effects upon the sealanes, of which the North Atlantic Ocean was by far the most important for British trade.

Inland canal construction and the improvement of river navigation did play a part in the opening of several colonies. Navigation of the St Lawrence was made possible through the construction of canals to avoid the rapids and to link the lakes for small vessels. Ocean-going vessels could proceed no higher than Montreal before the completion of the St Lawrence Seaway in 1959. However, the majority of mid-latitude colonies lacked the rivers and often the rainfall regimes to support extensive navigable river and canal systems. Australia's internal waterways were severely limited by water availability and the Murray River transport system did not develop as the equivalent of that on the Mississippi River as its promoters suggested. Indeed a parallel paucity of resources and exportable goods in the catchment areas rendered the system of minor importance. The situation was even more acute in Southern Africa with low, seasonal waterflows and major rapids and waterfalls on all the main rivers.

In the tropical colonies river and canal systems assumed greater importance, although canals were built primarily for irrigation works. The Ganges Canal thus had limited transport usage. The rivers, however, were used extensively. River communications dominated the administration and commerce of several colonies and provinces. The Irrawaddy was navigable for some 1,650 kilometres above Rangoon and the trade and passenger service on this prime artery was dominated by the Irrawaddy Flotilla Company throughout the colonial period (Chubb and Duckworth, 1973). Similarly the Brahmaputra provided the main means of access to Assam from Calcutta as did the Niger for Nigeria before the construction of the railways. Bulky goods continued to be transported by river owing to costs. In central and East Africa the great lakes provided the basis for an internal transport system similar in concept to the Great Lakes of North America, but without the opportunities which the St Lawrence offered for reaching the sea.

ROADS

Routes on land present no lack of ready recognition. One of the great feats of the British colonial authorities and commercial concerns was the provision of road and railway systems for their possessions. Inland transport was essential for the promotion of trade and security, and therefore received high priority in many colonies, with direct government intervention in construction.

Roads were the first priority, before the coming of the railway. Thus up until the 1860s–1880s road building programmes were vital to colonial economic and political expansion, whether to cross the Blue Mountains from Sydney and link up the potential agricultural lands of New South Wales with the port, or to expand the Indian Grand Trunk Road from Calcutta to Lahore (Figure 3.1). Major feats of road and bridge building were undertaken by the military authorities throughout the Empire to facilitate troop movements, more especially the systems of frontier roads developed in India, Canada and South Africa. Even after the railways had been built, the

Figure 3.1: Howrah Bridge, Calcutta, the beginning of the Indian Grand Trunk Road

construction of new roads in the more inaccessible parts of the British Empire continued. Nowhere was more famous for its roads than the frontier regions of India. Road building on the borders with Afghanistan and China together with internal roads in such rugged terrain as the Assam and Burma borderlands resulted in a major transformation of accessibility from the plains, with all that this implied in the movement of men, goods and diseases into the hill tracts.

Prior to the development of the motor car, colonial road systems were designed as Roman roads had been, for armies on foot and wagons carrying goods and supplies. Road surfaces improved in sophistication as fast coaches were introduced to trunk roads early in the nineteenth century. In the early years of the twentieth century more carefully graded roads were constructed to cope with the demands of the motor car. Initially many such improved roads acted as feeders to the railway lines which carried the main bulk long distance transport during the late nineteenth and early twentieth centuries. Significantly road construction led to a boom in mass movement in tropical colonies where the bicycle provided a means of transport for people previously without even baggage animals. Integrated motor road systems were constructed after the First World War, but the accumulated state investment in railways, which would be prejudiced by such systems, often led administrations to slow construction. Thus in Palestine trunk roads in competition with the railways were usually upgraded late in the building programme (Biger, 1979). However, a sign of the changing times was the decision in 1920 by the British North Borneo Company to build a metalled road rather than extend the railway line (British North Borneo Company, 1929).

In Australia large parts of the pastoral regions were not linked to the railway, neither were graded roads a feasible proposition over the distances involved. The problem of the movement of stock to market, as of people, was overcome by the introduction of Travelling Stock routes, along which animals could be driven from watering point to watering point on Crown Land, thus not affecting the pasturage of adjoining ranchers. The provision of organised stock routes together with government watering points was adopted in other semi-arid regions including Bechuanaland Protectorate.

The colonial transformation of the road pattern has been the subject of some enquiry. One detailed study of the Niagara peninsula of Ontario suggested that the early European penetration of the area was effected through the use of Indian trails (Burghardt, 1969). Once settlement began certain key routes were improved and with the establishment of administrative centres, linked roads were built to integrate outlying areas (Figure 3.2). Finally as the full settlement process was completed the road pattern was increasingly linked to the survey pattern and extended to a network of graded roads of varying quality. Many earlier roads and trails, particularly those along the rivers, declined in importance or were abandoned. The construction of graded, later paved and finally asphalted, roads paralleled improvements in the means of communication, notably the introduction of coach services prior to the development of the railway network and in the twentieth century the introduction of the motor car. The last development resulted by the 1920s and 1930s in the surveying and construction of new trunk roads linking the main centres rather than villages and rural service centres. The new main roads were built without reference to the rectangular survey system. Similar patterns of road construction in the colonial era have been distinguished in non-settler colonies, notably the Gold Coast and Nigeria (Taaffe et al., 1963). However, this involved no major reorientation of the minor road pattern to adjust to a new settlement

Figure 3.2: Road development in southern Ontario

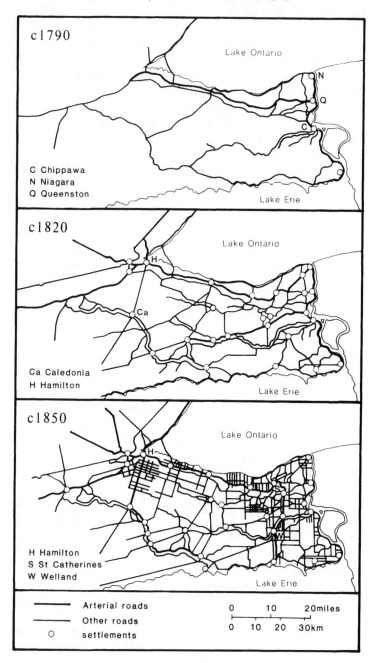

pattern, but the building of routes to link administrative centres and later indigenous settlements already in existence.

RAILWAYS

Railways are one of the major legacies of colonial rule. Few developments excited so much debate in the pre-Great Depression era as the construction of the major colonial railway lines, nor such political bargaining as the building of the branch lines. High priority was given to the laying of lines which were considered essential to colonial progress or indeed to colonial prestige.

Economic motives were most usually put forward to support plans to build a railway line. Typical of such promotion was the calculation that Nigerian railways reduced the cost of transportation of goods from the interior to the coast to one-fifteenth of previous levels when undertaken by head porterage (Ijere, 1973). Similar calculations based on the relatively high costs of road transportation and the savings in time which railways could afford were universally expounded. Some lines were laid for political reasons, hence the Canadian Pacific Railway was built as part of the price for British Columbia acceding to the Canadian Confederation. Expenses were partly defrayed through the government grant of extensive tracts of land to the Company and the anticipation that land sales would help to offset anticipated running losses in the early years of operation and high costs of construction in difficult terrain (Figure 3.3). The Uganda Railway from Mombasa to Lake Victoria was similarly built for political purposes, although ostensibly for humanitarian reasons, to eliminate the slave trade. The British government was criticised for undertaking the enterprise, dubbed the 'Lunatic Express'. Others, notably the Khyber Pass line built in the 1920s over a length of 42 kilometres for a cost of more than £2 million, could only be justified on strategic grounds.

Many of the grand plans, however, did not come to fruition. Thus the projected Cape to Cairo Railway and the Trans-Australia line from Darwin to Adelaide were never built. Others proved to be financial liabilities and were closed after only a few decades of use, such as those on the islands of Zanzibar and Labuan.

Plans for colonial railways were drawn up on a grandiose scale during the 'Railway Mania' in the British Isles in the 1840s. However, only Jamaica executed its plans and constructed a line in 1845, extending some 22 kilometres from Kingston. It was only in

51

Figure 3.3: Canadian Pacific Railway embankment

the 1850s that the railway systems of India, Canada and Australia were commenced and in the 1860s in South Africa and New Zealand, while Western Australia opened its first line in 1880. Nevertheless, most colonial authorities considered the construction of railways and the majority had done so by 1930 when, in addition to the dominions, some 35 colonial lines were in operation and two had already been dismantled. The systems ranged from the extensive networks of Canada and India with approximately 70,000 kilometres a piece to 13 colonies with less than 250 kilometres of track. By 1930 a total of 236,000 kilometres of railway line had been laid in the British Empire outside the British Isles (see Table 1.1).

Integrated systems were few outside India and those Dominions where there were interior focuses of political and economic power. Most colonial lines were built as links between the port and interior resources, whether agricultural regions, mining centres or strategic points, with a view to facilitating trade with the metropole. In the majority of cases little else was accomplished, although subsequently more than one line might be opened to focus upon the port and further emphasise its primacy. Thus the Jamaica railway was extended in the 1890s with new lines crossing the island to link the north coast settlements of Montego Bay and Port Antonio to Kingston (Eisner, 1961). The pattern of separate colonial lines attained its most confused state in Australia where no agreement on a standard gauge was reached, so that the various colonial authorities developed their lines on differing gauges, making intercolonial transportation difficult. Accordingly the railway system of each colony focused the trade of that colony on the capital, even when some settlements were close to a rival colony's capital in terms of distance. The costs of physical transshipment of goods at colonial borders was such as to emphasise economic as well as political separateness. Thus the trade rivalry between Adelaide and Melbourne in the middle Murray River region was largely determined by the rail lines of differing gauges laid by the South Australian and Victorian governments. Indeed crossing the Murray River between New South Wales and Victoria was compared to crossing an eastern European frontier, so separate were the two systems, particularly before 1901 when the Victoria government maintained customs posts at the crossings.

Many of the smaller lines were financial liabilities to their owners, and frequently their assets were acquired by the government as the only means of ensuring their survival. The Jamaican railway system was subject to several changes of ownership, ultimately ending as a government liability. Even in the 1890s an official commission of enquiry reported that the Jamaica railway had 'no reasonable prospect of obtaining from traffic such a sum sufficient or nearly adequate to meet the interest and the cost of management and maintenance' (Great Britain, 1899: 6). Indeed state ownership or financial guarantee of colonial railways was common, often from the inception of the systems, as private investors demanded security which only the government could provide. The infamous Nyasaland government guarantee to stockholders on its railway system from the Mozambiquean port of Beira is a case in point (Vail, 1975). Payment of interest took precedence in the colonial budget placing a severe strain upon the entire Nyasaland economy in periods of depression, while the line benefited only one section of the economy, the European plantations, during periods of prosperity. Railways also experienced increasing problems of deterioration and competition from road transport, and by the 1930s the smaller lines were being closed. The Barbados line only opened in 1881 suffered from rail corrosion and frequent washaways on embankments, which resulted in unprofitable operations (Fletcher, 1961). In 1916 it was acquired by the government and was finally closed in 1937 in the face of successful and cheaper road haulage competition. Similarly the short (13 kilometres) Malta Railway between Valetta and the second city of Medina could not survive competition from the motor car and was terminated in 1931.

The development of the railway systems of India on the one hand and southern Africa and Canada on the other illustrate two trends in Imperial railway construction, strategic and economic. Although plans for Indian railways had been launched in the early 1840s, it was only in 1853 that the first short line was opened in Bombay, followed by the other presidency towns, Calcutta (1854) and Madras (1856). In each case the strategic importance of linking the bases of British power in the interior to the administrative bases on the coast was dominant, particularly after the rising of 1857. The engineering problems confronted in crossing the Ghats or the Bengal swamps and rivers were immense, but overcome at considerable financial outlay. The cost of engineering works on the line crossing the Ghats in the 1850s was £11,000 per kilometre. By 1870 some 7,634 kilometres of railway had been laid and India was traversed by lines linking Lahore and Delhi in the Punjab to both Bombay and Calcutta.

Construction of the Indian system continued, to reach over 69,000 kilometres by 1936, with the most active period of expansion in the 1890s and 1900s. In 1870 the Indian States, starting with Hyderabad, began to build their own systems linked to the British system. Also in 1870 as an economy measure, narrow gauge (1 metre) lines were approved for branch lines, but broad gauge (1.68 metres) was retained for all main lines. The 1870s were also significant for linking railway building to famine relief, when the famine of 1874–9 had to some extent been alleviated by the transfer of grain from surplus to deficit regions. This produced the intriguing calculation from the Indian Famine Commission of 1880 that 'one train in a day of sixteen hours was found to do the work which it would have required 2,500 camels to do in a fortnight' (Sahni, 1953: 23).

The Indian railway system became one of the major employers in India with nearly 750,000 employees by the 1920s. Separate railway towns were established adjacent to the main centres, further adding to the complexity of the Indian city. Workshops were constructed, initially with the Great Indian Peninsula Railway Company's works at Byculla near Bombay, but paralleled by others, including the extensive Howrah coachworks also founded in the 1850s. Locomotive construction began in the 1890s and the industrial plants of Jamalpur and others pioneered heavy engineering for the railway companies, encouraging the formation of local iron and steel works in the first decade of the twentieth century. The insatiable demand for coal similarly stimulated the Indian mining industry to replace imports from the British Isles.

The massive engineering works required from the inception of the Indian railway system posed problems which were tackled on a grander scale than in England. By 1930 some £65.3 million had been invested in railway construction and two-thirds of the public debt of the Indian government had been incurred for use on the system (India, 1945). Engineering feats such as the railway bridge at Patna over the Ganges, built in 1900, was some 3,064 metres in length divided into 93 spans and clearly involved design and construction work of a high order. Bridges were not always so well designed or appreciated. The Landsdowne Bridge over the Indus at Sukkar, constructed in 1889, although ingenious, has been described as 'perhaps the ugliest ever built', as the basic double-decker, road-rail bridge was held together by an apparently unattractive linking of iron girders (Morris and Winchester, 1983: 124). In facing the challenge of ascending the Himalayas, the Darjeeling Railway (1878) climbed over 2,000 metres in 60 kilometres with gradients of up to 1:19. Construction problems were solved through the employment of an intricate system of loops and reversing stations, which remain today as one of the most spectacular monuments to the Imperial railway engineer. Such intricacies as the 'Agony Point' loop on the Darjeeling line or the 8 kilometres of tunnels on the Kalka-Simla line (1903) illustrate some of the most splendid solutions to railway building in mountainous terrain, facilitating the linking of the hill stations with the plains.

Indian railway companies directed much attention and capital to the erection of the principal railway stations, which were, as a result, often the most spectacular public buildings in Indian cities in the late nineteenth and early twentieth centuries. The massive, dual-purpose, crenellated fortress station at Lahore is an indication of one motive in design. In general, companies were intent on proclaiming their stability, wealth and Imperial interests. The Victoria Terminus of the Great Indian Peninsula Railway in Bombay was completed in 1887 at the then enormous cost of £250,000. The architect, Frederick William Stevens, employed an exciting and essentially Victorian blend of Venetian-Gothic design and Indo-Saracencic motifs, which epitomised the search for a new Anglo-Indian Imperial style (Figure 3.4) Philip Davies (1985: 175) describes the effect as 'proclaiming British supremacy to the world at the zenith of Empire. It is Xanadu conceived through very English eyes'.

In southern Africa the first lines constructed in 1860 were designed to link the ports of Durban and Cape Town with their immediate farming hinterland. Lacking any strategic impetus to railway building, only 99 kilometres had been laid in the subcontinent by 1870. Economic expansion associated with the revenues derived from the Kimberley diamond mines and pastoral produce, quickened the pace of development (Table 3.1). However, it was only with the discovery of gold on the Witwatersrand in 1886 that a concerted programme of railway construction was undertaken. Within ten years Johannesburg was linked by rail to the ports of the Cape of Good Hope and Natal, and to the Portuguese port of Lourenço Marques in Mozambique.

As the colonial economic system of southern Africa was expanded through the opening of new territories to exploitation, particularly mining, so the main line system was extended northwards. In the 1890s the British South Africa Company extended the line into its territories in Southern Rhodesia where a 'Second Rand' was anticipated. By 1910 Rhodesia Railways had reached as far as its directors' latest objective, the Copper Belt in the Belgian Congo. In addition to the trunk lines, branches were constructed, particularly in the first 30 years of the present century, to link mines

Figure 3.4: Victoria Terminus, Bombay

Table 3.1: Railway construction in southern Africa, 1860–1930

Years	Cape of Good Hope	Natal	Kilometres opened Orange Free State	Transvaal	Rhodesia & Bechu- analand	Total
1860–70	91	8	–	–	–	99
1871–80	1,370	152	–	–	–	1,522
1881–90	1,387	320	194	66	–	1,967
1891–1900	704	347	514	1,333	1,008	3,906
1901–10	1,978	680	877	1,331	2,344	7,210
1911–20	1,530	605	566	1,483	234	4,418
1921–30	1,493	312	467	1,006	173	3,451
Total	8,553	2,424	2,618	5,219	3,759	22,573

Source: Annual reports of South African Railways and Harbours and Rhodesia Railways. The figures may not tally with those in Table 1.1 as lines lifted by 1930 remain in totals.

and more especially developing and potential agricultural regions. The maize-producing regions of the eastern Orange Free State and the irrigation settlements of Natal were all linked to the national network of southern Africa. The system being almost entirely state owned and planned was built on economic principles. Furthermore the operation and development of the harbour system after 1910 came under the same administrative department, resulting in a highly integrated transportation network, which through the manipulation of tariffs was able to influence the spatial pattern of economic development in southern Africa.

Similar patterns emerged in the other settler colonies and dominions. The planning of branch lines and stations in the Canadian prairies by the Canadian Pacific Railway and other lines was designed to bring the entire cultivable area within economic cartage of a railway siding and its silos. Agricultural development and the provision of railway facilities were inseparable. The competition between the Canadian Pacific and Canadian National Railways in the 1920s resulted in the construction of some 6,678 kilometres of branch lines in the Prairie Provinces and a marked northward shift in Canadian Pacific interests (Figure 3.5) (Lamb, 1977). Competition for railway links was also a notable feature of many colonies where competing local service centres sought to boost the local economy at the expense of their neighbours through the detailed routing of the line of rail. Political considerations were often significant in explaining the precise lines chosen as parliamentary committees and cabinet ministers in charge of railways dispensed political

Figure 3.5: Branch line construction in the Prairies in the 1920s

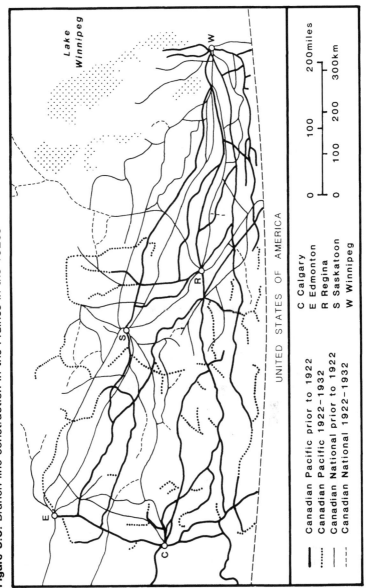

Lake Winnipeg

UNITED STATES OF AMERICA

—— Canadian Pacific prior to 1922
········ Canadian Pacific 1922–1932
—— Canadian National prior to 1922
--- Canadian National 1922–1932

C Calgary
E Edmonton
R Regina
S Saskatoon
W Winnipeg

0   100   200miles
0   100   200   300km

favours to supporting communities. The famous 'Octopus Act' of Victoria in 1884, which authorised the laying of 65 new lines some 1,870 kilometres in length, abandoned economic calculation as the basis for the approval of new railway lines (Rimmer, 1975). Thus often speculative building led to an oversupply of lines, but through competition and abandonment in the slump of the 1890s some rationalisation was achieved. Here the American model of railway construction as a precursor of settlement and economic development was adopted in Australia. As in America, however, not all railway schemes were successful.

The railways were to remain the subject of the utmost controversy as befits such significant precursors of social and economic change and tangible symbols of Imperial expansion. Popular views often reflected the nineteenth century literary hostility to industrialisation. Thus, writing of East Africa, Karen Blixen (1937: 153) considered that 'when the first stream engine was constructed, the roads of the races of the world parted, and we have never found one another since'. However, this is contrary to the Indian experience where the railways were rapidly assimilated into the daily life of the indigenous population. By 1920 some 1.2 billion passengers and 90 million tons of freight were carried annually on the Indian system, which today remains one of the most powerful forces for national integration. In academic debate the 'civilising rails' were initially deemed to be one of the most important elements in the opening of Africa to Western influences and modernisation. While more recent revisionist interpretations have presented a case for the 'decivilising rails' leading to dependency and decay notably among southern African indigenous societies (Pirie, 1982).

POSTAL SERVICES

The dissemination of information throughout the British Empire was an essential part of the political, economic and social systems upon which it was based. Knowledge of political events, government policies and colonial reactions were vital for the administrative functioning of the colonies. Traders and producers similarly required information on prices, production and prospects for the profitable conduct of commerce, and hence the various import and export activities of the colonies. Finally individuals in the metropole and colonies desired personal information on the progress of relatives and friends separated by considerable distances. The volume of such communication increased rapidly in the nineteenth and twentieth centuries paralleling the increased complexity of administration and the growth of bureaucracy on the one hand and the growth of trade and the organisation of international markets on the other. In addition rising literacy among the English-speaking population, particularly in the late nineteenth century as a result of the introduction of compulsory education in Great Britain and some of the colonies, generated massive increases in communication flows.

Until the nineteenth century the postal systems of the Empire were rudimentary and expensive. Use of them was limited to the wealthy and the official and commercial correspondence for administration and commerce. Ships carried the mail subject to the same vicissitudes as passengers, while urgent official despatches might be sent by the Royal Navy. Once post had arrived in the colonial ports and capitals the internal distribution was limited and often relied upon the communication systems of Colonial Secretaries for the despatch of letters and other materials, including newspapers and Government Gazettes to magistrates, district commissioners and other officials. The army ran a parallel system of field offices and distribution to military units.

The increased demand for postal services led to a number of major reforms. The British postal reforms introduced by Sir Rowland Hill in 1840 were emulated throughout the Empire in the following two decades as the British Post Office relinquished control of many colonial systems. The colonial dependence upon a regular mail system was echoed by the weekly *Eastern Province Herald* in 1855 which on noting that no mail from England had arrived since the last issue, declared that there was no news to print! Regular shipping made available through the development of steam vessels enabled speedier communication with England. The colonial governments awarded contracts to shipping lines which undertook to maintain regular weekly mail services, taking a set number of days. The shipping lines thereby gained assured revenues and often subsidies for the service. The growth of such services may be measured by the flow of postal items from Cape Town to Southampton. In 1873 some 300,000 items were sent to England by ship, whereas 35 years later the number had increased to 8,900,000. Internal communication was improved through the introduction of the coach services and postal couriers in the more densely settled parts of the mid-latitude colonies where road systems were upgraded. Later the railways moved the bulk of mail.

Expanding private demand for mail services from an increasingly literate population resulted in the establishment of separate colonial postal departments, and incidentally from the 1840s onwards, distinctive colonial postage stamps; which in virtually all cases depicted the sovereign's head, adding a sense of unity to the Imperial postage system. Post offices were erected in the main centres and a network of specialised postal buildings was built throughout the Empire in the second half of the nineteenth century. Competition between communities for new post offices was often stiff. Although colonial governments regarded postal services as a public non-profit-making service, the communities for whom postal, savings bank and money order facilities were introduced had to show that they would be financially viable (Osborne and Pike, 1981). Factors such as literacy rates, ethnic background, occupation and even political persuasion all influenced the decision as to whether to establish a post office in a particular centre. Thus in Canada, post office provision in Quebec lagged far behind that of Ontario reflecting differing rates of usage and cultural background. At micro-level regarding the location of post offices within a community in Quebec location was sought close to the church while in Ontario location near the centre of commercial activity was chosen — a reflection of differing attitudes in regions of dispersed settlement with no village cores.

Within cities, sub-post offices were established as well as a system of collection boxes. These minor features of street furniture remain as reminders of the Empire in the present time, even if they are no longer painted pillar box red, nor indeed if the royal cyphers have been removed. The internal city systems introduced house-to-house delivery thereby speeding up the dissemination of information, financial accounts and statements as well as private letters. The rising flow of correspondence was only stemmed with the introduction of the telephone system, which introduced yet another aspect to the city-scape prior to the laying of underground cables.

Increased use of the postal system led to the reduction of postal rates and finally in the late 1890s to the introduction of Imperial Penny Postage, whereby a letter could be sent from one part of the British Empire to another for the cost of an internal letter. The flow of letters and parcels was thus cheap and delivery was guaranteed, if not initially to the recipient's front door, as in the cities, at least to the nearest post office in the rural areas. Rural services improved as newspapers and later mail order catalogues became significant elements of the service. These helped to reduce the disparity between rural and urban living standards through facilitating the flow of information and goods into the rural areas.

In order to administer these services the colonial governments ran the postal services. Post offices were among the largest of the government buildings being erected by the end of the nineteenth century, rivalling town halls and administrative offices for grandeur. The extension of postal services was such that by 1930 there were over 53,000 post offices in the Empire outside the British Isles, as well as a number in other countries including Morocco, Kuwait and Oman which were closely integrated into the Imperial system. The British postal systems in China and Turkey had been dismantled in the 1920s while the extensive network in Latin America and countries such as Thailand had been closed following the inauguration of the Universal Postal Union in 1874. It should be noted that 24,000 post offices were situated in India, more than the number for the United Kingdom. In terms of post office provision the dominions of Canada, Australia and New Zealand each had more than one post office per 1,000 inhabitants, indicative of the need felt by settler societies for communication and links with relatives, friends, news and markets.

TELEGRAPHS

The search for improved and more rapid forms of communication was successful in the early nineteenth century with the invention of the telegraph, which enabled signals to be sent along wires over short distances (1837). Improved technology increased the distances which could be traversed, but it was the development of the submarine cable which was to revolutionise Imperial communications. The first cross Channel cable was laid in 1850 and Ireland was linked three years later. Improvements in cable manufacture, laying facilities and signal booster techniques enabled the Atlantic to be crossed by the end of the decade. The possibilities of a worldwide all-British network of telegraph cables were realised in the remaining decades of the nineteenth century — a reality evident to the Germans at the outbreak of the First World War.

The telegraph system was essentially of two parts, the intercolonial, usually submarine system and the internal land systems. The latter were erected rapidly to link up the various administrative centres of the colonies and particularly to link the more remote and militarily sensitive frontier zones, notably in India. In 1854 Calcutta was linked to Agra some 1,300 kilometres distant, and in the following decade to virtually all the centres of the subcontinent, facilitating the control of the Empire from the summer capital at Simla. Although the telegraph system was initially expensive, government officials made substantial use of it. Ministers in self-governing colonies and dominions in the nineteenth century at times used the system as virtual government monopolies to transmit long reports and instructions. The result was a much tighter rein being applied to remote officials and officers who were instructed more rigorously and subject to instant supervision. Internally too the major commercial houses and banks could solicit information, transfer credits and supervise their trade systems on a day-to-day basis. The telegraph thus contributed to the increased centralisation of the trade and finance firms.

It was the international implications of the telegraph which were particularly long lasting. The intercontinental links concentrated initially on communication with India in 1865, Australia (1872) and the Cape of Good Hope (1880) (Barty-King, 1979). Thereafter Imperial ambitions increased to lay all-British lines, most spectacularly demonstrated in the Pacific cable from Canada to New Zealand and the Indian Ocean telegraph from Natal to Australia, both laid early in the present century. Consequently by 1929 when the various British lines were grouped in one company, Cable and Wireless controlled 164,400 nautical miles of submarine cable, over half the world total (Figure 3.6).

The sudden increase in the speed of communication between Great Britain and the Empire resulted in a number of significant changes in relationships. Just as local officials became more directly answerable to the government in the colonial capital, so the Colonial Office in London became more closely concerned with the detail of colonial administration. Governments in Australia which might have taken six weeks to reach by steamship could be questioned or answered in a matter of hours. The flow of Colonial Office telegrams increased dramatically from 800 in 1870 to 10,000 in 1900 while letters increased from 13,500 to 42,700 in the same period (Blakeley, 1972). Similarly the commercial firms of London could obtain trade information from the colonies and plan accordingly. Hence the individual wholesale firm in the colonies was reduced to little more than a handling agent for the Imperial concern. Local knowledge built up through local contacts and judgements of the state of the market were available to the Imperial head offices which were able to direct commodity flows on a worldwide basis. Centralisation tendencies in administration were paralleled in trade.

Figure 3.6: British submarine cable system, 1929

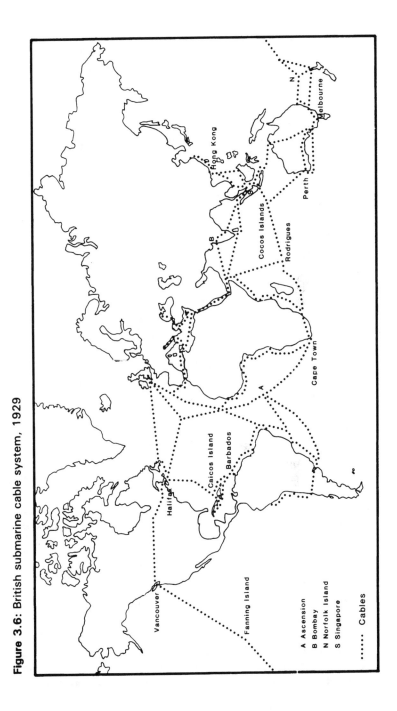

Hong Kong

N

Melbourne

Perth

Cocos Islands

Rodrigues

B

Cape Town

A

Caicos Island

Barbados

Halifax

Vancouver

Fanning Island

A Ascension
B Bombay
N Norfolk Island
S Singapore

..... Cables

The telegraph system required the maintenance of extensive land works. These included the various stations such as Fanning Island in the Pacific or the Caicos Islands in the West Indies, which represented the oceanic hubs of the systems. Ascension in the south Atlantic was considered to be of such importance to the Imperial system that it was administered by the Admiralty until 1922. In 1929 Cable and Wireless maintained some 253 cable and wireless stations manned by over 8,000 operators in their worldwide network. On land the wires had to be maintained and repaired, a particularly difficult job in states where the indigenous inhabitants valued the copper wire for other purposes, or where hostility resulted in frequent breaks in the line.

INVESTMENT

One of the more important linkages within the British Empire and beyond was the complex web of investments emanating from the London financial markets. The evolution of efficient means of investing in overseas ventures was slow and prior to the eighteenth century London followed, rather than led, Amsterdam in the practice of placing money in what was essentially a highly speculative enterprise (Wallerstein, 1980). Few individuals were able to bear the expenses of overseas colonisation and exploitation and recourse was made to chartered companies with defined rights and duties subject to the grant of a royal monopoly in which only a few participated. By the nineteenth century public limited liability companies spread the investment net more widely both in terms of the greater numbers investing and in the wider range of projects undertaken.

Chartered companies formed to exploit the resources or conduct trade with foreign land were significant participants in the age of British expansion and proved to be exceptionally adaptable to change ensuring a remarkable longevity (Griffiths, 1974). The first English chartered companies were formed in the late sixteenth and seventeenth centuries to trade in defined areas of the world. Thus the East India Company obtained a monopoly on English trade with India and the East Indies and the Levant Company on trade with the Ottoman Empire and adjacent regions. The latter company failed to obtain a territorial base, but the former, together with a number of other companies, notably the Hudson's Bay Company, became military and administrative powers in their own right. They constitute one of the distinctive factors in Imperial development where the local authorities were responsible not to the British government but to a board of directors in London, whose primary concern was profit for their shareholders. The quasi-independent chartered companies require a special investigation regarding the impact of imperialism (Moodie and Lehr, 1981).

The chartered company remained an instrument of British economic penetration even after the ending of Company rule in India (1858) and the establishment of Dominion control over Rupert's Land in Canada (1870). A number of single-purpose chartered companies were formed in the nineteenth century to undertake tasks of a limited nature. These objectives ranged from agricultural settlement in Canada and Australasia to trading and ranching in the Falkland Islands. Significantly they lacked the administrative powers appropriated by many of the earlier companies. However, a new generation of administrative chartered companies was formed in the 1880s to act as agents for Imperial expansion where the government had no desire for direct involvement, notably in Africa. The British South Africa Company was the most important of the new group of governing chartered companies, although the British North Borneo Company was more long lasting as an administrative power.

The formation of public limited liability companies was streamlined as a result of the reforms introduced by the Companies Acts of 1858–62. The results were dramatic, with a series of company flotation booms and a vast outflow of investment capital from Great Britain to the rest of the world. In the period between 1870 and 1913 investors in Great Britain placed some 5.2 per cent of the country's Gross National Products in overseas lending (Edelstein, 1982). This was a unique occurrence. No other country approached this level of external lending and it has not been repeated since. Some 69 per cent of all new issue capital exported from Great Britain was invested in public utilities. Railway systems were the major recipients with 41 per cent of the total, while a further 28 per cent was directed towards tramways, docks, telegraphs, telephones, gas, electricity and waterworks. Such a massive investment in infrastructure clearly had profound effects upon the countries involved. The remainder was directed towards agriculture and mining (12 per cent), land trading companies (15 per cent), while manufacturing industry attracted a mere 4 per cent. The selective nature of British overseas investment reflected not only the early stages of development in which many of the recipient countries were

Table 3.2: British overseas investment, 1914

Country	Accumulated capital invested	(£ million)
A. British Empire:		1,780.0
Canada and Newfoundland	514.9	
Australia	332.1	
New Zealand	84.3	
South Africa	370.2	
West Africa	37.3	
India and Ceylon	378.3	
Malaya	27.3	
British North Borneo	5.8	
Hong Kong	3.1	
Other colonies	26.2	
B. Foreign countries:		1,983.3
United States	754.6	
Argentina	319.6	
Brazil	148.0	
Mexico	99.0	
Chile	61.1	
Russia	110.0	
Egypt	45.0	
China	43.9	
Other countries	402.1	
Total British overseas investment		3,763.3

Source: Fieldhouse, 1984; Platt, 1986, based on estimates produced by Sir George Paish between 1907 and 1914.

placed, but a recognition of the relationship between an industrial heartland in the British Isles and the colonial Empire supplying the raw materials for that industry.

After the First World War, British overseas investment was directed to a greater extent towards new industrial projects, as the opportunities for infrastructural investment declined, and towards new oil fields and rubber plantations, reflecting technological change (Kindersley, 1932). No strict comparisons are possible between pre- and post-1914 figures owing to differences in calculation and interpretation of results.

Approximately 68 per cent of the £3,800 million invested overseas by 1914 was placed in regions of recent European settlement (Table 3.2). The United States secured the largest inflow of capital (20.1 per cent), although Canada (13.7 per cent) was the major recipient in the 20 years before the First World War. India (with Ceylon), South Africa and Australia each absorbed approximately 10 per cent. It is noticeable that little preferential attention

Figure 3.7: Distribution of British investment in colonial land, 1913

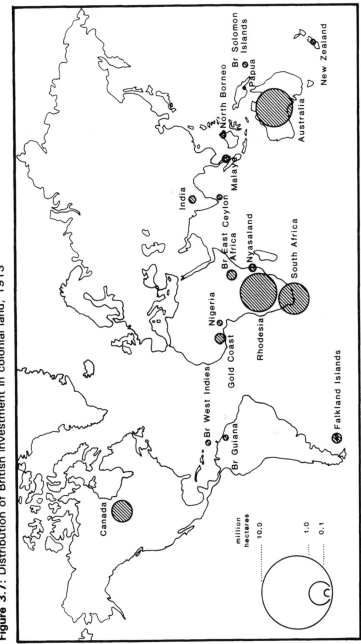

was directed towards British possessions as capital was exported widely to regions such as Latin America and Russia prior to 1914 (Fieldhouse, 1984). The figures have been subject to scrutiny as representing a nominal flow through the British capital markets and therefore representing totals which take little account of foreign investments placed through the London Stock Exchange, or subsequent purchasing patterns in bonds and securities (Platt, 1986). However, examining the direct investment in land by British registered companies, only half the land owned in 1913 lay within the British Empire (Christopher, 1985). This was initially concentrated in the mid-latitude dominions, but after the Rhodesian 'Age of the Fortune Hunters' (1890–6), became markedly African in concentration (Figure 3.7).

British capital entered all aspects of colonial production and commerce, often down to the direct ownership of the land involved in agricultural and pastoral production. The early phases of colonial exploitation were often undertaken by individuals or syndicates with limited financial resources. However, the demands for greater capital resources and the greater organisation of trade and production rendered such enterprise obsolescent, giving rise to the development of the major merchant banking firms, notably Rothschild and Baring Brothers (Chapman, 1984). London-based finance was linked to colonial financial and commercial expertise which initially was often locally controlled. Colonial banking facilities were at first locally owned, but due to their small size liable to failure in periods of economic depression. Thus banks in the colonies were either taken over in the 1860s and 1870s by banks based in London or driven out of business. In the Cape of Good Hope the rapid ascendancy of Imperial banks is evident as they used their superior financial resources to exploit the opportunities offered by periods of financial stringency (Mabin, 1985). Thereafter they were able to establish chains of banks in all the main and many minor towns, in order to offer loan capital, usually against the security of fixed property. London finance was thus intimately involved in the detailed planning of colonial ventures and the direction of colonial economies.

The penetration and control of colonial economies is illustrated by the change in the ownership of pastoral leases in New South Wales between 1865 and 1900. In the former year only 0.2 per cent of land was controlled by banks and a further 1.4 per cent by financial institutions. By 1900 these figures had increased to 21.3 and 43.6 per cent, respectively. Banks and companies exercised the supervision of pastoral holdings through the employment of inspectors, resulting in the reduction of the majority of New South Wales pastoralists to the status of tenants or occupiers-at-will, liable to eviction or dispossession at any time for not pursuing the farming practices prescribed by banks or investment companies. Significantly the banks and financial institutions did not eliminate the individual pastoralist, and amalgamate his holdings or run the enterprise through managers, they merely controlled him and restricted his freedom of management (Butlin, 1950).

Even more clearly the plantations of Malaya were controlled by finance companies through the agency system, and by the linking of individual plantation boards of directors through complex webs of interlocking directorships. The system was well developed by the First World War and was applied to other plantation regions, notably Ceylon and India. In Malaya the managing agency firms had their origins in the major merchant houses which dominated Singapore's commercial life in the late nineteenth century and later invested in and managed rubber plantations. Others began as commercial ventures in Great Britain and Europe and established links with Singapore-based firms. There were by the 1920s some dozen agencies which 'link together the agricultural and mining activities of the mainland, with the commerce of Singapore, the technical expertise of the Midlands and North Britain and the finance of London' (Puthucheary, 1960: 52).

The relative profitability of colonial investment is a matter of debate. Returns on capital invested declined after the 1870s more rapidly on colonial ventures than for home or foreign investments, resulting in comparatively unfavourable terms for much of the immediate pre-First World War era (Davis and Huttenback, 1982). As in so many ways the perceptions of colonial riches were not matched by reality. The host of bankruptcies in colonial enterprises attests to the speculative nature of many investments. Even the British South Africa Company failed to pay its shareholders a dividend for over 30 years, and was maintained financially as much for national prestige as for the hope of profit.

4

The Colonial Bases of Power

The linkages described in the previous chapter were operated by a substantial personnel who manned the naval and military bases, ran the trade system and carried out the administration of the colonies and dominions. The Imperial system was based first and foremost on naval power and intercontinental trade. In this respect the major arteries of Empire were virtually invisible except where they converged at strategic points or routes, such as the Suez Canal or Singapore. The naval bases constituted one of the essential chains of control for the maintenance of British freedom to trade and for the transportation of armies across the world to meet threats to British colonial interests. The bases were thus outward looking with little link with the territories in which they were situated, beyond the supply base towns. Naval bases were frequently not centres of commercial power and the major entrepots which played a vital role in British territorial expansion and colonial trade development required different sites.

Within the colonies control was exercised through the army for external and often internal security and through police forces which might on occasion be para-military in organisation and character. The main military effort was directed towards maintaining the security of the colonial borders. Hence most military bases and constructions tended to be in the frontier zones and in the chain of bases leading back to the ports securing the supply lines. However, in India and other tropical colonies the indigenous towns and cities were frequently regarded in official circles as zones of potential subversion and hence were overawed by the construction of major military cantonments adjacent to them, within which the army was housed to support the civil authorities.

Civil control was exercised through a colonial administration which was urban based and depended upon the police, judiciary and bureaucracy. The civil bases of administration were more evenly spread across the colonial territory, reflecting the population distribution and priorities assigned to the government. In this respect the administrative pattern tended to reflect the system of commercial enterprises, and commerce and administration were often closely linked. Civil power, being hierarchical in character, established an urban hierarchy of command which was often accepted by the merchants as the system for their transactions, although the administration might occasionally follow the traders to healthier or better situated sites.

NAVAL BASES

The British chain of naval bases established throughout the oceans of the world was the most comprehensive network created by any world power. The major naval bases had been founded over a long period of time at the ports of call of commercial and later Royal Naval vessels on the trade routes of the Empire. The struggle for supremacy waged by the Royal Navy until the end of the Napoleonic Wars resulted in the construction of a series of protected harbours with naval dockyards at a number of sites in the West Indies, Canada, Australia and India. This network was enlarged through the acquisition of strategic islands and towns on the main trade routes such as Gibraltar, Malta and Aden. Strategic importance was differently assessed in different ages as sailing techniques and technology altered naval requirements. Thus St Helena acquired in 1659 by the East India Company as a staging post on the route to India, was adversely affected by the acquisition of the Cape of Good Hope in 1806, with its superior site for a naval base at Simonstown, and later in 1869 by the opening of the Suez Canal. St Helena's strategic importance was thus severely undermined with disastrous consequences for its economy. Similarly Antigua in the nineteenth century ceased to be of major significance to the Royal Navy as its strength was reduced in the Americas.

Changing technology affected the need for bases in other respects. Steam power revolutionised transportation but introduced new demands. Regular coaling ports were required for vessels to operate on the high seas. Coaling stations for naval and merchant vessels were thus established in the nineteenth century throughout the Empire, and were generally strategically placed. Coal, notably

Welsh, was exported and stockpiled at such stations as Labuan on the South China Sea, to keep the Royal Navy mobile. In the early twentieth century similar facilities were organised for petroleum products as the Royal and merchant navies converted to oil for propulsion.

The range of facilities required at a naval base became more complex through time. Accordingly the early protected beach where careening and repair work could be carried out was replaced by more complex facilities where major repairs and even partial rebuilding of masts and rigging could be effected in the nineteenth century. Royal Naval dockyards in Halifax, Nova Scotia and Gibraltar and the East India Company yard at Bombay were equipped to undertake full fabrication and repair of vessels. The dockyards were refitted and extended according to defence plans at intervals, to provide facilities for vessels operating for long periods of time away from Home Waters, around the British Isles.

The bases established on islands such as Malta and Singapore were designed to offer a full range of facilities from revictualling to repair and construction. The size of their defence works was such as to secure large numbers of vessels from enemy attack and provide a base from which offensive operations could be launched. The dependence of the local economy upon the naval base was well illustrated on Malta where a third of the workforce was dependent upon the government for employment. The fortress image of the islands deterred any attempt to introduce alternative industries, leading to massive unemployment and out-migration (Blouet, 1984).

Valetta provided a vital link in the route to India, and in the build up to the First World War the naval facilities had been extensively rebuilt prior to the late decision to reduce the size of the Mediterranean fleet. Grand Harbour, with its adjacent inlets, provided sites for storage, repair and supply facilities as well as a large protected anchorage for the fleet. A permanent garrison equipped with hospitals, barracks and recreation facilities catered for the transient nature of the remainder of the naval population. In order to defend this major base, the town had been heavily fortified by the Knights of St John prior to the British occupation in 1800, and the process of fortification had been continued thereafter (Figure 4.1). The defence included the Victoria Lines constructed across the main island to protect Valetta from attack in the event of an enemy landing elsewhere on Malta. Malta accordingly presents a veritable museum of every type of defence construction devised from the sixteenth to the twentieth centuries (Figure 4.2).

Figure 4.1: Fortifications around Valetta

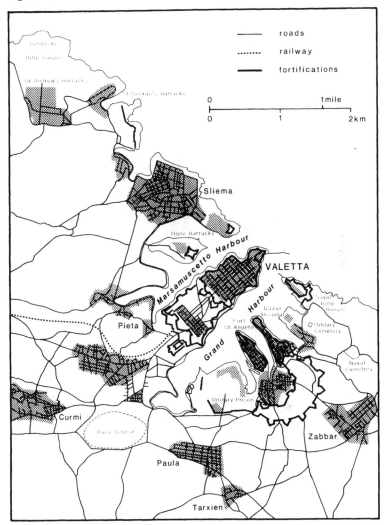

The majority of bases were smaller and lacked the massive defence works which surrounded Valetta. In the main this was because landward attack was not anticipated, an assumption which was to have such disastrous consequences for the defence of Singapore in 1942. The interior country behind the bases was assumed to be either in British hands or at least neutral. Further the physical detachment of the base areas from populated zones was

75

Figure 4.2: Fort St Angelo, Valetta

viewed as an advantage for defensive purposes. At Aden, acquired in 1839, the neighbouring sultanates retained a high degree of independence until the end of the colonial era, providing a landward *cordon sanitaire* against the intervention of other powers. The same basic assumptions applied to Hong Kong and Wei-hai-wei in North China. The latter was an ephemeral holding (1898–1930), abandoned as political conditions changed, and was not a precursor of Imperial expansion.

The manpower of the Royal Navy shrank by a third between 1914 and 1931 and reliance on home-based facilities became more marked. The exception to this was Singapore. The decision to build the Singapore naval bases was taken in 1921 in view of the possible naval threat from Japan which rendered Hong Kong and Wei-hai-wei untenable. In the words of the First Sea Lord, Singapore possessed 'the finest strategical position in the whole world' (Neidpath, 1981: 52). However, by 1930 few of the facilities had been constructed as the British government operated stringent economic policies on defence.

ENTREPOTS

Naval bases were not necessarily suitable sites for trade development, although many were so used. The principal British aim had been to secure trading stations through which goods could be exchanged and transferred for shipment between Great Britain and the colonies, and indeed independent states. The acquisition of such entrepot sites was often seen as vital to the expansion of trade by the traders and companies involved. The initial 'factories', later fortified storehouses, such as those built at Surat in India or Cape Coast in West Africa, were transshipment points designed to provide warehousing for incoming and outgoing goods. The latter, however, was but one of a line of slave depots established in the seventeenth and eighteenth centuries to supply the West Indies and adjacent mainland with a servile labour force, while the former fulfilled more closely the needs of a two-way trade initially between equal trading partners.

The bridgehead position was clearly significant among the sites chosen for many colonial cities, whether for small islands such as Bridgetown, Barbados, or Charlestown, Nevis, or as trade bases for major regions of the world such as Hong Kong or Singapore. The local configuration of coastlines, assessments of the potential communication systems into the interior of the trading area, or the centrality within a maritime trading system, all played their role in determining the selection of the site for an entrepot. Some sites selected after initial surveys were found to be unsuitable when interior communications were more realistically assessed, such as the changes in the position of the trading bases at the mouths of the Niger River (Ogundana, 1972). Burutu, established by the Royal Niger Company, replaced the less favourably situated Akassa (Fieldhouse, 1978) (Figure 4.3). Changing technology and changing physical conditions, particularly on rivers liable to silting, also led to the abandonment of bases in favour of new sites. In the Anglo-Egyptian Sudan, the historic Arab port of Suakin was abandoned in favour of the purpose-built Port Sudan, as the former was unsuitable for adaptation for the larger size of shipping in the early twentieth century and for the adequate provision of railway facilities on the island site (Hoyle and Hilling, 1970). However, in the vast majority of cases the early explorers and pioneers proved to have undertaken their investigations thoroughly and relatively few changes occurred.

Entrepots varied in character from the pure trading base to the colonial administrative capital (Figure 4.4). The majority of colonial

Figure 4.3: The port of Burutu, Nigeria

capitals were coastal in location and the link between commerce and Empire was always strong. The entrepot function of cities such as Sydney and Calcutta were merged with numerous other functions. However, in many cases the trading function remained dominant. In the early colonial period not only the prime capital sites were selected but also numerous smaller trading stations, to serve the main port of the colony and also to export directly overseas. However the technological changes wrought by the Industrial Revolution transformed the pattern of entrepots, initially pre-industrial in character.

In the course of the nineteenth and early twentieth centuries the technology and organisation of the shipping industry underwent a number of profound changes reflected in the ports. First, ships were converted from sail to steam and ultimately to oil power (Headrick, 1981). This enabled vessels to sail faster and on set courses without reference to the wind systems. For example, in the early nineteenth century and up to the 1850s, the time taken to travel from Plymouth to Sydney was approximately 100 days. Steam vessels in the second half of the century further reduced the time to 30 days (Jeans, 1972). Not only were sailing times reduced but reliable timetables of

Figure 4.4: St John's, Newfoundland

regular arrivals and departures could be drawn up. Motorised vessels revolutionised transport on rivers enabling light launches to penetrate at will far into the systems.

Secondly, vessels were constructed in iron instead of timber, with a resultant increase in size as the engineering problems were solved. Merchant as well as naval vessels could thus be built with tonnages of 20–30,000 tons by the twentieth century, enabling larger quantities to be transported and at reduced costs. The revolution in transport costs for Canadian grain exports to the British Isles is but one example of the worldwide change in transport economies (Perry, 1974).

Thirdly, the increased capital investment per vessel resulted in the organisation of a number of large shipping companies, which in turn in the 1880s initiated the formation of cartels. The shipping conferences sought to reduce competition and rationalise sailings and trade rates in different sectors of world trade (Solomon, 1982). Hence the shipping lines offered regular sailings between certain destinations and as a result abandoned smaller ports and concentrated their efforts upon a number of major centres with the facilities to handle the ever increasing size of vessels. This rapidly reduced the time spent in port and therefore the unprofitability to its owners.

Simplification of port systems resulted. The concentration of Australian trade in the colonial capitals and the decline or abandonment of most of the remainder is a case in point (Rimmer, 1976). The more complicated history of the Malayan port system illustrates the shifting provision of facilities related to government initiatives and private corporate responses. Malacca was replaced by Penang and later also by Singapore in the nineteenth century as the main port of the colony of Straits Settlements. Nevertheless, the development of tin mines in Perak and Selangor in the late nineteenth century prompted the government of the Federated Malay States to develop its own port at Port Swettenham, with full ocean vessel handling facilities in the first decade of the present century. However, the shipping lines with vested interests in Singapore and Penang resisted the move. They imposed heavier surcharges on trade bound to and from Port Swettenham than on that bound for Penang and Singapore and so effectively crippled the port (Lim, 1978).

Singapore illustrates particularly strongly the varied aspects of the importance of communications for an entrepot city (Tregonning, 1967). Established by Sir Stamford Raffles in 1819 as a potential trade and transit port, it depended upon its local coastal and wider oceanic links between India, under whose government it fell until

1867, and China. Its growth was rapid as traders and financiers utilised government encouragement and the facilities offered to them. By 1871 the population had reached 67,752 and in 1931 it totalled 445,719. Although initially designed as a trade centre for the East Indies and the Malay Peninsula, the opening of the Suez Canal in 1869 reduced the journey to England by some 5,300 kilometres and the tonnage of ships entering harbour increased markedly. In 1869 some 0.6 million tons were recorded, while in 1876 the figure reached 1.5 million tons. Extensive harbour works were initiated and in 1905 the government took over direct control of the port facilities. Trade increased rapidly as a result of the rubber and tin booms. The value of the port's trade stood at £61.3 million in 1911 but had attained £221.8 million in 1925. Furthermore inland communications were improved with the completion of first the west coast railway on the Malay mainland in 1909 and then the east coast line in 1931. The causeway linking Singapore with Johore Bahru in Malaya was completed in 1923, bringing the landward trade of the Peninsula even more effectively into the city's hinterland. The economy was however heavily dependent upon external trade and the depression of the 1930s was particularly severe for the city. The value of trade in 1930 had fallen to under half the 1925 figure. Symbolic of the entrepot role was the arrival of some 100,000 to 250,000 Chinese every year between 1900 and 1930, passing through Singapore to work in Malaya, and the smaller number who returned to China. Hong Kong as the southern entrepot for southern China developed along similar lines after its annexation by Great Britain in 1841 (Keswick, 1982).

A unique form of entrepot in the Imperial system was the botanical garden, which acted as a base for the introduction of new plants into the colonies, as well as the export of indigenous plants to Great Britain and other colonies. The primary purpose of the network established throughout the Empire was well expressed at the founding of the Royal Botanical Gardens at Calcutta in 1787 as:

> not for the purpose of collecting rare plants as things of curiosity or furnishing articles for the gratification of luxury, but for establishing a stock for disseminating such articles as may prove beneficial to the inhabitants as well as the natives of Great Britain and which ultimately may tend to the extension of the national commerce and riches (Brockway, 1979: 75).

The key link in the system became the Royal Botanical Gardens at Kew, which despatched explorers to locate new plants and return with examples of plants and seeds. The Andes and the Himalayas proved to be remarkably rich sources both for government and private collectors, contributing not only commercial plants including cinchona but decorative garden species and flowers which were also dispersed throughout the world, including such 'English' plants as rhododendrons and many species of rose. The plants collected were examined, researched, and where suitable sent to other gardens in the Empire for investigation into their commercial possibilities. Accordingly tea bushes were sent to Jamaica, tobacco and cinchona to St Helena, rubber to Adelaide and Pietermaritzburg and pine-apples to the Straits Settlements. Botanical gardens were laid out in virtually all the colonies beginning with St Vincent in the mid-eighteenth century. They were established not only in the capital but often in a range of climatic conditions in order to test the climatic suitability of the plants. Thus Ootacamund at an altitude of 2,210 metres complemented sea-level Calcutta, and Kampala in Ceylon was established specifically to propagate rubber plants at a higher altitude than the pre-existing garden at Peradeniya.

In time, extensive botanical gardens formed an integral part of the plan of many of the larger colonial cities. Exotic plants were propagated 'as things of curiosity' and for the beautification of the city. Tropical houses to exhibit the rare plants of various parts of the world were also erected, virtually as municipal status symbols, encouraging an even wider dissemination, just as the conservatories attached to the houses of wealthier residents reproduced on a smaller scale the exotics of the government-run institutions.

MILITARY OUTPOSTS

The army had a far more all-embracing role within the colonies than the navy. Securing the boundaries and maintaining internal security were tasks which often required a wide deployment of personnel with marked influences upon the spatial organisation of the country and the cities. Security had been one of the chief concerns of colon-ial administrators and merchants from the inception of colonial enterprise. The factories established in India and the trading stations on the West African coast had initially been fortified. Indeed the West African establishments have been referred to as 'trade castles' (Von Dantzig, 1980). Cape Coast Castle and Fort George, Madras, were both founded to protect the trading community and their merchandise. Initially the whole British community lived within the walls of the forts. In the West Indies and in Canada forts were built to guard the ports and the major settlements. In the main the purpose of the forts was to protect British traders and settlers from attack from other European powers, and only secondly from the indigenous population. Inevitably, though, with the long period of European peace in the nineteenth century, the role of the fort changed to that concerned with the internal security of the colony and defence against indigenous enemies.

Chains of forts were erected on the main routes within colonies which experienced threats to British security, as well as in the frontier zones. Hence on the Canadian Prairies police posts were established at strategic points to regulate movement and control activity. In South Africa forts were erected along the eastern borders of the Cape of Good Hope to secure the boundary with the neighbouring Xhosa peoples. It was, however, in India that the concept of security and the position of the army assumed greatest significance and one of the few areas where British garrisons remained after the First World War.

The Indian Army was politically separate from the British army and not subject to the same parliamentary controls as its metropolitan counterpart. Although largely raised in India and officered by British personnel, it had been official policy since the Indian rising of 1857 to station British regiments in India to maintain a ratio of at least one European to every four Indian troops. Thus at any given time there were over 200,000 troops in India in the first third of the twentieth century. The Indian Army accordingly constituted a major element of the British presence in India and also a considerable source of trained manpower for deployment elsewhere in tasks ranging from surveying to road construction, in colonies as widely spread as Nyasaland and North Borneo.

One of the features of all major Indian cities and a fair number of minor ones was the cantonment. This was a separate, often physically detached district, devoted to the army. Within a cantonment the military authorities from the commander downwards were responsible for the organisation, planning and construction of the suburb. Not only were the officers' quarters, barracks, messes and lines of European troops segregated from Indian troops, but the infantry, artillery and other units were also segregated, as were the storage, repair and manufacture sectors. The cantonment was noticeable for its spaciousness. Extensive polo, football and cricket fields, together with race courses, golf courses and parade grounds

Figure 4.5: Frontier road and fortifications, Khyber Pass

resulted in a remarkably low density settlement. Because of the level of segregation between Indian and British, and even within British society between civil and military, the cantonment acted as a separate township with its own shops, places of entertainment and churches.

Cantonments varied substantially in size from the relatively small bases attached to some of the early British towns or hill stations, to the major establishments at Poona and Dehra Dun where the army effectively dominated the town. The latter housed the Survey of India which was responsible for one of the largest mapping projects undertaken prior to the introduction of air photography: the production of a one inch to one mile map of the Indian subcontinent. Even New Delhi, planned for the civil administration of the Indian Empire, included a cantonment as an integral yet physically separate part of the plan. The Commander-in-Chief of the Indian Army might stay in New Delhi at Flagstaff House, now the Nehru Museum, but the Commander of the Delhi garrison lived elsewhere, on the cantonment.

In contrast to the cantonment, the frontier districts, more

especially the North West Frontier, were active military zones throughout the period of British control. An intricate network of roads linked a series of forts to the bases at Peshawar and Quetta. The militarised nature of the landscape was apparent from the density of fortifications guarding routes such as the Khyber and Bolan passes (Figure 4.5).

The cantonment was transferred to Africa in the organisation of colonies following the partition of the continent. Many officers with Indian experience participated in the military occupation and administration of the African colonies and adopted Indian solutions to the problems which they encountered in their new situations. Thus Lord Lugard designed Northern Nigerian towns, including the capital at Kaduna, with the segregated cantonment. The British South Africa Company similarly laid out large blocks of land adjacent to the towns planned in the 1890s for the para-military British South African Police.

ADMINISTRATIVE CAPITALS

Colonialism involved a high degree of administrative regulation and the imposition of a substantial bureaucracy. Each colony from its inception was controlled and ordered by a government established either by the Imperial authorities in London, or acting on behalf of the British government. Thus a chain of command extended from London to the most remote outpost of Empire, operated through a civil authority based in the colony. British colonies tended to be less subject to detailed regulation by the metropolitan authorities than the French and Portuguese colonies and hence the Colonial Office was a relatively insignificant department of state until Joseph Chamberlain's assumption of responsibility in 1895. Accordingly, with notable exceptions, colonial authorities were rarely subjected to grand colonial theories and local administrations conducted their affairs within the general ethos of British policy rather than subject to the direct political control of parliament in Westminster. This provided greater scope for adjustments to local conditions and greater opportunities for local bureaucracies to impose their wills upon the population and upon the detailed planning of the landscape. This is not to suggest that civil services were vast and cumbersome. Even the largest, the Indian Civil Service, with the other agencies of local government and government controlled agencies only employed some 4.5 million people in 1911. In total 10.9 million were then supported by the state — a mere 3 per cent of the population, and noticeably less significant than the position in the modern state.

In each colony the authorities established a capital city. The site was usually determined before occupation, although the example of Sydney suggests that instructions could be overruled in the light of the assessment of the situation by local officials. The selection of a site for a capital was important as often the largest group of Europeans, whether administrators or settlers or both, would be concentrated within the primate settlement. Considerations of communications, both internal and external, water supply, health and economic development were of significance in determining the choice of a site. Communications with England were usually a dominant consideration, hence the majority of colonial capitals established by British authorities were on the coast, and only occasionally was the seat of government moved inland. Internal communications within the colony were also of significance, although not always as important, as roads and railways could be built after the town pattern had been laid out to overcome locational problems, and only rarely the other way around. Hence Victoria on Vancouver Island remained the capital of British Columbia after the centre of economic development moved to the mainland and Vancouver became the focus of trade and industry. Improvements in communication lessened the apparent disadvantages of Victoria's situation.

Health also played a role in site selection, and in tropical areas elevation was taken into consideration. Thus in Sierra Leone the establishment of Hill Station as a residential retreat above Freetown played a significant role in creating a healthy environment in the capital. Considerations of health led to some of the few moves in colonial capital sites, notably in Africa (Christopher, 1984b). Hence in 1850 when Great Britain purchased the Danish West African possessions, Christianborg Castle at Accra was acquired and was chosen as the capital in favour of Cape Coast, on account of its better health record. Similarly the move by the Kenyan administration from Mombasa on the coast to Nairobi in the Highlands was undertaken as much for the sake of the health of the administrative officers as to questions of promoting economic development. However, despite investigations undertaken with a view to relocating the Nigerian capital from Lagos to the interior, notably at the time of the unification of Northern and Southern Nigeria in 1914, no move was undertaken in the colonial era and the proposals of the British authorities were only acted upon in the 1980s. Conservatism thus led to the retention of a number of capital sites which proved to be inconvenient as regards communications, and were plagued by problems of health and flooding. Belize in British Honduras, with its propensity to flood, was only abandoned as the capital after the hurricane disaster of 1962. The ultimate administrative anomaly, Mafeking, remained until the end of the colonial era. A portion of the town, the Imperial Reserve, acted as the administrative capital of the Bechuanaland Protectorate although the remainder of the town lay within the Cape of Good Hope, some 29 kilometres from the Bechuanaland border.

A major problem of capital selection arose when colonies were merged or when federal groupings were established. The British government had at various times promoted a number of federal states, notably among the settler colonies, to establish the dominions of Canada, Australia and South Africa. It had also grouped non-self-governing colonies together for the sake of administrative convenience. Nigeria, the Leeward and Windward Islands and the extensive Gilbert and Ellice Islands group were cases in point. Other colonies had been merged with their larger neighbours such as Tobago with Trinidad or Labuan with Straits Settlements. No question of change in capital city had arisen as Scarborough, Tobago and Victoria, Labuan, lost their status to the substantially larger Port of Spain and Singapore, respectively.

The administrative system of Malaya presented one of the most complex patterns outside India (See Figure 7.2). The British settlements which formed the colony of Straits Settlements had been annexed piecemeal in the late eighteenth and early nineteenth centuries by the East India Company, and subsequently in 1867 separated from India. Singapore had been proclaimed the capital of the British Malayan possessions in 1832 as it was the largest and most important port on the Straits of Malacca. The various Malay sultanates accepted various degrees of British protection from the 1870s onwards as a measure of restoring internal order disturbed by external pressures and the advent of tin mining. In 1896 the four states of Negri Sembilan (itself a federation of several smaller states), Pahang, Perak and Selangor were linked to form the Federated Malay States. The capital of Salangor, Kuala Lumpur, was chosen as the federal capital as a result of its proximity to the main centres of mining and communication routes. In 1909 the four northern states of Kedah, Kelantan, Perlis and Trengganu were ceded to Great Britain by Thailand, but they chose not to join the federation.

Finally in 1916, Johore became a British protectorate but the Sultan also chose to become an 'unfederated' state. Attempts to link the various formal and informal administrative structures were unsuccessful prior to the Second World War with the result that Singapore and Kuala Lumpur shared the functions of the capital of British Malaya.

The federal dominions constitute a special feature of British rule. Inevitably the politicians examined the United States of America as a model. Consequently Canada, after much internal wrangling in which four existing towns were successively chosen as the seat for parliamentary sessions, followed the American example and selected the neutral site of Ottawa on the boundary between the two provinces of Quebec and Ontario, representing French and English speaking communities, respectively (Knight, 1977). The Dominion of Canada widened to include additional members after 1867, endorsed the choice. The Australian government similarly rejected existing colonial capitals in favour of a neutral federal site. The final choice of Canberra, sufficiently distant from both Sydney and Melbourne, provided the compromise of a city whose business was designed to be government, on the model of Washington. New Zealand, although not a classic form of a federation, similarly adopted a compromise between the rival claims of Auckland in the North Island and Christchurch in the South Island, to select Wellington on Cook Strait. The neutral site solution to selection of a federal capital did not appeal to the founding fathers of the Union of South Africa. In 1910 the somewhat unusual compromise of establishing three capitals was adopted. Cape Town became the legislative capital and the seat of parliament. Pretoria, in the Transvaal, became the administrative capital in which were situated the various ministries and departments of government; while Bloemfontein in the Orange Free State, became the judicial capital and site of the Supreme Court. Only Pietermaritzburg failed to retain the status of a capital city.

Non-self-governing colonial groupings did not incur such expense. Existing capitals were selected to fulfil federal functions. Accordingly St Johns in Antigua became the capital of the Leeward Islands and St Georges in Grenada served the same purpose for the Windward Islands. Lagos similarly retained capital status in the administrative re-arrangements effected in Nigeria between 1900 and 1914.

The capital city as the seat of the governor, however designated, acted as the centre for administration. The elements of parliament house, if self-governing, government house, law courts, cathedral, government offices, together with police and prison facilities, were built into all capital city plans. It is perhaps salutary to note that the prison was often the first public building to be erected — 'the first requirement of a civilised society' (Purcell, 1928: 89). Thus in Georgetown, Penang, the jail was built in 1805–6 but St George's Cathedral only in 1817–19. The range of government buildings expanded rapidly with the increasing complexity and nature of administrative functions in the twentieth century, thereby creating distinct government precincts. New educational facilities, schools, universities, archives, art galleries and museums were added to the administrative function. Whereas government departments had initially only provided the framework for development, notably surveys, communications, customs and protection; by the late nineteenth century administrations were increasingly involved in social issues, necessitating welfare, housing and other service departments. Social services, indeed, were more advanced in the Australasian dominions and states than in Great Britain.

Capital cities were thus designed to include substantial arrays of government buildings, or where little provision was made, major adjustments were implemented. The key elements of government offices and housing were arranged in great variety from the apparent unplanned situation in many capitals established in the seventeenth century, to the formal designs of nineteenth- and twentieth-century capitals. In general the design of government buildings was linked to a generous provision of open space. Entire city blocks were set aside for the major official functions while frequently vistas were designed to close upon prominent public buildings or monuments (Figure 4.6). Government offices were often designed to be impressive, even if this meant no more than being larger than the shops and houses around them. Government Houses were similarly designed as country villas with spacious surroundings, but rarely were they designed to be palaces capable of competing in grandeur with the major country houses of England. Only India provided examples of opulence for governors and officials, elsewhere it was the need for public economy which frequently intervened to prevent grandiose designs being carried out. Possibly the fact that Government Houses were rarely occupied by their incumbents for lengthy periods tended to reduce the urge to expand which affected private housing.

A range of smaller administrative centres for lower tiers of government ranged from major provincial cities with many of the

Figure 4.6: Government buildings in Sydney

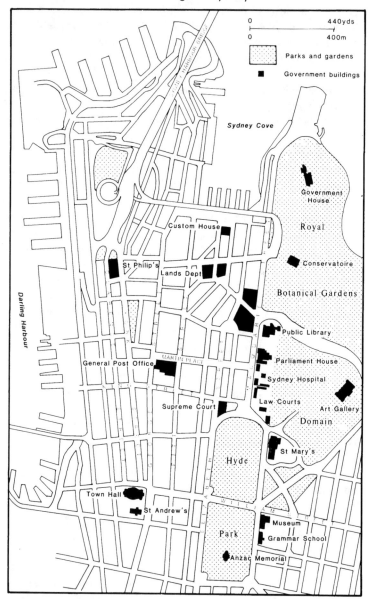

capital's functions and features reproduced, if on a smaller scale, to the minor centre with an all-purpose office housing the versatile District Commissioner or magistrate, who provided a complete government service, acting in a range of capacities from lawgiver to postman. The internal structure of local government was more flexible than the pattern of colonies and hence susceptible to frequent changes. In settler colonies local authorities, more especially city and town councils, gained a range of civic powers which were reflected in the often flamboyant town halls, which became all-purpose offices and meeting places symbolising municipal importance. Owing to the general fragmentation of local authorities in the late nineteenth century consequent upon urban expansion, many of the major metropolitan areas included several municipal governments. Greater Melbourne, for example, included some 24 separate jurisdictions by 1890, each with its own administrative offices and services separate from its neighbours (Dunston, 1984). Even planning regulations varied, leading to differing townscapes on either side of municipal boundaries, reflecting differing housing and road regulations. Only slowly were metropolitan-wide services established, beginning with the Melbourne and Metropolitan Board of Works in 1891, for the purpose of overseeing water supply and sewage systems. The administrative example of the London County Council, formed in 1889, was not emulated in Australia.

HIERARCHIES

The system of linkages together with the bases of power discussed in Chapter 3 and in the earlier sections of this chapter provide the basis for an examination of the urban hierarchy of the Empire. In 1931 London, with a population of over eight million was nearly six times the size of the next largest city, Calcutta — an extreme example of metropolitan dominance if the Empire as a whole is considered as a single system. However, the same relationships of dominance often existed within the colonies, and within the component parts of federations and unions. Hence in small colonies the capital was often the only settlement of any size. Thus in Barbados, Bridgetown was the only urban settlement and several times the size of the villages elsewhere on the island. At the other end of the scale the Australian state capitals dominated the hierarchies of their respective states.

Owing to their histories of separate political existence the ten

Figure 4.7: Urban networks in Southern Rhodesia and the Orange Free State, 1936

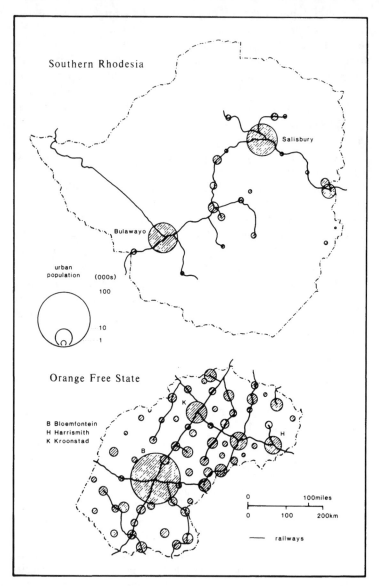

largest cities of the Empire included the three Presidency cities of India, namely Calcutta, Bombay and Madras, two of the Australian state capitals, Sydney and Melbourne, two of the Canadian provincial metropolitan cities, Montreal and Toronto, and one island base, Hong Kong. Only Toronto was not a seaport, although it was an inland port city and the commercial hub of the economically most advanced province of Canada.

Two different forms of urban hierarchy and network are present. The first is related to the colonies of settlement where the towns were planned and organised by settlers and colonial governments. The second was based on the mercantile principle propounded by Vance (1970) and structured to facilitate the import and export of goods according to the basic model of exploitation. In the former case a Christaller pattern of urban places was elaborated, notably in the agriculturally based regions including the Orange Free State in South Africa (Figure 4.7) and the Prairie provinces of Canada. In the latter case substantial areas remained basically unincorporated into the colonial economy and economic development was concentrated along the lines of communication, as in Kenya and Southern Rhodesia.

At the lower end of the hierarchy it has been noted that the small village and hamlet so common in Europe is lacking in most of the colonies of settlement. In the main this reflects a difference in settlement history where grouped agricultural settlement was rare, so that villages either were not planned at all, or died as settlers moved on to their own plots of land. The small service town thus was often the smallest urban place in the hierarchy in areas settled after 1840.

5

Settler Cities

British colonial authorities were faced as first priorities with the foundation of towns and cities. The networks of commercial, administrative, transport and military centres revolved around an urban concept of society in the first instance. Accordingly the initial acts of a colonial government involved the establishment of at least one town to fulfill these functions. Thus port cities were in general the foremost feature of the urban system. As the economy expanded so new towns were established, but usually the first foundation remained the most important city, became the colonial capital and developed into the largest urban centre in the colony. In many cases the first city plans had been conceived in England prior to settlement, at least in outline, while the later towns were planned in the colony itself.

The majority of British colonial cities were designed for a British or European population, on a site chosen for the purpose. Only in the later phases of British expansion in Asia and later Africa were pre-colonial towns adapted to colonial usage. Consequently two components may be distinguished: the unified settler city and the dual colonial city of tropical areas. Hybrids are evident where settler cities were modified in character through the migration of indigenes to the settler city and where the initial dualism was systematically broken down through replanning and social change. Inevitably the vast expansion of most cities since the end of the colonial era has profoundly affected their character, but often their origins are clearly distinguishable in the city centres and inner suburbs. It is proposed to deal with the settler colonies and the tropical colonies as two separate entities, although clearly there is an overall unified system.

The settler cities were created by British administrators and settlers for British settlers. As in many cases attempts were made to reproduce the English townscape, but on a more spacious scale. Few settler cities were cramped and in the majority of cases, space for expansion was viewed as presenting no problem for the town planners. Hence low-level buildings and sprawl were characteristics of colonial cities. These were noticeable first in the plans of the towns. The provision of open space and, by European standards, large building plots characterised cadastral plans. With no pressure on space, architects were not obliged to expand vertically except as prestige projects. The development of most settler cities also coincided with the revolutions in transportation of the nineteenth and twentieth centuries, and these concepts were built into their plans.

Government planning was clearly of the utmost importance in the colonial era, and plans and regulations were accepted constituents of colonial life. However private enterprise was not forgotten, and private towns were established to compete with government towns, although rarely as successful. Nevertheless, much of the urban expansion took place on lands already alienated by the government, and hence was dependent upon private initiative. The massive sprawl of settler cities was fueled by the same financial motives as in the United States city. Government planning also had comparatively little input into the mining camp and township. The various mineral rushes affected several parts of the Empire in the second half of the nineteenth century, but the resultant settlements were alien to the tidy minds of colonial administrators, who could do little beyond regulating the more disorderly features which appeared.

The growth of the settler city paralleled many features distinguished in the United States and West European city, yet colonial settler cities had different constraints related to their colonial status and the hierarchical society they embodied (Ward and Radford, 1983). Growth both in population numbers and in area were remarkable, yet the resultant cities were small by world standards. Indeed by 1931 only Sydney and Montreal in the temperate zone had attained a population of one million. However, the processes of internal differentiation were marked, with the development of distinct Central Business Districts and economic segregation in suburban areas, although the latter was less well defined than in England, as a result of the more equitable distribution of wealth in the colonial settler city.

PLANS AND URBAN DESIGN

Although governmental input into the planning and layout of the towns and cities in the colonies was substantial, blueprints for such settlements were rarely suitable for reproduction throughout the world. No grand design for a British colonial city, equivalent to the Spanish model, was ever evolved. Even such planning as was undertaken in London for the initial urban centres in a new colony was often changed as pioneers were confronted with the colonial reality. Thus the site of Sydney was revised after the arrival of the first fleet. However, a number of families of towns and cities may be distinguished, based upon their primary functions. Firstly, there were the major metropolitan cities, designed to be colonial capitals and hence including the major government buildings. Secondly, towns were designed to facilitate trade and administration beyond the capital. Thirdly, agricultural towns were planned to serve settlement schemes, and often lacked other aspects of urban facilities. The British administrations called upon experience in the British Isles and from existing colonies in the planning and construction of the settlements. Additional aspects were included with the annexation of territories occupied by other European settler communities, notably in Canada and South Africa, with their own colonial town planning heritage.

Early British colonial town planning was confined almost entirely to the West Indies and the mainland of North America. Indeed the colonies of the American South were closely related in terms of economy and society to those of the West Indies. Thus there was a constant interchange of ideas between them, resulting in a number of marked similarities (Reps, 1965; 1972). In common with the mainland colonies, the early British colonial town plans in the West Indies in the seventeenth century exhibited substantial variation. The initial island proprietors saw little need for town planning and the precedents of Spanish colonial urban design in the Americas were ignored. Towns such as Bridgetown, Barbados, had little overall scheme and were expanded from the initial harbour site as individual needs were perceived. The result was an irregular street plan, reminiscent of the unplanned towns and villages of England. Bridgetown and similar settlements were the earliest towns, laid out with a minimum of urban functions and designed to house only a few hundred inhabitants. The essential elements of harbour, fort, square, government building and church were all that they had in common.

However, the scope of town planning changed dramatically in the course of the seventeenth century as larger populations were anticipated and a more significant governmental presence became an influence upon colonial development. Late in the century comprehensive schemes with ubiquitous grid plans were adopted, which with some variation were to be reproduced throughout the British Empire until virtually the end of the colonial era. Kingston, Jamaica, founded after the destruction of Port Royal in 1692, was the most important of the early examples (Clarke, 1975). The initial town plan covered 100 hectares divided into a grid of streets and blocks, subdivided into rectangular plots. The focal point was the central parade, the equivalent of four blocks, around which the main buildings of church and state were constructed. Eighteenth-century extension adhered to the general design.

The contrast between the early proprietary settlements and the planned colonial governmental towns is well illustrated by a comparison of the two successive capitals of Bermuda (Figure 5.1). St George, founded with the colony, was irregular in plan. The fort, Town Hall, King's Square and St Peter's Church occupy apparently haphazard positions within the settlement. In contrast, Hamilton was planned on a grid pattern with town blocks set aside for the Sessions House, Secretariat and Cathedral. In common with many later colonial capitals, Government House is located outside the town grid in extensive gardens.

British town planning for the colonies became more exact in the later seventeenth and eighteenth centuries. The main direction was towards the 13 North American colonies where the designs for Philadelphia and Savannah indicated a break with the cramped medieval design of towns in favour of the grand plan of the Renaissance. Colonial governors were issued with Royal Instructions on appointment, which until the early nineteenth century included the principles of town planning, often in some considerable detail (Wood, 1982). The Board of Trade and Plantations in London, and its successors, provided a measure of continuity in plan and order, although the Board's officials had no first-hand knowledge of the colonies they were planning.

The layout of British settler towns in North America became steadily more elaborate. The organisation of the new Canadian provinces in the second half of the eighteenth century illustrate the problems raised by the attempts in London to exercise direct control over officials in the colonies. The layout of Charlottetown and Georgetown on Prince Edward Island in 1768 illustrate the imposition of a grid plan with open spaces and publicly reserved lands.

Figure 5.1: Plans of St George and Hamilton, Bermuda

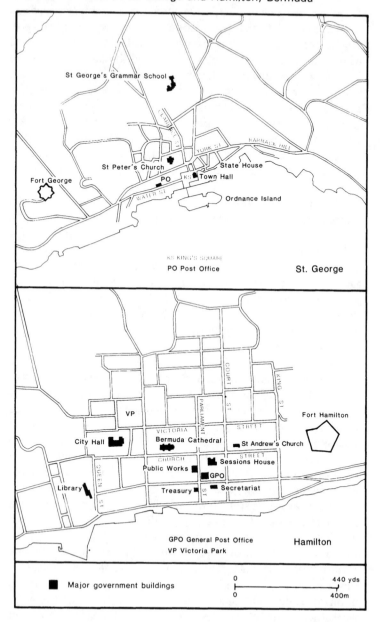

However, the Surveyor-General was able to translate the official model town into the urban plan on the ground with an eye to aspects of spaciousness, defence and ease of communications derived from his own practical experience. The resultant towns were therefore not copybook reproductions of the London-based model. However, in the layout of towns in Upper Canada in the 1780s the Royal Instructions were more precise and attempts were made to carry out the London plan in all its detail. Requirements provided for a chequerboard of square street blocks. The central square was to be an open space flanked on its four sides by the church, courthouse, school and workhouse. Other regularly spaced parks and public buildings occupied set places in the plan. Cornwall, on the St Lawrence River, was one of the few towns to be planned in detail according to the colonial model, but even here the scheme broke down. Few other towns were laid out adhering so closely to the model and a greater degree of flexibility was introduced to allow for the physical peculiarities of the sites.

Detailed planning of settler towns in England was not confined to the North American experience. In the settlement of Australia not only the capital cities were designed in advance, but some of the smaller towns as well (Gentilli, 1979). However, by the mid-nineteenth century local colonial experience was drawn upon to a much greater extent than in the previous century. This found its most notable expression in the family of 'parkland towns' laid out in South Australia and Victoria. George Goyder, the Surveyor-General of South Australia, produced in 1864 the sketch of a parkland town which became the model of urban settlement in the colony. The design made provision for a standard layout of public spaces and buildings, as well as commonages and suburban lots. Between 1865 and 1909 some 218 government townships were surveyed and 179 were either complete or partial reproductions of Goyder's design (Williams, 1966). The speed with which new towns were laid out to provide for an expanding frontier of settlement inevitably led in the later nineteenth century to the reproduction of a successful design which was easy to survey and which provided set areas for town plots, smallholdings and public spaces. Familiarity among urban pioneers with the survey system paralleled familiarity with rural surveys and standardised farm sizes.

One of the largest town planning schemes, outside India, to be undertaken in the twentieth century was the establishment of a capital for the Australian Commonwealth. Under the Australia Constitution Act a new, neutral, site for the federal capital was to

Figure 5.2: Canberra, *c.* 1930

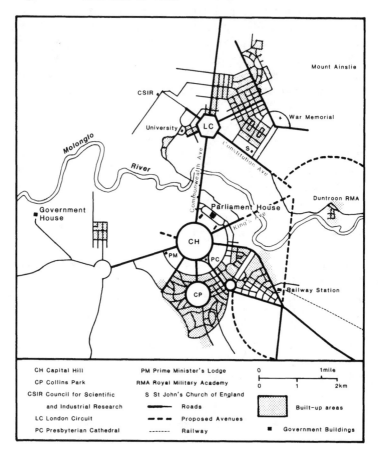

be selected at least 160 kilometres from Sydney, but within the State of New South Wales (White, 1945). In 1909 the site was selected at Canberra and in 1911 an international competition was held for the design of the city. The first prize was won by Walter Burley Griffin of Chicago, not by British or Australian entrants. The plan provided for Capital Hill to be the focal point of the city from where the main avenues, 60 metres wide, were to radiate outwards (Figure 5.2). The principal focus was to be upon the Parliament House, the symbol of Australian democratic government and political independence. Around this were located the other organs of government, the Prime Minister's residence, the ministries, Canberra

University College, Council for Scientific and Industrial Research and the Royal Military College. At the second focus, London Circuit, the civic and commercial sectors were concentrated. Significantly Government House, the residence of the Governor-General, was situated in extensive grounds outside the main urban area.

Considerable attention was paid to the garden city aspect of the project. An artificial lake was designed for the centre of the plan, while extensive tree planting within the city was complemented by afforestation of the neighbouring mountains. This concentration on government and gardens prompted considerable criticism and elicited the comment that it was 'a garden without a city' (Higgins, 1951: 88). The Federal administration had expanded since its inception in 1901 with new functions and therefore new departments handling matters including old age pensions (1908), the administration of the Northern Territory (1911) and health (1921). However, in 1927 when the official move from the temporary capital at Melbourne was effected, the Federal government only employed 1,700 people at its headquarters offices. Thus in 1930 the population of Canberra was a mere 8,719 and the area covered by the initial town plan was only filled out as federal government functions and its bureaucracy multiplied during the Second World War and thereafter.

MINING SETTLEMENT

The organised system of settlements, planned and laid out by the authorities, was interrupted by private settlements with less organisation and design. The major group of such settlements were established by mining communities. By the very nature of the activity little anticipation of development was possible and the level of government control was often limited. In the course of the nineteenth century a series of gold rushes, beginning with Australia in 1851 and concluding with the Yukon in 1898, resulted in the creation of new towns and the influx of large numbers of settlers not attracted by prospects of colonisation in a new land, but by the hope of acquiring instant wealth. As in the case of California in 1848 so men and women were attracted to the money to be made not only from mining but also from the provision of services. Towns thus formed the basis of the settlement, and only later were rural activities added if the mining settlements proved to be permanent and failed miners turned to agriculture for a living; or in the case of the Yukon abandoned the area altogether.

The British Empire contained areas of considerable mineral wealth. Gold was the most significant in terms of the ability to attract adventurers. Small quantities were traded from indigenous production in India and West Africa, but it was not until the discovery of gold in Victoria in 1851 that any significant source was found to be worked by European miners. The growth of these initial mining towns was spectacular. Some 250,000 prospectors came to Australia in the five years following the first strike. Indeed the population of Australia more than doubled in the course of the 1850s. Ballarat and Bendigo became notable towns. The boom, however, subsided and many miners left the goldfields for other cities and for the rural areas of Victoria. Rushes also attracted miners to British Columbia and New Zealand in the 1860s, with the same results.

Southern Africa proved to be the richest part of the Empire regarding minerals, although this fact was only discovered later. The first major mining rush took place as a result of the discovery of diamonds on the banks of the Vaal River in 1869 and subsequently the location of the kimberlite pipes in the vicinity of the future Kimberley. The initial widespread alluvial works along the terraces of the river were superseded by the exploitation of the diamondiferous pipes in the early 1870s. By 1877 some 20,000 people were enumerated on the diamond fields. The alluvial workings and the diggings on the claims on the main pipes required little initial capital. However, as the diggings became deeper so the problems of mining, removal of the diamond-bearing blueground and its processing, became more expensive. Problems of floodings, mining unweathered rock and collapse of neighbouring claim walls, allied to the expense of power and labour, led to a severe rationalisation of ownership during the economic boom of 1878–81 and the subsequent depression as the smaller and less capitalised claim owners were displaced.

The increasing centralisation of ownership and the depression in prices led to a number of significant changes in the mining industry which were to have a profound effect upon the subsequent development of southern Africa (Mabin, 1986). By 1889 the mines had come under the control of one company, De Beers Consolidated Mines Limited, and a central selling organisation was able to manipulate the market to maintain the price of gemstones. The mine owners also sought to consolidate their control over the workforce, which had proved to be highly restive during the depression. Here the force was composed of European miners, who had been reduced to paid employees of the major companies in the course of the 1870s, and a substantially larger number of Africans who sought work to obtain funds for goods and particularly firearms. In the period 1877–85 a series of wars had led to the consolidation of colonial control over the indigenous populations of southern Africa forcing increasing numbers to seek work. Company control over the workforce was regarded as vital to reducing costs through the maintenance of a steady, sober workforce and through the control of the illicit diamond trade which undermined world prices.

Company control was introduced in such a way as to establish the model company town in southern Africa which was to be emulated elsewhere, most noticeably on the Witwatersrand and in the Rhodesias. Closed segregated compounds were introduced for the control of the African workers who were restricted in movement for the duration of their work contract. Within the compound the worker was housed (at high density), fed, clothed and only given access to company facilities. This resulted in a reduction in absenteeism and rigid control over the labour supply and its wages, which could be depressed in times of abundant demand for work. The European labour force was controlled through the construction of a company village, Kenilworth, where tied company housing was provided for both married and single mine workers. A range of facilities was offered including a club and school, to create a self-contained community dependent upon the mining company. The company town devised in Kimberley in the 1880s was the model which was copied by other enterprises where corporate ownership dominated, particularly in the mining industry, but also in the agro-village of the colonial sugar plantations.

The development of the diamond fields was but the preliminary to the discovery of the gold-bearing reefs on the Witwatersrand in the Transvaal in 1886. This discovery led to the most profitable of the gold rushes, but due to the lack of alluvial gold, the individual prospector was soon displaced by the major capitalised mining houses. Shafts were sunk to considerable depths requiring both substantial capital outlays and specialised technical innovation (Scott, 1951). Thus in 1897 the Robinson Deep Mine had penetrated 730 metres below ground level and in 1917 Village Deep Mine had attained a depth of 1,675 metres. The value and scale of workings may be gauged from two sets of statistics. In 1898, the last full year of production before the outbreak of the Anglo-Boer War, the volume of production had reached 100,000 kilogrammes, worth

£16.2 million. The mines employed some 9,000 White and 88,000 Black workers. Thirty years later some 290,000 kilogrammes, worth £49 million, were produced by 216,000 workers, of whom 21,000 were White.

The resultant settlements were more akin to Kimberley than Australia in organisation, as most of the strenuous manual labour was undertaken by Black workers. These workers were recruited on contract terms to serve for short periods, usually under one year. The Transvaal Chamber of Mines appointed a Native Labour Commissioner in 1893 and in 1896 the Witwatersrand Native Labour Association was established to recruit workers from the Portuguese territories in Mozambique. The transitory labour force was housed in compounds on the mines, although the product was not of a portable nature as that on the diamond fields; which had been the reason put forward for enclosed compounds in the first place. The White labour force lived in the regularly laid out towns established along the 70 kilometre outcrop ranging from Krugersdorp in the west to Springs in the east.

The mining village was an essential part of the Imperial urban system, illustrating most clearly the exploitation of resources (Figure 5.3). The spectacular boom towns associated with the gold rushes or the discovery of diamonds were subject to marked fluctuations, as veins were exhausted or alluvial workings declined in profitability. However, mining for coal was often a more long-term business with the transfer of technology and manpower from Great Britain to the colonies. Consequently the development of coal mining in Australia and Canada soon took on many of the attributes of British mining, including the preponderance of English and Welsh mining names (Figure 5.4). The isolated mining villages located along the outcrops of coalbearing rocks became a feature of the colonies (Ironside and Hamilton, 1972; Wilson, 1968). Railways were laid to the collieries from the beginning of exploitation in most cases, as the railways were themselves initially one of the major users of colonial coal. The colonial mining settlement was, however, more spacious than its British counterpart. Back-to-back housing was not exportable for colonial European workers who generally enjoyed higher wages than their British counterparts. This nevertheless did not apply to mining activity in India, where Indian miners were more controlled, as were their African counterparts, and were housed at high densities in separate mining villages.

Figure 5.3: Broken Hill, New South Wales

Figure 5.4: Colliery settlements, New South Wales

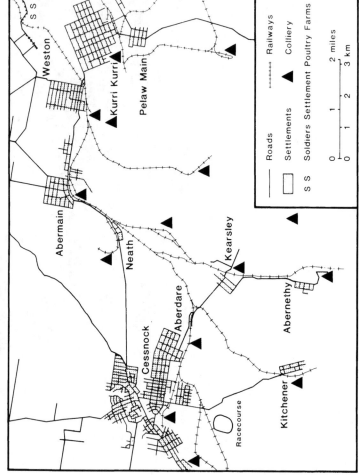

INTERNAL DIFFERENTIATION

The initial plans for largely undifferentiated cities were modified as the processes of growth and increasing complexity of the economy exerted an influence upon land use patterns. Within most major settler cities, and some of the smaller ones, government sectors had been established in the plans, with sites for churches, official residences and offices both for central government and municipal administrations. Otherwise central areas were little differentiated and the margin between city centre and suburbs undefined. However, paralleling developments in the British and North American cities change occurred in the nineteenth and early twentieth centuries in both the development of Central Business Districts and a range of economically segregated residential suburbs.

Settler cities were essentially mercantile in their origins and early development. In the majority of colonies, industrialisation, other than service and processing of local products, was little advanced until after the First World War. Manufacturing, even in the dominions, only became a major contributor to the economy once a reliance on imported goods was seen to be hazardous under wartime conditions. Thus the major towns developed their wholesale and retail trades together with the financial institutions required to facilitate economic functions. It was the wholesale trade which first developed a distinct quarter in the port cities, related to the port and internal transportation facilities. Warehousing was required for the bulk exports of sugar, wool, grain and later meat which the colonies sent to Great Britain and other parts of the world, and also for the storage of the great variety of manufactured goods imported in return (Figure 5.5) (Aplin, 1982). Given this degree of storage it is remarkable that comparatively little processing was undertaken to increase the value of exports. Wool washeries and sugar refineries made some contribution to colonial economies, but grain and meat exports did not lend themselves to preprocessing.

The other Central Business District functions remained comparatively undifferentiated compared with major British and American cities because of the limited scale of operation. Cities such as Sydney only developed retail and financial institution areas in the second half of the nineteenth century (Edwards, 1981). The Central Business District usually developed around the public buildings and market square which were features of the majority of town plans. This became the hub of communications and the location of business firms as colonial economies began to expand. Upward growth was

Figure 5.5: The development of the Sydney Central Business District

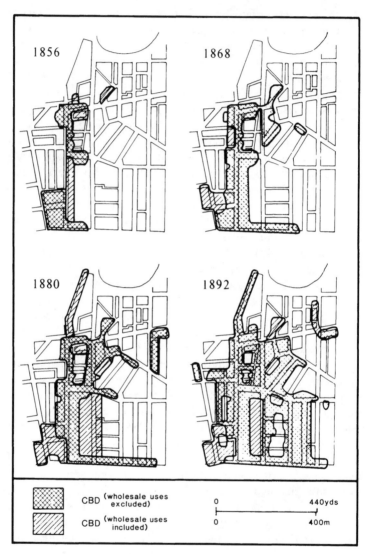

restricted until the 1880s by the problems of building techniques and communications. However, the introduction of reinforced steel frames and the improvement of lift technology enabled architects to erect higher and more demanding edifices. In this respect the colonies emulated the United States rather than Great Britain and a cycle of skyscraper building was only brought to a halt by the 1929 slump (Roth, 1979). As may be expected it was Melbourne in the boom of the 1880s which pioneered many ideas within the British Empire. In 1885 Prells Building — some 30 metres and ten storeys high — marked a significant development in design. It was superseded four years later by the 53 metre (12 storey) Australia Building which was to remain Australia's tallest until the 1950s (Wilson and Sands, 1981). Planning restrictions in the form of a height limit prevented any further upward growth in Melbourne. Other, Canadian, cities were not so inhibited.

TRANSPORTATION

The introduction of public transportation systems and the technical innovations applied to both private and public systems profoundly affected the course of the development of settler cities in the nineteenth and early twentieth centuries. The physical constraints upon expansion imposed by the walking city as evident before that time in Europe were not evident in colonial cities, which in the early nineteenth century housed only small populations with few appearances of overcrowding or cramped conditions. City authorities and private individuals adopted transportation innovations designed for larger, more populous centres, which when applied to low-density urban areas in the colonies resulted in virtually continuous suburbanisation. Technical innovation therefore made the sprawl of the nineteenth and early twentieth century settler city possible on a scale far beyond that experienced in the British Isles. Transportation systems were thus more influential upon the development of youthful cities which were generally without any well entrenched physical or social structures, or which were planned to incorporate the new systems within their fabrics.

Although horse-drawn buses and suburban train systems were introduced to a number of settler cities, it was the tram which was the major influence upon decentralisation prior to the mass ownership of the motor car. Trams introduced cheap transport and the means of carrying people several kilometres relatively rapidly. The colonial experience may be judged from New Zealand where some nine towns constructed urban tramways (Bloomfield, 1975). The length of line varied from 86.2 kilometres in Christchurch to lines of only 1.6 kilometres in Nelson and Devonport (North Auckland). After the initial burst of activity in the late 1870s and 1880s, lines in the main centres were extended slowly until a renewed period of construction following electrification in the first decade of the present century. Major programmes of expansion followed the electrification of the original steam or horse-drawn network as loads and speeds could be increased and gradients previously insurmountable could be tackled. Usage and profitability reached a peak in the period 1926–31 and although the Auckland system continued to be extended until 1932, most systems were virtually complete by 1920. Auckland, however, through the combination of an expanding economy, the development of housing estates adjacent to lines and special recreational facilities, continued to be profitable when other lines began to show deficits.

Lines were constructed often ahead of building activity in the expectation of a rapid rise in population densities in the suburbs and economic activity in the streets served by the trams. However, in some cases the housing densities were insufficient to generate the passenger numbers to establish profitability. In 1926 Auckland recorded a population of 105,000 living in an area already in excess of 100 square kilometres. Ten years later the population had increased by only 10 per cent, but the urbanised area had been extended far more rapidly. In the 1920s motor buses, which could operate without the capital expenses of constructing and maintaining the tram lines and the overhead wires, were able to serve low-density suburbs, enabling sprawl to continue at an accelerated pace. However, between the 1880s and 1930s the tram was the major influence on town development both in the suburbs and in fashioning the Central Business District. Bloomfield (1975 : 117) claimed 'The rise of the central city department store, large capacity cinema, and speculative office blocks for rental, owe much to the mass transportation provided by the tramway'. Certainly the focus of the lines on the central part of Auckland, notably Queen's Street, is a case in point (Figure 5.6).

If the tram was the colonial means of urban transport *par excellence*, then the train opened up prospects for even greater mobility over longer distances and for more people. However, few cities embarked upon programmes of suburban railway construction in the colonial era, as cities lacked the population numbers for

Figure 5.6: Auckland tram network

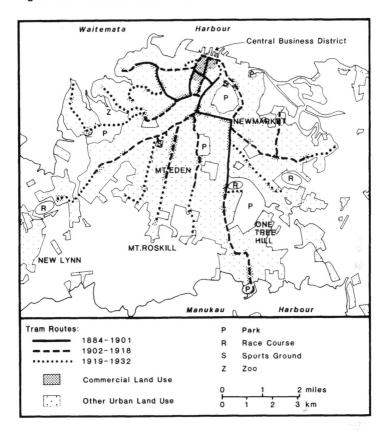

financial viability. Commuter services were offered on lines built for other purposes and occasional branch lines were provided. Thus settlements several kilometres from the city centre were developed as residential areas initially for the wealthy, but later to serve a wider social spectrum. Melbourne in the course of the boom in the 1880s was one of the few cities to plan and partially construct an integrated suburban railway system designed to cater for both existing and projected residential areas. The provision of closely spaced railway stations and an integrated plan for railways and suburbs although most carefully designed in Melbourne, was repeated in several other major cities.

It was the revolution brought about by the motor bus and motor car which freed public transport from the need for tracks and the

111

inflexibility which this imposed and offered the prospects of independent private transport. Dominion levels of car ownership were high by the late 1920s, although substantially lower than those in the United States. Those with independent transport were free to live further from the city centre or the railway station, as residential township developers ensured the layout of graded motorable roads in their suburbs. The full appreciation of the implications of these advances led to a massive subdivision of suburban plots and the beginning of accelerated sprawl in the 1920s, leading to a major transformation of the settler city beyond the scope of the present work.

EXPANSION AND SPRAWL

The areal extent of settler cities was limited, prior to the 1930s, by the means by which people could be transported to work in the burgeoning city. The massive potential for urban development brought about by the motor car age had only begun to be realised in 1931. However, this did not mean that cities in the colonies had been subjected to the same constraints as cities in the British Isles. Residential sprawl was a feature of most major settler cities and indeed the majority of settlements of over 1,000 inhabitants by the 1930s. The initial town plan, in successful urban ventures, was rapidly filled and extensions begun along the main highways, notably roads with tramlines, and at new nodes around railway stations. Areas of suburban planning often went far ahead of demand in a series of speculations, some of which were built upon and others left as little more than townships on paper in Surveyor-Generals' offices.

The majority of government town planning schemes had failed to provide a reserve of land around the town for expansion. Accordingly most urban growth was controlled by private landowners subject to little official oversight. Privately-owned smallholdings adjacent to the initial town were usually acquired for speculation rather than intensive agriculture as planned. The planned smallholdings were designed to supply provisions to the townspeople, and in the case of the port cities provisions for ships and garrisons. City expansion, however, could only take place as a result of the subdivision of such holdings and the laying out of streets and residential lots. The main framework of trunk roads predated this process so that an often radial road pattern was supplemented by the division of intervening blocks of land on a variety of grid patterns (Johnston, 1968).

The size and layout of such subdivisions depended upon the calculations of the township proprietor as to the class of person to whom he was going to sell the land. A wide range of economic classes, from the merchant aristocracy to manual labourers, was present in the settler colonies from their inception. Wealth derived from agricultural and industrial development widened the range thereafter. Residential segregation of classes became marked in the nineteenth century and was more apparent in the larger centres. A tendency which has been noted to coincide with the change from the purely commercial base of the early colonial cities to the industrial city of late Victorian times (Harris, 1984). This parallels changes in the English city, but took place at a later date. In Canada marked economic segregation was noted by the 1880s in the larger eastern towns (Harris *et al.*, 1981).

All the major port cities developed extensive suburban zones in the second half of the nineteenth century. Areas were divided into plots of 1–5 hectares in extent and there the major mansions were constructed. Class and elevation were usually coincident and the speculative process ensured the acquisition of the more desirable areas by those with the capital to pay for them. Asa Briggs (1968) selected Melbourne as the sole overseas representative for his book, *Victorian Cities*, as a consequence of the dynamic processes of expansion and development which it exhibited in the second half of the nineteenth century. This was fuelled by a massive influx of population associated with the gold strike of 1851 in Victoria and the rise of processing and manufacturing industries under a series of protectionist governments. The encouragement of local industry was also facilitated by the general preference afforded local production in government contracts. The Government of Victoria, for example, allowed a 10 per cent margin over external tenders, which provided a significant stimulus to local producers. As a result 75 per cent of all orders for railway locomotives and rolling stock were placed with local firms by 1890 (Linge, 1975). The concentration of colonial capital investment in the Melbourne metropolitan area was entirely disproportionate (Urlich Cloher, 1979). The resultant rate of growth was such that Melbourne exceeded the population of Sydney until the First World War, reaching nearly 500,000 in 1901, and 996,000 or 55 per cent of the population of the entire State of Victoria by 1931.

Urban expansion exhibited two main forms, the suburban villa or more substantial terrace house which often through time declined in status, and the built semi-slum which began its urban existence near the bottom of the social scale. That suburbs could be built blighted is significant for the development of many colonial settler cities. Thus Sydney's first suburb, the Rocks, was built to the north of the city centre on land too steep and rocky for road transport or for the provision of sewerage, and took the overflow of convicts and others in the early nineteenth century. Plague scares in 1900 and then the construction of the Sydney Harbour Bridge resulted in the demolition of large parts of this blighted suburb in the late 1920s. Melbourne also illustrated the problem of differential growth. The city centre laid out in 1835–7 was surrounded by a regular grid of rural divisions one mile (1.6 kilometres) square. Adjacent to the city there were carved 10 hectare suburban lots. In the late 1840s subdivision for town development commenced. Each owner divided his lots with little reference to his neighbours, resulting in an unintegrated road pattern and a noticeable drainage and sewerage problem in the lower areas adjacent to the Yarra River.

The physical environment thus influenced the development of two inner suburbs, Fitzroy and Collingwood (Barrett, 1971). Fitzroy, adjacent to the city centre, occupied a hill, while Collingwood, further from the city, was lower in elevation on the flat plain above the River Yarra. Subdivisions in Fitzroy were larger, streets wider and buildings more substantial than those in Collingwood. The latter was built as a poor working-class district from the start in the 1850s. Industries were also attracted to cheap land adjacent to the river which acted as a vast industrial and domestic refuse drain. Thus tanneries, soapworks, wool washeries and breweries were established, intermixed with poor single-storey housing, often only accessible through alleyways rather than roads. By contrast Fitzroy developed a middle-class image with some substantial villas. In 1891 one-fifth of housing in the suburb contained seven or more rooms compared with only a twelfth of Collingwood's housing stock. However, just as the rural smallholdings had been converted to housing estates so in the 1880s Fitzroy underwent another change. The tramways enabled people to move further out into more congenial conditions. Terrace houses, even substantial edifices, were no competition for the lure of the villa sites offered in more distant suburbs developed in the boom period of the 1880s, and the suburb became more working class in occupation.

The majority of the Melbourne inner suburbs were more modest in dimensions with terrace housing persisting as a construction form, but usually of only a single storey. Resulting densities were still low. Thus Northcote, some 3 to 5 kilometres from central Melbourne, expanded from the 1850s onwards to a population of 21,000 by 1911, which had doubled by the census of 1933. At that date some 11,000 houses had been constructed, nearly half since 1914. The suburb by this stage was fully occupied with little room for expansion except through the subdivision of housing plots (Lemon, 1983). The gross housing density amounted to a mere 7 houses per hectare or 25 persons per hectare, and this for a suburb of working- and middle-class population.

The same process took place around all the larger colonial settler cities and indeed many of the smaller ones as smallholding development attracted people to live in semi-rural conditions. The amenities of low-density housing, country living styles and freedom from urban taxation levels were conducive to many whose occupation remained tied to the city. Others were attracted to smallholdings as a means of earning a living from horticulture and smallscale farming. In both cases the motor vehicle made such a course of action possible. Sprawl therefore dominated colonial urban development producing a notably lower density pattern than that in the United Kingdom where land values were higher. The provision of subdivisions far exceeded demand leading to low densities and extensive unoccupied tracts between pockets of higher density occupancy, usually adjacent to the main roads and railways. The south-westward spread of Sydney in the 1920s to link up with Liverpool some 28 kilometres from the city centre illustrates the process of irregular development (Figure 5.7).

SEGREGATION

Not all settler cities remained exclusively the preserve of European settler communities. The West Indies provide an early illustration of a multi-racial population living in an urban framework designed for British settlers. During the era of slavery the unfree Black population was residentially integrated with the Whites, although slave labour in the industrial and port quarters was segregated in barracks. The free Blacks were socially and geographically separated from White citizens. Following emancipation in the 1830s economic class and race coincided to a large extent and this was translated into the townscape with the building of new, cramped, poor suburbs for the freed slaves. Social and physical mobility was slight in the colonial

Figure 5.7: Urban sprawl, south-west Sydney

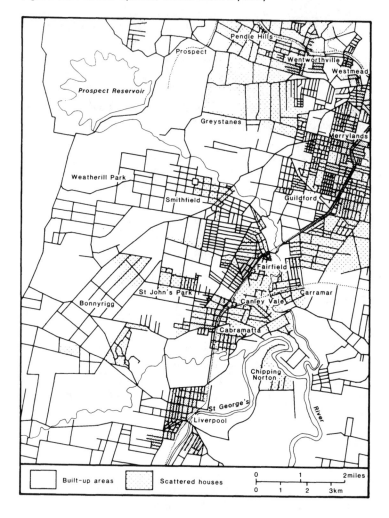

era, when the upper echelons of commerce and administration remained in White hands, and the middle ranks and suburbs were occupied by other immigrant groups and those of mixed parentage. The result was the emergence of a complex city characterised by marked racial sectors, but with an overall unity of design and function as exemplified by Kingston, Jamaica (Clark, 1985).

Segregationist, indeed exclusionist, pressures built up within White settler societies in the second half of the nineteenth century, severely limiting the scope of Asian activity within the Empire (Huttenback, 1976). Residential restrictions were placed upon Indian and Chinese communities in all the dominions and in a number of settler colonies. Attempts were made to prevent Asian immigration as White colonial and dominion governments gained greater powers. Laws aimed at repatriating Asian peoples whence they had come were placed on the statute books of several colonies in the late nineteenth and early twentieth centuries. The Chinese as non-British subjects were in a weaker political position than the Indians. The influx of Chinese miners to the Australian and New Zealand goldfields in the 1850s and 1860s brought the segregationist tendencies in colonial society into tangible form. Restrictions on Chinese mining activity were introduced, preventing them from obtaining claims and later from living in certain of the mining settlements. As early as the 1870s the town of Lawrence, New Zealand, framed regulations forbidding Chinese miners from living in the town. As a result a separate Chinese shanty settlement was erected at a distance from the main, exclusively White, town (Salmon, 1963 :113).

It was in Africa that the most complex reaction to the multi-racial character of the settler city was apparent, reflecting the more diverse composition of the population (Table 5.1). In South Africa after the emancipation of the slaves in 1834, distinct quarters inhabited predominantly by freed slaves were built within the framework of existing cities, notably Cape Town and Port Elizabeth. These overlapped European-occupied areas in a manner similar to that distinguished in the West Indies. However, the indigenous population which had not been reduced to slavery, was largely excluded from the organised structure of the towns as a result of a lack of urban background on the one hand and an official reluctance to precipitate large-scale urbanisation, except through the mediating activities of missionaries, on the other. Accordingly the first settlement for indigenous people adjacent to Port Elizabeth was established by the London Missionary Society in 1834, only 19 years

Table 5.1: Population of selected African colonial cities, 1931-6

City	European (%) population	Asian and (%) Coloured population	African (%) population	Total
Johannesburg	252,718 (53.2)	31,284 (6.6)	191,032 (40.2)	475,034
Port Elizabeth	48,608 (49.2)	24,296 (24.6)	25,800 (26.1)	98,704
Durban	88,062 (36.8)	87,903 (36.7)	63,540 (26.5)	239,512
Salisbury	9,619 (34.9)	848 (3.1)	17,112 (62.0)	27,579
Nairobi	5,177 (10.8)	15,988 (33.3)	26,800[a](55.9)	47,956

Note: a. Estimate.
Source: Census reports for South Africa (1936), Southern Rhodesia (1931), and Kenya (1931).

after the survey of the initial town. In general, municipal authorities regarded the indigenous population as temporary residents and the towns as the domain of the White Man — an attitude which lasted beyond the colonial era until the 1980s (Christopher, 1987).

Disease was prevalent in the poorly laid out and frequently crowded nineteenth-century urban locations. It was the outbreak of bubonic plague in the first decade of the twentieth century which prompted municipal authorities to institute a new system of permanent locations for the indigenous population at some distance from the European town. The 'sanitation syndrome' developed in Cape Town and Johannesburg was the argument raised for the segregation of the indigenous population. It revolved around the settler belief that the mixing of the races led to incidence of disease, while separate housing areas for settler and indigene would result in the eradication of disease. South African towns were thus replanned with separate locations 5–10 kilometres away from the European area. Accordingly Ndabeni in Cape Town, New Brighton in Port Elizabeth and Pimville in Johannesburg, the precursor of modern Soweto, were established between 1900 and 1904 and subsequently enlarged. In 1923 the statutory obligation was placed on all South African municipalities to establish separate Black locations. The degree of actual segregation differed as employers still housed a number of their workers on their premises, while some Africans had been able to purchase land in the towns, prior to the legal removal of that right after the formation of the Union of South Africa in 1910. The resultant South African city was a marked variant upon the settler city with its separate segregated indigenous townships or locations outside the main urban framework (Figure 5.8) (Davies, 1971).

Figure 5.8: The segregated South African city, Port Elizabeth, 1936

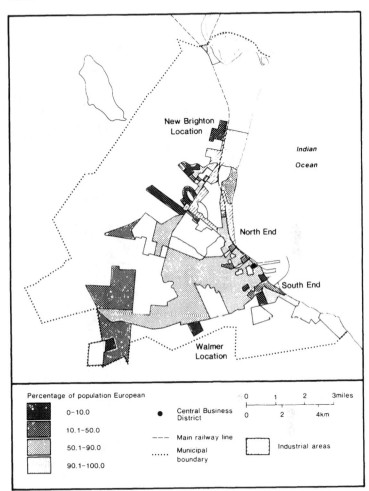

Percentage of population European

0–10.0
10.1–50.0
50.1–90.0
90.1–100.0

● Central Business District

– – – Main railway line

...... Municipal boundary

Industrial areas

0   1   2   3miles
0   2   4km

Within the main framework of the city the post-emancipation pattern of partial economic and social, but not legal, segregation of the various non-indigenous groups continued. Later immigrants, more especially Indians, added an extra dimension to the South African city (Figure 5.9). Although the majority of Indians came to South Africa as indentured labourers to work on the sugar plantations, some came with capital as traders. They successfully

Figure 5.9: Grey Street, Durban

competed with European shopkeepers, establishing stores particularly attuned to the requirements of the African population, as well
as supplying the settler population. The result was the European
settler attempt to segregate, even to dispossess, the Indian traders
through the introduction of discriminatory laws. Separate bazaar
areas were set aside in certain towns and the general practice was
to create secondary Indian business areas.

The central and east African colonial towns evolved on similar
lines. Nairobi was planned as a segregated city on the basis of the
sanitation syndrome, prior to its official rejection in 1923 (White *et
al.*, 1948). However, by that time separate European, Asian and
African areas had been established and restrictive racial covenants
written into property deeds ensured the perpetuation of the design.

The pattern of European planning and the mixture of European,
Asian and African populations thus produced a cross between the
settler and the colonial city. An examination of the town plans of
cities from Durban to Salisbury and Nairobi reveals the ancestry
inherited from settler town planning. However, the organisation of
space within the cities exposed not only economic but also structural
segregation, akin to colonial cities without permanent settler populations. The question thus arises as to where such cities should be
classified. Based on origins, they are settler cities. Based on resultant patterns the tropical colonial model appears and strengthens its
position through time as the indigenous population became
urbanised. However, large-scale urbanisation is mainly a post-
Second World War phenomenon. In the 1930s these cities were still
small and the indigenous proportion of the population still relatively
low, when compared with the post-Second World War explosion
which is still continuing.

STYLES

British settler and colonial cities exhibited a great variety of architectural styles. As late as the 1930s though the majority of colonial
architects and planners followed British ideas and often consciously
emulated British practices. Thus a distinctively British character was
impressed upon the towns and cities of the Empire. The search for
the development of an Imperial style proved to be elusive and indeed
was never achieved, although the aim to create a distinctive British
Imperial style, particularly in the early twentieth century was powerful. The editor of *The Builder*, writing on 'Imperialism and

Architecture', commented:

> An empire can nurse no finer ideal than the cohesion of its domin-
> ions in cities erected in one style of architecture recognised
> throughout the world as the expression of its own imperial ideals.
> The encouragement of such an empire-pervading style throughout
> colonies, dependencies, and protectorates will tend to annihilate
> distance and conduce to an imperial liberty, equality and frater-
> nity (27.9.1912).

The translation of these ideals into reality, whether they were for
domestic or public architecture, broke down under the strains
imposed by differing climates and social environments within the
Empire. It is also worth noting that at the very time Imperial unity
in tangible form was being promoted, the beginnings of separate
nationalisms in the dominions, translated into architectural form,
may also be discerned (Addison, 1910; Gowans, 1966). Yet the
development of distinctive regional styles did not have to be forced
deliberately. The emergence of a West Indian, notably Jamaican,
vernacular style in the eighteenth and early nineteenth centuries
illustrates the problems of maintaining an Imperial style. In the West
Indies Georgian style houses were modified to suit local climatic
conditions, although maintaining the essential ethos of classical
design. However, the hurricanes which destroyed Bridgetown,
Barbados, in 1780 and 1831, and Kingston, Jamaica, in 1907 largely
obliterated this heritage although lesser evidence in Spanish Town
and Falmouth, Jamaica, survive (Acworth, 1951).

It is noticeable that the classical, Georgian, style proved to be
remarkably long lasting in the colonies, due largely to its simplicity.
Thus in the colonies, buildings of this nature were constructed long
after its abandonment in the British Isles (Stacpoole, 1976;
Lewcock, 1963). The elaboration of High Victorian architecture was
difficult to achieve with the materials available and with the general
level of income in many colonies. It was only through large-scale
importation that some of the more fanciful excesses of the period
were constructed through the ability to obtain cast-iron and other
ornamentation from factories in England and Scotland by mail
order.

PUBLIC ARCHITECTURE

In the early stages of colonial development the army was a major influence upon style. The officers concerned with the design and construction of public buildings had frequently lived in many parts of the world and introduced to colonial government architecture a tropical style derived from the West Indies or India, while the domestic architecture built by immigrants was closer to English provincial models. Thus the early major public buildings in Sydney were Georgian in style with touches which belied Indian influences, derived from their architects' and indeed governor Macquarie's periods of service in that country (Herman, 1970). In Western Australia the experience of personnel previously serving in the southern United States and the West Indies have been suggested for the importation of colonial designs (Morison and White, 1979).

Public architecture in the colonies and dominions ranged from the major parliamentary buildings to minor schools, police stations and offices. Government Houses rarely achieved the prominence and distinction of those built in the tropical colonies and so tended to be designed as a large villa within the overall town plan or were situated in the rural-urban fringe rather than in the town centre. Styles, as in the neighbouring privately owned villas, ranged from neo-classical (Brisbane) to Scottish baronial (Hobart). A regional variation was the adoption of Cape-Dutch designs for Government House in Salisbury, Southern Rhodesia, symbolising the links which existed between the British South Africa Company's administration and the Cape of Good Hope.

However, it was the parliamentary buildings which were most lavishly designed, built and landscaped, as symbols of the independence and political rights of the dominion, state or province which they served. The individual colonial structures were again mostly classical in style, dating at least in inception from the major period of granting representative and responsible government in the middle of the nineteenth century. Accordingly, the major parliamentary buildings in Cape Town, Sydney and Melbourne resembled American state capitols in form, although the symbols and decoration were very different, emphasising the new community's link with the Crown. However, the first dominion, Canada, chose to erect a gothic edifice, emulating the detail of Augustus Pugin's and Charles Barry's new Houses of Parliament at Westminster. The Parliament Building for British Columbia in Victoria illustrated a more pragmatic, if massive, treatment of the gothic theme (Figure

Figure 5.10: British Columbia Parliamentary Buildings, Victoria

5.10). This diversity of style was transferred down the scale to town halls, post offices and other major official buildings. In all cases the relatively more spacious design of the town plan enabled buildings to be seen to greater advantage than was possible in London or the British provincial cities.

Architectural styles in the nineteenth century were perceived to have political content when applied to public buildings. Thus in the pursuit of national styles the self-governing colonies were faced with problems of identity. Canadian architects designing the Ottawa parliamentary buildings were confronted with the difficulty of linking architectural style to nationality (Gowans, 1968). In the United States at independence this had been relatively simple as Roman republican styles were deemed to convey republican virtues. The Virginia state capital at Richmond, designed by Thomas Jefferson in 1785, was based on the Maison Carrée in Nîmes. Later as the Romanism of the French Revolution became associated with the Napoleonic Empire so the United States moved towards classical Greek republican styles of architecture to express national sentiments. In reaction the United Kingdom turned towards gothic to express national parliamentary and ecclesiastical ideals. Consequently once Ottawa had been selected as the Canadian capital in 1858 the style of its parliamentary buildings had to be neo-gothic, in marked contrast to the contemporary construction of the Capitol in Washington. Gothic thus distinguished Canadian public buildings from American and preserved a sense of separate identity and a link with Great Britain. This even filtered down to private houses where the gothic revival found a more responsive mood in British settler cities than in the United States.

Public buildings were significant elements within the townscapes of settler cities as the state played and always had played a more interventionist role in the economy and social make-up of the colonial society. Schools occupied prominent places within the design of towns, rather than being added as afterthoughts. It was, however, the churches which presented the most noticeable element in many skylines as well as key positions within many town plans. Colonial populations tended to have a greater diversity of religious adherence than in England and Scotland, and the state Church of England, although occupying the prime site within a town or city plan, was surrounded by many rivals for the Methodist, nonconformist and Roman Catholic populations. The comparatively simple classical style of the eighteenth century gave way in the mid-nineteenth century to an explosion of designs with a predominance of neo-gothic churches and chapels. British architects designed churches for the colonies as well as for the British Isles and styles were essentially contemporary with Great Britain, conditioned only by the availability of local building materials.

Public buildings and churches in the later Victorian era in the colonies became ever more elaborate. Nowhere was this more evident than in the colony of Victoria, which until the financial slump of the 1890s led the way in many aspects of Australian development. Rising church attendance and the fragmentation of organised religion into numerous sects resulted in a boom in church and chapel erection, effectively transforming the skylines of colonial cities. Thus whereas there were 39 churches in Victoria in 1851, by 1871 the number had risen to some 2,602. In the early 1870s a peak of 250 churches a year were being opened for worship. The boom in building was aided by the generous terms offered under the Church Building Act of 1836 which provided for the ecclesiastical acquisition of land at a nominal price and a pound for pound grant towards building costs for new churches (Freeland, 1968). Within other spheres of public endeavour colonial and municipal authorities provided for education. In 1872 Victoria introduced compulsory education resulting in a spate of school building. Public libraries and institutes were also erected as part of the programme of public betterment so enthusiastically pursued in the nineteenth century. Civic offices to house the burgeoning municipal bureaucracy were constructed on an ever increasing and grandiose scale emulating similar developments in England (Cunningham, 1981).

Clubs and societies also erected halls for meetings, theatricals and social gatherings of various types. The gentleman's club as an institution was transferred to all parts of the Empire and few towns of any size were without at least one. Similarly masonic lodges were established as part of British society and their temples were erected in the major centres. Even the more localised Orange Order kept the memory of Ireland alive through a colonial organisation. The Orange Order halls were a noticeable feature of Ontario where 'it was the Orangeman's hope that the thin red line of empire might be inset by an orange stripe' (Houston and Smyth, 1978 : 262).

The government structures, churches and other public buildings were often constructed in flamboyant styles which still present a highly distinctive element in colonial cityscapes. The extravagances of the High Victorian era often exhibited the taste of men who had made money themselves when the colonies offered opportunities for rapid riches, and wished to show off that wealth. The exuberance is all the more surprising when it is considered that it took place (until 1901) in an apparent period of sombreness while the Empire was in mourning for Prince Albert, causing Freeland (1968 : 171) to suggest:

> The successful man could not adorn his wife, let alone himself, with jewels, furs and brightly coloured silks, while a touch of grey or mulled lavender was the only relief permitted to the universal and gloomy black or brown suits and dresses. He found

the answer to his frustration by dressing his buildings in a way which in other times he would have dressed his wife.

DOMESTIC ARCHITECTURE

In the range of domestic buildings, the colonies did not emulate British design so closely. Even the early settler cities built before the transport revolution of the 1860s and 1870s were rarely so constrained for space that high-density multi-storey housing was deemed necessary. The inner terrace housing of Sydney, Toronto and other settler cities was rarely as extensive or cramped as schemes undertaken in London or English provincial cities. The availability of space enabled those with only moderate means to acquire a plot which provided a garden. Thus terraces were often only single storeyed, while where possible houses were completely detached. Consequently even working-class suburbs took on a more spacious aspect than their British counterparts. At the other end of the scale the movement to villadom was virtually universal, with most of the more important towns and cities developing the highly exotic styles of the late Victorian and Edwardian eras. The bungalow, originating as a peasant's hut in Bengal, became the house for European residence in India, and through complex transfers of ideas became accepted as the house style for Europeans in the colonies, whether in Kenya or Australia (King, 1984). Thus even the colonial concept of a 'house' changed from that of the metropole.

In outward appearance buildings thus departed from British styles fairly rapidly. Building stone presented a problem in many cities, while bricks were often of poor quality requiring plastering and painting. Wood was extensively used for construction in parts of Australia, Canada and New Zealand, while corrugated iron proved to be a valuable addition to building materials in regions deficient in suitable wood, stone or clay. Roofing in slate was rare, although the major wool ports such as Sydney and Port Elizabeth imported slate in ballast from vessels returning to Great Britain with colonial cargoes. However, timber and corrugated iron dominated as roofing materials. Other adopted building features such as verandahs in hot climates and pitched roofs for snowy winters resulted in a marked range of styles developing from the single origin.

Within the settler colonies comparatively little was adopted from the experience of the majority of indigenous peoples for the construction of permanent as opposed to temporary houses. Maori motifs and timber construction methods are an exception to this statement. It was other immigrant peoples, other Europeans and the Asian communities which contributed to the diversification of styles. The two most important non-British European overseas communities were the French in Canada and the Dutch in South Africa (Picton-Seymour, 1977). Both, in the course of the seventeenth and eighteenth centuries, had developed building styles derived from their countries of origin but adapted to the conditions of the colonies. Thus French mansard roofs and turrets and Cape-Dutch gables were adopted as distinctive features by other settlers in Canada and South Africa, respectively. French styles in Canada made few concessions to the dominant Anglo-Saxon culture of the continent, in order to preserve a distinctive identity. The Château Frontenac Hotel in Quebec built in 1890 with its later central tower provided a model for subsequent Canadian Pacific Railway hotels across Canada, effectively reinforcing a Canadian style, often incorporated into domestic architecture. Other immigrant communities, particularly the Indians and Chinese, influenced styles in their own quarters into which they were frequently segregated, but by 1930 little of this heritage had been introduced into the mainstream of settler taste.

Settlers frequently found that new and strange environments required new building techniques. The prefabricated house developed for North American conditions at the end of the nineteenth century as a 'Pacific' style was transported across Western Canada and also across the Pacific Ocean. Australia and New Zealand were thus influenced by styles and techniques adopted in California and British Columbia. The need to develop new styles led to the conscious attempt to promote distinct Canadian and Australian architecture as part of a national awakening in the two countries. However, as in many other fields of endeavour, it was only after the Second World War that such attitudes were more generally accepted and promoted.

Greater space was required as styles changed. The construction of verandahed houses necessitated wider frontages in the nineteenth century. In the motor age, driveways for cars, or at least leading to where the owner expected to garage his car, were required. Only the wealthy continued to build double storey houses in Australian suburbia in the twentieth century as a demonstration of status, elsewhere single storey, extensive ground plan dwellings were the norm. Individual home ownership in settler towns and cities became the accepted rule, whether the owner was at the top or near the bottom of the social scale. Building societies were established to aid this ideal and had a greater influence in the colonies than in the metropole in promoting private ownership. In 1854 the Metropolitan Permanent Society was formed in Melbourne to erect workers' cottages and provide a means of financing individuals desiring their own houses. Other societies followed throughout the British Empire. Schemes such as the Australian War Services Homes Scheme after the First World War similarly encouraged individuals to own their own houses by providing the means to do so — a marked piece of social engineering with geographical implications for the sprawl of the cities.

6

Colonial Cities

In contrast to the settler cities discussed in the previous chapter, a substantial part of the British Empire was occupied by well established indigenous peoples with urban cultures. Accordingly in India, Malaya and parts of Africa, colonial cities were designed either as additions to existing cities or as entities which would be multi-ethnic from their foundation. The resultant patterns and organisations reflect the concepts of colonial administrations in the conduct of relations with other peoples. British colonial governments were largely segregationist in their approach to town planning. A dualism is apparent within virtually all colonial cities in tropical Africa and Asia, with distinct quarters for the immigrant and indigenous populations. Often this dualism was further enhanced by the division and segregation of the immigrant groups into separate quarters. The military cantonment and the Civil Lines of Indian cities are the most noticeable examples.

Dualism was based on the assumption that contact between different ethnic groups had to be reduced to a minimum to ensure the smooth running of administration and flow of trade. There was a resulting contrast between the indigenous and European quarters, built adjacent to one another but having little social contact. Frequently social distance was converted into physical distance. In cities planned entirely by the British, the core was occupied by Europeans and periphery by the indigenous population. Thus the walled city of Bombay, built by the East India Company, overlooked the indigenous suburbs (appropriately named 'Black Town'), separated from one another by an open field of fire, the future Maidan. Indeed the walled settlement and segregation which it implied reflected the organisation of medieval English colonial towns on the Celtic fringe (Christopher, 1983). In contrast the major pre-colonial Indian cities such as Delhi and Agra not only possessed a fort or citadel, but the entire indigenous city was walled, effectively containing the indigenous population. The British colonial town was then laid out adjacent to the walled city with the fortification and walls separating the two societies. Hence the two British Indian capitals, Calcutta and Delhi, took on very different colonial images, reflecting their histories and age of British building.

TOWN PLANNING

British officials who controlled and planned the colonial cities were constrained by the overall framework of colonialism. The central social fact of colonial planning was the maintenance of power. Social engineering was enforced in the attempt to retain the colonial structure with the minimum of effort and expense. Segregation was one aspect of social engineering and was practised principally, though not exclusively, on racial lines (Ross, 1982). Ethnic groups were accepted by colonial authorities as basic elements in the planning of urban centres. Town planning was primarily designed to ensure 'orderly' development and a healthy environment for the European population (King, 1980). As the majority of colonial towns were commercial and administrative in function, rather than industrial, plans were flexible with extensive provision for government functions. In metropolitan society urbanisation was closely linked to industrialisation. However, in a dependent relationship colonial urbanisation was also linked to industrialisation in the metropole through trade (Simon, 1984). Colonial industrial development beyond primary processing was neither desired nor anticipated in many official quarters. As a result industrial zones grew with as little administrative forethought as in the British Isles, in spite of the opportunities afforded town planners in the colonies to learn from the mistakes of the British experience of industrialisation.

The colonial city planners tended to be military men until the last few decades of the colonial era. Town planning in the form of the layout of cantonments as well as building principles and the elements of architecture were taught to the Royal Engineers at Chatham and Woolwich, and in India from the mid-nineteenth century at Thomason Engineering College (Roorkee University) and the Madras Engineering College. Later in the nineteenth century surveyors and civil engineers were attached to town boards to organise urban designs and layouts. The results frequently, though not always, reflected the military desire for regularity and order, with everything and everyone in their place. Personal experience was often called upon in executing basic town planning; for example Dr William Montgomerie, military surgeon in Singapore from 1819 to 1842, had obtained considerable practical experience as the secretary to the Singapore town committee during the town's formative years. He was consulted on the layout of Rangoon in 1852 (Pearn, 1939). Not unnaturally his proposals emphasised both ethnic separation and health regulations, two of the key issues at Singapore.

The Public Works Departments in India were established in the 1850s and other colonies followed later. These departments attracted permanent professional staffs concerned with the layout and servicing of towns, together with official architecture. Town plans as such were late in appearance. In 1921 the government of the Federated Malay States appointed a professional town planner and other administrations followed suit. It was only at the end of the colonial period that professional town planners were employed in any numbers and exerted noticeable influence. Nevertheless the military hold remained influential. As late as 1896 it was a sergeant of the Royal Engineers who laid out the regular but cramped Nairobi, eliciting the comment that 'the same mistakes of overcrowding and insanitary conditions as existed in England in the early nineteenth century have a tendency to repeat themselves in new countries' (White et al., 1948: 1). Indeed the overall plan and siting of Nairobi prompted Winston Churchill to write 'it is now too late to change, and thus lack of foresight and a comprehensive view leaves its permanent imprint upon the countenance of a new country' (Churchill, 1908: 19). Such a comment could have been applied to many colonial foundations, yet other military men produced contrasting results. Colonel William Light's design of Adelaide must be rated one of the successes of colonial urban planning. Most towns lay somewhere in between the two, which through the passage of time tended to have more in common than initial responses might suggest.

DUAL CHARACTER

The dual nature of colonial cities only appeared either after the acquisition of extensive tropical territories with established urban traditions, or through the attraction of substantial numbers of the indigenous populations to cities built in the British settler mould. In both cases dualism became structured into the design and pattern of the cities concerned. The latter case has already been discussed in the previous chapter, as it affected the African or West Indian settler cities. However, although in appearance very similar, the Asian colonial cities are dealt with here, as it was not a permanent settler society which was involved but transient commercial and administrative cadres who may be expected to have had different expectations and demands.

In the course of the nineteenth century Great Britain acquired extensive territories in Africa and Asia where urban civilisation was of some antiquity. In India in particular the pattern of towns, outside the three Presidency cities, was inherited by British rulers who adapted to new conditions by ignoring the presence of the urban indigenous population as far as possible. The object largely appears to have been to reduce contact with the indigenes except on a master-servant relationship. Thus new European towns were built adjacent to the existing Indian towns. These were laid out according to town planning principles of the time, usually with grid plans or more generous and irregular patterns for the early civil lines. The military cantonment under army control was built alongside. The new towns outside the walls of the old indigenous cities were virtually self-contained entities with all the administrative, commercial and social facilities of a town from club and church to shop and bungalow. Dualism is a misnomer as distinctions and segregation were carried to even greater lengths. Self-contained cantonments, railway settlements and industrial estates, together with the partial segregation of the Anglo-Indian (mixed) population, added to the complexity of the urban pattern (Figure 6.1).

In the African colonies the heritage of such traditions as the Hausa and Yoruba cities of Nigeria or the Swahili city states of the East African coast elicited the same response, namely the construction of a separate British settlement for the administration and such civilian traders and others as might be stationed with them. Again the most noticeable feature was the contrast between the high-density walled or severely circumscribed indigenous city and the adjacent low-density British suburbs. The small size of the European community and the presence of either Asian or indigenous trading communities modified the form of the African colonial city limiting the extent of the European sector.

It is significant that British authorities directed most of their attention to the European sector of the city, which was supplied with services and room for expansion. In contrast the indigenous city was

Figure 6.1: Cawnpore, *c.* 1930

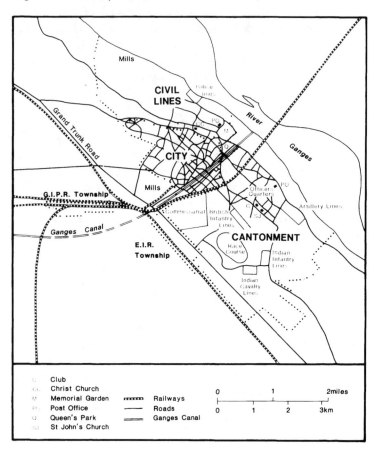

neglected and bereft of the financial support offered by the previous indigenous rulers. No philosophy of preservation akin to that prevailing among French administrators in Morocco was offered to maintain existing structures and styles. The results were spasmodic attempts to improve living conditions within the old cities, or at least to overcome the problems of rising population densities and attendant sanitary problems. The provision of services such as piped water, sanitation and electricity were rarely undertaken except in parts of the more important cities. Road improvements, usually the bulldozing of wide roads to replace alleys and winding streets, were often highly destructive to the urban fabric. Town planning in the old cities of India was thus fitful and inadequate resulting in the contrasts between the two major sectors of the cities widening during the later colonial period (Tyrwhitt, 1947).

Although the early British colonisers were impressed by the cultural heritage of Asia and initially sought to study and preserve it, this attitude did not last long. The architectural monuments of extra-European civilisations received little attention until the late nineteenth century. British officials in Egypt had been brought into contact with that country's heritage after the military occupation in 1881. Tourism to Egypt consequently led to increased appreciation of the history of other parts of the world. In India the nadir of British sympathy with indigenous achievements had been reached in the 1820s when Lord Bentinck's administration even proposed the demolition of the Taj Mahal at Agra to serve as a source of building stone (Ramaswami, 1979). Lord Curzon in the 1890s conversely reflected a new concern for the monuments of India and indeed personally contributed to the restoration of the Taj Mahal and subsequently established the Historical Monuments Commission.

If India and Egypt were early appreciated, other civilisations received little attention until much later. Great Zimbabwe, for example, was effectively plundered in the 1890s by a commercial concessionary company seeking the gold content of its relics. After the First World War greater consideration of other civilisations was apparent when cities such as Jerusalem, Baghdad and Mosul-Nineveh came under British control. This in turn provided greater impetus for the appreciation and conservation of the monuments of other colonies including Malta and Cyprus. By the 1930s National Monuments Commissions in a number of colonies and dominions were concerned with the artefacts of a wide range of histories from Stone Age rock paintings in southern Africa to the monumental architecture of Moghul and Hindu India.

The British capture of Jerusalem in 1917 brought the concept of conservation of other cultural heritages most clearly into focus (Shapiro, 1973). Indeed the city was captured and held more for prestige and for promoting a modern image of the crusaders than any political or economic benefit which accrued (Packenham, 1985). The spiritual significance of the city for a Christian country and indeed for many other subjects of the Crown led to the careful formulation of plans to preserve its special character and construction. In 1918 the first of many British plans were drawn up to prevent undesirable development and also to create open spaces around the walls. Most significantly the decision was taken to enforce construction in local stone. A series of plans thereafter sought to promote the religious character of the city and steer new industry and commerce away from the walled city which remained as a sacred but living museum. The new city was also closely controlled, developing a markedly different, dominantly Jewish, character.

CALCUTTA

Calcutta, the most important of the tropical foundations, dates only from 1690. Its site on the Hooghly distributary of the River Ganges was unhealthy, liable to flooding and periodically visited by cyclones. However, to its founders it provided the base for trade in Bengal, which, because of its wealth and proximity to the centre of power in India, was placed to become the port for the subcontinent and capital of British India. The first settlement was contained within the fort, Fort William, which was enlarged and improved in the eighteenth century as one of the major centres of British military power in Asia. The eighteenth-century fort was based on Marshal Vauban's concepts of fortification and cost over £2 million. Around the fort the field of fire was preserved in the form of an open space, the Maidan, extending over 5 square kilometres. Beyond this, building was permitted and merchants and officials built houses to reflect their wealth and prestige. The attempt to place a further line of fortifications around the city was never completed and uncontrolled sprawl became one of the major features of the town plan.

The city grew rapidly as the major port of northern India and the seat, until 1911, of the Imperial administration. The population had reached 180,000 by 1821, and grew to some 1.2 million by 1931 when the city covered approximately 8,000 hectares. The trade passing through the port increased, subject to the fluctuations of the economic cycle, and was worth £57.5 million in 1901–2 and increased to £168.8 million in 1925–6. However, the slump of 1929 resulted in a drastic reduction in the early 1930s. Expansion was made possible by a programme of municipal works including the construction of water storage and distribution facilities, sewerage and drainage works. Port works, notably the excavation of a series of docks downstream of the city, supplemented the early river moorings. Industrial development further resulted in the economic base of the city being widened in the course of the nineteenth and early twentieth centuries (Ghosh *et al.*, 1972). The jute industry occupied a significant place in the growth of the Calcutta region. The first jute spinning mill was established in 1855 and by 1900 some 31 mills were in operation, with a production exceeding that of the Scottish industry. By 1931 there were 93 mills in operation within the greater Calcutta region employing 328,000 people (Banerjee and Roy, 1967).

It was against this background that Calcutta underwent a major transformation in the early nineteenth century when its position as an Imperial capital as opposed to a mercantile enclave was manifested in structural form. The most prominent element of this aggrandisement was the building of a new Government House by Lord Wellesley, the Governor-General between 1798–1805. The architect, Charles Wyatt, chose Kedleston Hall in Derbyshire as his model, but adapted the residence to the Bengal climate (Figure 6.2). The result was a magnificent structure, which was to provide the impetus to general private building programmes causing Calcutta to receive the epithet 'city of palaces'. The expense of the project (£167,000) resulted in Lord Wellesley's recall by the directors of the East India Company on charges of extravagance. However, Lord Valentia, a visitor to Calcutta in 1803, supported the change of attitude which Government House symbolised:

> The sums expended upon it have been considered as extravagant by those who carry European ideas and European economy into Asia, but they ought to remember that India is a country of splendour, of extravagance and outward appearance; the Head of a mighty Empire ought to conform himself to the prejudices of the country he rules over . . . In short I wish India to be ruled from a palace, not from a country house; with the ideas of a Prince, not with those of a retail-dealer in muslins and indigo (quoted in Davies, 1985: 68).

In the late eighteenth and nineteenth centuries central Calcutta was beautified through the construction of a suite of government buildings ranging from the Writer's Building of 1780, which under a new 1880s Victorian gothic façade still stands, to the Mint and Library. The latter in the early nineteenth century contained one of the largest book and manuscript collections in the world (Moorhouse, 1983). St Andrew's Scottish Church vied with St John's Anglican Church as models of classical buildings. On the Maidan numerous monuments were erected, notably the 46-metre-high column raised in 1828 in honour of Sir David Ochterlony, the

Figure 6.2: Government House, Calcutta

Figure 6.3: Plan of Calcutta

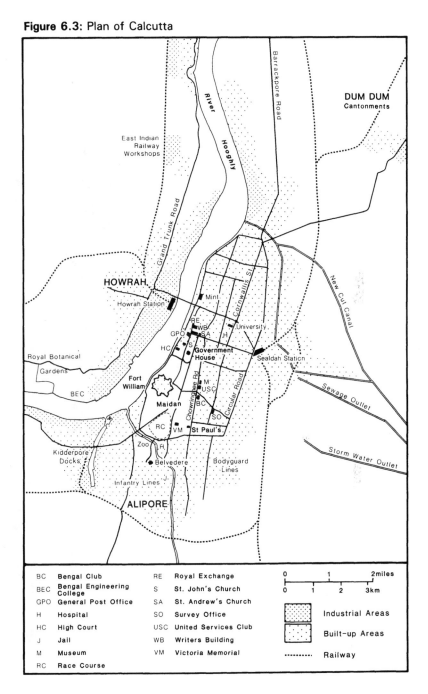

BC	Bengal Club	RE	Royal Exchange	
BEC	Bengal Engineering College	S	St. John's Church	
GPO	General Post Office	SA	St. Andrew's Church	
H	Hospital	SO	Survey Office	
HC	High Court	USC	United Services Club	
J	Jail	WB	Writers Building	
M	Museum	VM	Victoria Memorial	
RC	Race Course			

Industrial Areas

Built-up Areas

.... Railway

Figure 6.4: The Victoria Memorial, Calcutta

Figure 6.5: European suburb of Calcutta

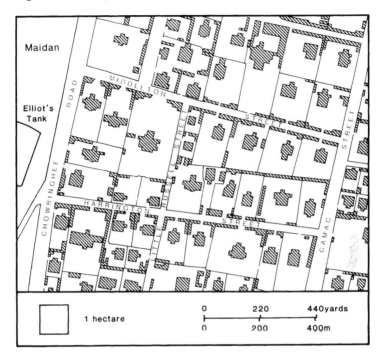

victor of the campaign against Nepal. The resultant townscape was a remarkable blend of English classical design with Indian modifications. The plan provided for extensive open spaces and grand ceremonial vistas yet lacked the rigidity imposed by a grid system (Figure 6.3). On the Maidan the race course occupied the southern sector, while in the present century the Victoria Memorial complex has carried the monumental skyline to the south of the open space (Figure 6.4).

Although the main lineaments of Calcutta were planned by the British, no formal scheme of segregation was imposed on the areas beyond the Maidan. However, the division of the town blocks between the main streets reflected differing concepts of town planning among British and Indian merchant classes. British suburbs were planned on an expansive scale, with many plots exceeding one hectare. Large mansions and bungalows were erected in the centre of the plots, with servants' quarters at the sides and back (Figure 6.5). Town planners in Calcutta anticipated the garden suburb, with

141

Figure 6.6: Indian suburb of Calcutta

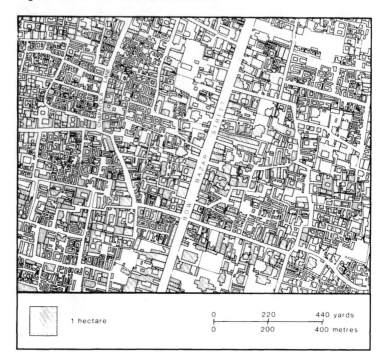

an emphasis upon individual often single storeyed houses set in their own grounds, as opposed to the classical terrace houses with communal gardens built in contemporary London and Edinburgh. Indian-occupied areas of the city in contrast were far more densely settled with a close network of alleyways and courtyard buildings (Figure 6.6). It was only in the nineteenth century that a few of the wealthier Indian merchants called attention to their wealth through external show, emulating British styles of architecture and urban design. However, in 1931 some central wards of the city enumerated over 1,000 persons per hectare, indicative of conditions of extreme overcrowding.

Even the low-density European suburbs were abandoned in the late eighteenth century by those who could afford a seasonal summer retreat from the heat, odours and diseases of the capital. Thus Warren Hastings erected a country house, Belvedere, at Alipore to the south. Later Governor-Generals built a summer residence at Barrackpore to the north for use in the era before the annual migration of the administration to Simla. Barrackpore, as its name suggests, was initially established as a military cantonment in 1775 some 25 kilometres from Calcutta. It is now the repository for a host of monuments to British heroes originally erected at the settlement and more recently others displaced from other sites in the Calcutta region as a result of nationalistic fervour. Closer to Calcutta further cantonments were built at Dum Dum, which became the site of the major ordnance factories.

BOMBAY

The authorities in Calcutta, through its prestige as the capital of the Indian Empire prior to 1911, created one form of planned British Indian city based primarily upon administration. Bombay through its trade and industry developed a distinct variation on the theme as a result of the relative unimportance of the military and the absence of an Imperial government. The army adopted upland Poona as the main base in western India early in the nineteenth century, while the Bombay Presidency rarely undertook the grandiose schemes so noticeable in Bengal. Bombay became the main port of India through the development of the Mediterranean-Red Sea route and later the opening of the Suez Canal. Allied to this the development of the cotton industry related to increasing demand and the ability of cultivators in the adjacent Deccan to supply raw cotton, provided an industrial base for the city.

Bombay was built initially as a new British base on the west coast of India (Tindall, 1982). In common with other settlements the first building was a trade castle. In the eighteenth century the castle proved to be inadequate and a walled town, the Fort, was constructed with elaborate fortifications. It is interesting to reflect that the walls of Bombay were demolished in the same year, 1864, as those of Vienna. Beyond the walls the Esplanade, now the Maidan, was cleared of trees and buildings to provide a field of fire some 1,000 metres wide. North of the Esplanade an Indian settlement, Black Town, became the nucleus of a steadily growing suburban area. It should be noted that the walled city was not exclusively inhabited by Europeans as many of the traders and manufacturers were Indians. The Parsee and Sephardic Jewish communities played a significant role in the commercial development of the city. In the early nineteenth century European suburban development began beyond the Esplanade, adding to the complexity of land use and occupation.

In the 1860s and 1870s a series of major transformations took place in Bombay, which resulted in the emergence of the industrial and commercial city recognisable over a century later. The cotton boom attendant upon the American Civil War gave impetus to local cotton manufacture. The governor, Sir Bartle Frere, and later India's first elected civic council embarked upon a major programme of urban improvement (Emery, 1984). The developments in shipping prompted renewed dock construction and land reclamation. For all these transformations the technology was available and was applied by ambitious and optimistic people looking to the economic gains to be made.

One of the most spectacular transformations was the erection of a row of new public buildings in place of the walls (Figure 6.7). Local, mostly military, architects were presented with the opportunity to design a large number of major government edifices, which became the finest assemblage of gothic revival buildings anywhere in the Empire. The local architects adopted the eastern-influenced Venetian gothic style for the Secretariat, Public Works Offices, Post Office and massive Law Courts, as it was considered most suitable for the city occupying the position of 'Gateway of India'. However, the University was a more purely English gothic-style structure, designed by Sir George Gilbert Scott, and it is clearly a relation of those erected in Toronto and Sydney. Other public buildings continued to use the Venetian gothic style though with increasing indigenisation towards Indo-Saracenic, exemplified by the Municipal Buildings erected in the 1890s. The highly spectacular Victoria Terminus of the Grand Indian Peninsula Railway has already been mentioned in Chapter 3. It was challenged a few years later by the Churchgate Station of the Bombay, Baroda and Central India Railway erected to the west of the Maidan. The transformation continued with the construction of new mansions for wealthy merchants and financiers, together with seaside villas.

There was another side to the growth of Bombay. The expansion of trade was linked to the new docks which were extended northwards from the Fort on land reclaimed for the purpose. Adjacent to this development and growing from the original Black Town, new suburbs and industrial works were built. Most significantly cotton mills were erected to capitalise upon the opportunities which the railway link with the cotton growing regions of the Deccan and the rest of India presented for the location of industry and the distribution of finished products. In 1865 some 10 mills had been

Figure 6.7: Plan of Central Bombay

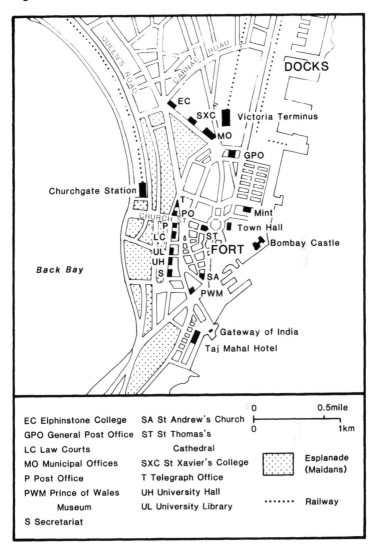

EC Elphinstone College	SA St Andrew's Church	
GPO General Post Office	ST St Thomas's	
LC Law Courts	Cathedral	
MO Municipal Offices	SXC St Xavier's College	Esplanade (Maidans)
P Post Office	T Telegraph Office	
PWM Prince of Wales	UH University Hall	
Museum	UL University Library	Railway
S Secretariat		

erected employing 6,000 workers. By 1900 the number had increased to 82 mills employing 73,000 workers. Housing of a very different nature to that in the south of the island was built for the rapidly growing labouring population. Tenements and high-density dwellings became the main form of housing in Bombay, to the horror of British municipal officials who viewed such overcrowding as undesirable and unhealthy. However, at a time when municipal by-laws, local improvement schemes and cheap workmen's railway fares assisted the decongestion of working-class suburbs in London and other major British cities, Bombay officials lacked the financial resources materially to alter the course of events. By 1931 some 1.2 million people were crowded on to Bombay Island, often at densities in excess of industrial England.

The Bombay municipality was active in the provision of services and illustrates many of the parallels between British and colonial cities. The civic improvements of late Victorian and Edwardian England are paralleled by similar schemes in this the most complex of the colonial cities. Health was a major concern of the European population. The provision of piped water from the mainland to replace the open tanks on the island, including those in graveyards, was among the first municipal engineering works. The laying of sewerage systems, but without treatment plants, was another civic priority. As a result, through the late nineteenth century Bombay's health record was better than that of London. Other improvements included the tram system to link the two sides of the island and a host of civic developments recognisable in any other Western city of like size at the time, ranging from public street lighting to model company villages. Many of the projects were based on enterprises undertaken in London, which provided the inspiration for all colonial metropolises.

SINGAPORE AND SUCCESSORS

In other town planning schemes the element of segregation in multi-racial communities was more evident. Thus when Singapore was planned, British, Malay and Chinese towns were drawn up together with separate administrative, commercial and military sectors. The result was a town of the utmost complexity from drawing board to reality. The various quarters took on their predetermined characteristics ranging from the spired cathedral to the pagodas of Chinatown. Every community, even the Malays on the island, was one of immigrants, who re-created as closely as possible what they had left behind (Teo and Savage, 1985). The significant element of Sir Stamford Raffles' plan was the assumption that each group was likely to operate most efficiently within a recognisable familiar environment (Figure 6.8). It marks a departure from the more

Figure 6.8: Plan of Singapore

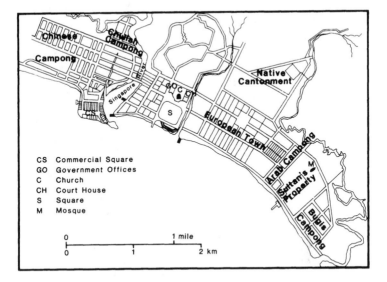

integrationist approaches of tropical town planning in the eighteenth century exemplified in Calcutta and Bombay, where social and economic segregation dominated town planning.

The process recognisable in Singapore continued throughout the nineteenth century and into the twentieth in new Asian and African colonies. Nigerian cities such as Kaduna (1917) were planned to provide a threefold division, for the Europeans, local Africans, and finally other African groups associated with the administration (Lock and Theis, 1967). Each group was separated from the other by extensive open spaces within a low-density town plan. The planning of parks, polo grounds and golf courses formed an integral part of urban design and the promotion of segregation.

In most colonial towns it was not only the British who were the immigrants to the country and the towns, as they were accompanied by substantial numbers of persons from other parts of the colony, and indeed often from other colonies and continents. Thus the racial ecology of the colonial city was often highly complex and this was frequently reflected in the town plan. Rangoon, for example, housed over 400,000 people in 1931 but only 31.9 per cent were Burmese while 3.6 per cent were European or Anglo-Indian. Over half the population (52.9 per cent) was Indian and 7.6 per cent was Chinese. Just as Europeans occupied the administrative niche in colonial

147

societies, so other immigrant groups occupied commercial or labouring sectors. Indian traders were a noticeable example throughout the tropical Empire, particularly where Indian indentured labourers had been sent in the nineteenth century to be followed by free businessmen. The other major migrant group were the Chinese who settled far beyond South East Asia to control among other enterprises, the grocery trade of towns as distant as Kingston, Jamaica, and Port Elizabeth, South Africa, by the early twentieth century (Clarke, 1985; Christopher, 1987).

NEW DELHI

Just as the settler cities, originally coastal in construction, achieved their apogee in the later interior settlements when many of the problems of a new environment had been overcome and new approaches were possible, so the colonial city in its most highly developed state needs to be examined away from the influences of the ports. In this respect, more than the settler city, the colonial city was most clearly demarcated and segregated in the planned capital cities. The centralisation of administration in most colonial structures was such as to concentrate a high proportion of the British officials and their dependent trades within the capital. Hence the major port cities which controlled government and trade grew to be the largest cities in the Empire. Tidy town planning, however, often broke down in a commercial environment but in the planned interior capital, planning principles could be most rigidly enforced. The government of India's decision in 1911 to move the capital from Calcutta to Delhi was a momentous one and as symbolic as the Australian decision to establish Canberra in the same year.

New Delhi, nevertheless, bears only passing similarities to Canberra, reflecting a very different ethos of the administration. The basic planning of New Delhi was implemented rapidly although its inauguration only took place some 20 years after the decision to move (Irving, 1981). The project as the largest and most monumental piece of planning and building in the British Empire, deserves some attention.

The decision to transfer the capital was dictated by the twin desires to emulate the magnificence of earlier capitals of India and to escape from the heat and humidity of Calcutta. The annual migration from Calcutta to Simla by the administration was clearly unsatisfactory, although the move to New Delhi did not result in the stabilisation of the government in one place. The idea of a major monument to British rule in India appealed to the spirit of pre-1914 Imperialism. Delhi, as the site of the 1877, 1903 and 1911 durbars, was the only serious contender for the position of capital, surrounded as it was by the ruins of numerous Imperial sites spanning over 2,000 years. The selection of a specific site also presented few problems as the plain to the south of Delhi (walled Shahjahanabad) was comparatively unurbanised (India, 1912).

The broad plan envisaged a new city covering some 25 square kilometres and accommodating 30,000–57,000 people. In this respect it was to be smaller than Canberra which had a city area of 65 square kilometres and a planned population of 75,000. However, New Delhi was regarded as a government quarter addition to the existing city, whereas Canberra was designed as a complete entity. The site was dominated by Raisina Hill some 4 kilometres to the south-west of the walls of Old Delhi, and as the site of the key public buildings was the core of the total design. Sir Edwin Lutyens and Sir Herbert Baker were commissioned to plan the city and design the main buildings. Lutyens had established an extensive architectural practice in England with numerous commissions for country houses and government buildings, while Baker had developed a considerable practice in South Africa designing offices, houses, churches and most significantly the Union Buildings in Pretoria. Both therefore had experience of designing monumental edifices and were influenced by the new trends in architecture and planning evident in the early twentieth century.

The grand geometrical plan anchored to the Raisina Hill site for Viceroy's House was clearly influenced by the spectacular temporary pavilion erected for the coronation durbars of King Edward VII and King George V (Figure 6.9). The initial concept of visually linking Old and New Delhi by focusing the main ceremonial way (Kingsway) on the Jama Masjid in Old Delhi was abandoned in favour of an east-west axis leading down to the Jumna River. Old and New Delhi therefore were now to be two separate entities with an open green belt between them. At right-angles to Kingsway a second axis, Queensway, provided another key element in the design of radiating vistas and axes with hexagonal blocks and open spaces. The avenues and roads were broad, with trees planted at frequent intervals to provide a verdant appearance to the city, particularly noticeable in the dry season.

Kingsway extended for 3 kilometres from Viceroy's House to the All-India War Memorial Arch and canopied royal statue. It was

Figure 6.9: Plan of New Delhi, 1931

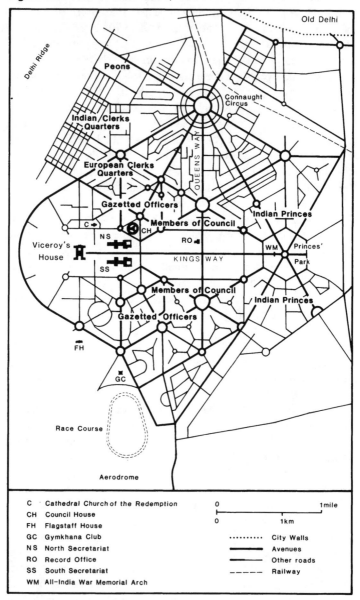

C · Cathedral Church of the Redemption
CH   Council House
FH   Flagstaff House
GC   Gymkhana Club
NS   North Secretariat
RO   Record Office
SS   South Secretariat
WM   All-India War Memorial Arch

0 ⊢————————————⊣ 1 mile
0 ⊢————————————⊣ 1 km

·········· City Walls
━━━━━━ Avenues
———— Other roads
— — — — Railway

Figure 6.10: North Secretariat, New Delhi

flanked by the twin Secretariats which shared Raisina Hill with Viceroy's House, all constructed in pink and cream sandstone (Figure 6.10). Extensive parks with water gardens completed the impressive design of Kingsway. However, the vista concept was partially negated by the decision for Viceroy's House to share the summit of Raisina Hill with the Secretariats. The ceremonial view of Viceroy's House, itself larger than the Palace of Versailles with an eastern façade some 200 metres in length, begins to be obscured some 800 metres from the Secretariats. At the base of the hill only the dome of the house is visible. Thus much of the impact of the vista is lost and it is Baker's Secretariats which dominate, not Lutyens' Viceroy's House, causing the latter to refer to it as his 'Bakerloo'. Perhaps the unwitting bureaucratic victory emphasising the true resting place of administrative dominance in the Empire was not inappropriate. The Hill was adorned with great attention to detail. British lions and Imperial elephants were placed in appropriate positions. The Jaipur Column was erected in the forecourt of Viceroy's House, while the four dominion columns presented by the governments of Canada, Australia, New Zealand and South Africa adorn Government Court between the two Secretariats. The dominion coats of arms at the base of each column emphasised the unity of the British Empire (Figure 6.11).

At the intersection of Kingsway and Queensway a complex of cultural buildings was planned but only the Imperial Record Office was built to Lutyens' design. Key sites in the city plan were occupied by Flagstaff House, the residence of the Commander-in-Chief and the Anglican Cathedral Church of the Redemption. It is notable that the Council House, for parliament, was fitted into the scheme late in the planning stage as a measure of self-government was conceded. Thus the parliamentary buildings do not form the major focus of the plan, in contrast to Canberra or Ottawa, where it was the ideal of self-government which was enshrined in urban design. The Viceroy's House was designed to dominate the entire plan, a concept of authoritarian government already obsolete when New Delhi was inaugurated in 1931 and certainly inappropriate for modern India's parliamentary democracy.

Most of the plan was occupied by housing, some 4,000 houses in total. A strictly hierarchical system was adopted with segregation of housing according to status in the administration (King, 1976). Accordingly senior civil servants occupied plots of over 1 hectare while juniors occupied smaller plots. The most senior were situated to the south of Viceroy's House, and seniority suitably declined

Figure 6.11: South African Dominion Column, New Delhi

with distance from the head of the government. In style the bungalow with simple pillared stucco design was adopted. The larger extended to a dozen or more rooms with extensive outbuildings, while junior Indian clerks were housed in more modest terraces and the messengers (peons) in hostel blocks. At the eastern end of Kingsway a section was laid out around Princes' Park for the mansions of the Indian princes. The Nizam of Hyderabad, the senior feudatory ruler, obtained the most prominent site and built a house costing over £200,000. The town plan provided for a maximum of 3 hectares for the princes' town houses, thereby preventing any of them building structures to rival Viceroy's House.

The northern focus of the road system, Connaught Circus, was designed as the commercial centre of the city. Originally it was intended to build the main railway station on the northern side, but this was never implemented. Connaught Circus was built in a wide circle of two-storeyed shop and office blocks, also constructed in white painted stucco with a marked classical pillared appearance. This became the business sector of the city and reduced dependence upon Old Delhi. It also represented the one sector which was essentially erected by private enterprise in an otherwise government city. The remaining section of the plan was the cantonment to the west of the administrative city. The plan was simpler but one of the most extensive ever laid out in India.

At the time of its inauguration in 1931 New Delhi recorded a population of 73,700 out of a total for greater Delhi of 636,200. At a cost of over £10,000,000 it is without doubt one of the great monuments of the British Empire. Philip Davies (1985: 15–16) noted 'the monumental conception and scale of New Delhi is the crowning achievement of British architecture in India'. This was particularly remarkable in view of 'the congenital meanness and philistinism of British government and bureaucracy' (Stamp, 1981: 372).

New Delhi was a model for the plan of Lusaka, the capital of Northern Rhodesia. In 1931 the administration decided to move from the peripheral site at Livingstone on the Southern Rhodesian border to a more central site, yet one still distanced from the rapidly growing Copperbelt (Collins, 1980). New Delhi, however, provided a poor guide as there were two significant differences between the new Indian and Northern Rhodesian capitals. The first was the lack of any long tradition of indigenous urban settlement in Northern Rhodesia and the second the presence of permanent White settlers resulting in Salisbury being regarded as a model by some of the officials. Plans assumed an eventual population of 8,000 Europeans and 5,000 Africans. Yet Livingstone in 1931 enumerated 7,930 Africans and 1,596 Europeans. There was thus from the start an inadequate provision for the indigenous population. The plan provided for a geometrical pattern of roads with the official buildings placed in prominent positions. The European residential areas were to be spacious in best garden city planning practice with substantial parks and sports grounds. However, the miscalculation over the anticipated African population resulted in the planning of a typical southern African location for the indigenous population as the area of Crown Land available for the capital city project was limited. The garden city image of Lusaka thus only applied to part of the town.

HILL STATIONS

Possibly some of the most unusual features of the colonial town system were the more than 80 hill stations developed in India. During the summer the heat upon the plains was such as to induce the administration and others free to do so, to seek relief in migrating to the relative coolness of the mountains. Consequently Darjeeling was built as a summer hill resort at an elevation of over 2,500 metres in the foothills of the Himalayas after its acquisition by the British authorities in 1838. The government of Bengal migrated annually to the town to avoid the summer heat, leaving only those officials in Calcutta whose work demanded their remaining there. Other hill stations were developed as summer resorts for civilian populations and for the various provincial, presidency and Imperial administrations. The most notable included Ootacumund in the Nilgiri Hills in South India, and Simla and Mussourie in the central Himalayas. Intriguingly, the government of Jammu and Kashmir prevented Europeans from purchasing land in the state so that conventional hill stations did not develop in the western Himalayas. However, resourceful businessmen overcame the problem by building houseboats on the Kashmiri lakes.

The hill stations presented particular challenges due to their terrain. There was little flat ground, so that buildings were constructed on steep slopes and communication within the town as well as with the outside world was difficult. The ridges on which Simla and Darjeeling were built offered suitable sites for the governor's or viceroy's residences and the main military cantonments.

The remainder of the town was strung out along a series of contour roads and connecting paths and stairways lined with hotels, clubs and bungalows, resulting in a most irregular form. The houses and other buildings emulated a wide variety of English and European styles ranging from Jacobean Renaissance to a Victorian vision of timbered Black Forest (Figure 6.12). Thus in Simla a Victorian Gothic church and a half-timbered Victorian-Tudor town hall were incongruously built next to one another on the Ridge. The range of public buildings was greatest at Simla which acted as the summer capital of the Indian Empire. The government offices made extensive use of corrugated iron and because of the site, cast-iron cantilevers produced a highly utilitarian even temporary appearance, which was often condemned by visitors. Sir Edwin Lutyens commented of Simla in general that it was 'a pure piece of folly such as only Englishmen can achieve', while reserving his full condemnation for the Secretariat which looked as though it had been put up by the resident monkey population which 'must be shot in case they do it again' (Irving, 1981: 46).

The main purpose of builders and architects in the hill stations was to design holiday resorts, which masked the administrative importance of the settlements. Houses and bungalows were given names reminiscent of England (Richmond Hill, York Villa, Windsor Bungalow) or of its plants (Oak Lodge, the Elms, Violet Dale), not only in Darjeeling, but repeated in the other stations. Active planting of a wide variety of imported species as well as the rich variety of Himalayan flowering shrubs increased the image of a resort far removed from the crowded plains below. Problems of space made the race tracks at Simla and Darjeeling short and hazardous and much earth removal was necessary to create polo grounds, sports fields and parade grounds.

Unlike other Indian towns the hill stations were designed to be nominally entirely European and small. This is well illustrated by Darjeeling where in 1931 only 20,000 people were enumerated, half of whom were European. The indigenous population was either housed by employers on their premises or, more generally, occupied some of the lower slopes of the town. The ambience was intended to be British from the Mall on the crest of the ridge down the slopes to the plantations below, and this was achieved in large measure both in the Himalayas and the Nilgiris.

Hill stations of lesser distinction were established elsewhere in the tropical Empire. The desire to escape from the heat and humidity of the coast led to a variety of administrations establishing upland

Figure 6.12: The Mall, Simla

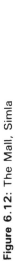

stations such as Rose Hill-Curepipe in Mauritius. Hill Station some 300 metres above Freetown in Sierra Leone was a rare example of a station built (in 1902) for daily commuting rather than on an annual basis. Hill Station provided the climatic advantages together with an illuminating example of the sanitation syndrome and racial segregation. At that date medical 'wisdom' suggested that the malarial mosquitoes were infected by Africans as carriers of the disease. Thus only after a mosquito had bitten an African could it transmit the disease to a European. As mosquitoes only bit at night, then segregation was only required for the night time (King, 1984). The settlement outlasted the exposure of this absurd fallacy.

Even in small island colonies the governors and officials adopted the same approach of seeking relief from the heat of the coast in the hills. Thus on St Helena, the governor abandoned the Castle in Jamestown for Plantation House at an altitude of 600 metres in the wooded upland interior of the island. Even the bishop moved his seat from St James' Church in the town to St Paul's, adjacent to Plantation House.

7

The Rural Division of Land

Within the British Empire there was a constant conflict of interest between the British, whether settler or administrator, and indigenous populations over the control and use of land. The result was the operation of a dualistic land policy in many colonies and territories, with a consequent effective partition of the land which profoundly affected the rural landscape. The attempt to separate immigrant and indigene, where they competed for land resources, was an early feature of English colonial policy and may be traced back to English experience in Ireland and Virginia.

The partition of land resources took several forms. In the early stages of colonisation when colonial governments were weak *vis-à-vis* indigenous polities, administrations sought to secure compact blocks of land for European immigrants, leaving extensive tracts for semi-independent indigenous societies. When power relationships had changed, European appropriation of most of a colony's land became possible, with the indigenous population relegated to small reserves conveniently located to supply labour for the European-dominated economy. Elements of protection, exploitation and control entered the policy which was subject to modification through time. Settler ethos also played a significant part. The contrast between Tasmania, with its harsh convict background and New Zealand with a free evangelical background was reflected in the development of colonial policies. In the former case Aborigines were systematically exterminated, removing any need to partition the island; in the latter a more systematic recognition of Maori rights ensured their survival and place in colonial society.

Rural land use planning was also apparent in the establishment of reserves for wildlife and scenic national parks, as an appreciation of the variety of fauna, flora and environments within the colonies

159

came into being. Similarly forestry reserves were promoted to conserve timber resources for commercial exploitation rather than felling to extend the agricultural area. Once more it was flexibility which was noticeable in the drawing of lines on maps prior to the First World War, although by the 1930s a certain degree of stability in demarcated areas was evident. In rural planning, the experience of the United States of America, in its administration of the occupation and development of its extensive public domain, was of significance for British colonial planners who shared a common cultural heritage and common problems with their American counterparts.

The most remarkable division within the tropical Empire was the partition of India between British India directly administered by the Government of India according to the laws of Great Britain and local amending legislation, and the Indian states under the personal rule of their princes (Figure 7.1) (Srivastava, 1979). The expansion of British power under the East India Company from the initial factory at Surat in 1609 had resulted in nearly two-thirds of the Indian subcontinent passing into the direct control of the British administration. However, the revolt of 1857 ended the period of active annexation policies. The Better Government of India Act effectively froze the pattern of states and British holdings at that date. Thus in 1928 there were some 562 princely states ranging in size from Hyderabad (214,013 square kilometres) to the smallest, Veja-no-ness in Kathiawar, covering only 100 hectares (Ashton, 1982). Subject often only to the concept of British paramountcy the rulers of the states were virtually free to pursue their own independent internal policies. The Indian states, however, suffered from a number of problems in that investment capital from the British Isles was almost exclusively directed towards projects in British India. In addition princely subjects were not legally British subjects and hence experienced problems when emigrating to other parts of the Empire. So far as the British government was concerned the princes presented a traditional counterweight to the rising level of Indian nationalism in the shifting politics of the Indian Empire, and little attempt was made to integrate their states into the framework of British India.

DEFINING THE 'NATIVE' RESERVES

British colonial policy regarding the indigenous population in the

Figure 7.1: India, political divisions, 1931

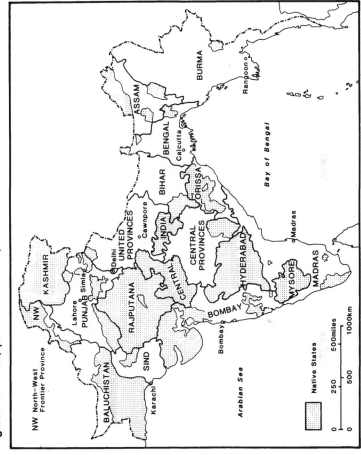

Table 7.1: Reservation of land for indigenous peoples in selected states, *c.* 1930

Dominion or colony	Total area (million hectares)	Area of reserves (million hectares)	Area in European hands (million hectares)
Canada	954.3	2.1	65.8
Australia	770.4	54.1	460.7
New Zealand	26.8	1.8	15.3
South Africa	122.2	8.9	82.8
Southern Rhodesia	38.9	8.7	13.0
Northern Rhodesia	75.2	29.8	3.6
Kenya	57.2	11.3	3.3
Malaya	13.2	3.4	1.2
Fiji	1.8	1.5	0.2

Notes: (1) Areas are often poorly defined with yearbooks of different origins providing contradictory figures. Some areas can be no more than estimates, providing approximately correct proportions.
(2) Reserves had different connotations in different territories. In Fiji virtually the entire colony remained under Fijian customary tenure with small concessions granted to European and Asian farmers, while in others reserves were specifically demarcated and remainders were declared Crown Land, some of which might be occupied by the indigenous peoples if not required for other purposes. In Malaya reservations were areas where only Malays might acquire land. Malays owned extensive areas outside the reservations.
(3) European areas include land held under licence on leasehold (Australia, 386.5 million hectares).
Source: Dominion and colonial yearbooks and blue books.

rural areas lacked any consistent direction. Attitudes ranged from impulses to convert and save souls on the one hand to exploitation and extermination on the other. Recognition of the land rights of the indigenous population similarly varied from the complete recognition of the pre-colonial land system to the assumption that all land on annexation became the property of the Crown. It was the latter which tended to predominate in the temperate lands and the former in the tropical areas of late incorporation into the Imperial system (Table 7.1).

Although no clearly defined policy was pursued, the resultant pattern suggests that segregation ideology was a powerful influence upon the practical implementation of land policies in the colonies. Where indigenous land rights did survive annexation, their territorial extent was clearly defined, and where possible and desirable from the settler point of view, they were legally circumscribed and reduced through purchase, treaty or confiscation.

Even in colonies considered unsuitable for European settlement, areas of direct British rule were carefully separated from areas of indirect rule, where the systems of the pre-colonial era survived, if in modified form. Mixed areas were generally discouraged. The official acceptance of the theory of friction between different groups was increasingly accepted. The statement, 'In the interests of all alike it is not desirable that Natives should acquire land indiscriminately owing to the inevitable friction which will arise with their European neighbours', appearing in the Report of the Southern Rhodesian Land Commission of 1925, would not have raised many objections (Southern Rhodesia, 1925: 3).

The major mid-latitude colonies and dominions, as the first to be subject to such a division of land resources, followed the experience gained by politicians and administrators in earlier English and Scottish colonisation ventures in Ireland. In the sixteenth and seventeenth centuries a *de facto* partition of the island took place as compact blocks of land were confiscated from their Irish owners and settled by immigrants. Parallel with this movement the settlement of North America began. The Charter of Virginia claimed all lands not belonging to a Christian prince as Crown Land, which conflicted with local pragmatic recognition of Indian rights of occupation. This contradiction in policy was to remain throughout the colonial era. The pattern of mistrust and intermittent conflict which ensued resulted in the suppression of land rights and the establishment of *de facto* separation of immigrant and indigene. *De facto* segregation was then replaced by *de jure* demarcation of reserves for the Indian population in Virginia and the founding of separate villages for Indians and Europeans in New England. The roots of colonial segregation are thus long and wide.

The general North American experience was the creation of a frontier zone separating the areas undergoing European colonisation and the areas still in Indian hands under traditional tenures. The line of 1764 defining the 13 colonies' area of settlement is but one example of the attempt to partition British dominions between areas for European settlement and areas for continued indigenous occupation. The mere imposition of the line was a source of settler grievance against the Imperial government and was profoundly unpractical as the pressures for settler territorial expansion built up. 'Permanent' divisions of the land resources between settler and indigenous populations proved to be no more than temporary as settler communities increased in strength and were able to ignore Imperial policy. The American experience was repeated elsewhere with more accommodating administrations in London, anxious not to provoke the final American settler response, namely the unilateral declaration of independence.

Accordingly in Canada, Australia, New Zealand and South Africa, settler communities expanded the areas available to them through measures ranging from annexation to purchase. Throughout the eighteenth and nineteenth centuries the expansion of the European settled area resulted in the contraction of the indigenous areas, whose land rights were extinguished. The result was the establishment of a series of reservations for the indigenous population, usually in areas of little settler interest, or where the Imperial government had considered an accommodation with the indigenous authorities to be of overriding importance. Thus on a map, the Indian and Eskimo areas of Canada or the Aboriginal areas of Australia appeared large for the number of people involved. However, the poverty of their resources and often unsuitability for the indigenous economy, rendered the population poverty stricken and wards of the dominion governments. Effectively reservations were excluded from the economy of the country and their populations from the political economy of the state. In Canada and Australia Indian and Aboriginal population declined as a result of the disruption of their economies and the importation of European diseases, and the reservations were consequently largely forgotten by the newly dominant immigrant groups (McQuillan, 1980). If numbers were higher in New Zealand and the measure of protection afforded Maori land rights more significant, the end result was still the partition of the Dominion into two land areas governed by two systems of land tenure.

The temperate dominion of settlement which did not follow this pattern was South Africa. Whereas Canada, Australia and New Zealand attained a European population majority within a relatively short time as a result of massive immigration, South Africa did not. Even after the peak of European immigration prior to the First World War, only a fifth of the population of the country was White. Other colonies of European settlement recorded even lower proportions (Table 7.2). Thus the division of land resources in southern and eastern Africa reflected a more complex pattern than in Canada or Australia (Palmer, 1977; Sorrenson, 1968). Initial sweeping land confiscations were followed by a complicated system of bargaining, albeit one-sided bargaining. In Swaziland the royal family and senior chiefs were incorporated into the colonial hierarchy through the restitution of their lands in the first decade of the present century, although two-thirds of the Protectorate remained in European hands

Table 7.2: Population composition of selected dominions and colonies, *c.* 1930

Dominion or colony	Total population (000s)	Indigenous population (000s)	European population (000s)	Other immigrants (000s)
Canada	10,378	100	10,278	—
Australia	6,449	62	6,837	—
New Zealand	1,443	73	1,370	—
South Africa	8,133	5,520	1,829	784
Southern Rhodesia	1,134	1,080	50	4
Northern Rhodesia	1,345	1,330	14	1
Kenya	3,041	2,972	17	52
Malaya	4,348	1,930	20	2,397
Fiji	183	90	6	87

Notes: (1) No uniform categorisation was used throughout the Empire. Thus people of mixed European ancestry were included in 'others' or in 'Europeans' depending upon territory. They have been included in 'other immigrants' where possible or estimates made for their numbers.
(2) Many figures are estimates rather than census returns. The figures for the indigenous population in Northern and Southern Rhodesia were estimated to the nearest 10,000, and subject to upward revision at subsequent censuses.

(Crush, 1980). In Kenya dominant tribes such as the Masai were confirmed in most of their traditional grazing and hunting grounds (Morgan, 1963).

Thus reservations ('Native Reserves') were defined and redefined in Africa as the European and African populations expanded and settled new areas. European dominance varied from the overwhelming 93 per cent of land ownership in the Orange Free State to lesser percentages elsewhere. The constant redrawing of boundaries, particularly in Southern Rhodesia, resulted in the attempt in the late 1920s and early 1930s to establish a permanent division of resources. The Kenyan, Southern Rhodesian and South African quests resulted in a hardening of racial land ownership boundaries consequent upon a hardening of racial attitudes, which were only partially softened at the end of the colonial era. The Southern Rhodesian Land Apportionment Act of 1931 was based on the premise of separation and parallel systems for immigrant and indigene, an approach adopted by several official enquiries into colonial matters elsewhere in the 1920s and 1930s (Christopher, 1971).

The balance between land deemed suitable and unsuitable for European settlement was a fine one. Thus Uganda in the early twentieth century was viewed as ideal for European colonisation. Yet despite initial optimism and the establishment of 130 plantations covering 20,000 hectares by 1913, the scheme failed. In 1923 the colonial administration decided that the agricultural sector of the protectorate's economy was best left in the hands of African cultivators (Mutibwa, 1976). In another marginal settler colony, Northern Rhodesia, the first Native Reserves were established for persons displaced from lands on either side of the railway lines, which were designated for future European settlement. The contrast between heavily populated reserves and unoccupied lands awaiting settlement was one of the anomalies which became of greater significance after the Second World War.

Within colonies considered unsuitable for permanent European settlement, the partition took other forms. Areas were reserved for European exploitation, notably for plantations in highland regions of the tropics or other territories with small indigenous populations and suitable climatic conditions. Within such areas it was often imported labour under European management which undertook the actual cultivation. Accordingly in India areas of Assam and the Nilgiri Hills in the south were acquired for plantation cropping and labour was recruited from other parts of India to work on the estates.

Reservations were also established to maintain indigenous land rights where threatened by other non-British immigrant groups. In 1913 the first of the Malay Reservations was established and the practice was extended throughout the Federated and 'Unfederated' Malay States (Figure 7.2). Land within Malay Reservations could not be alienated to other groups, notably the Chinese. The measure was designed to protect the Malay rural economy and also to prevent the cultivation of rubber on the Malay smallholdings, thereby ensuring the continued production of food staples. The result provided a complex pattern of Malay and Open Areas, each with its own distinctive pattern of agriculture and settlement (Figure 7.3). In contrast active colonisation by the Chinese was encouraged by the British North Borneo Company which offered smallholdings and free passages from Hong Kong for immigrant families. By 1928 nearly 1,200 families had arrived and a fifth of the territory's rubber cultivation was sited on the Chinese smallholdings.

Protection of indigenous land rights was extended in colonies where settlement by immigrant groups was viewed as politically undesirable. In Fiji customary land tenure had been guaranteed at the time of Cession in 1874, with the exceptions of concessions and land required for government purposes. Although the indigenous population was halved in the ensuing 30 years, this guarantee was strengthened in the face of Indian demands for land in order to

Figure 7.2: The Malay Reservations

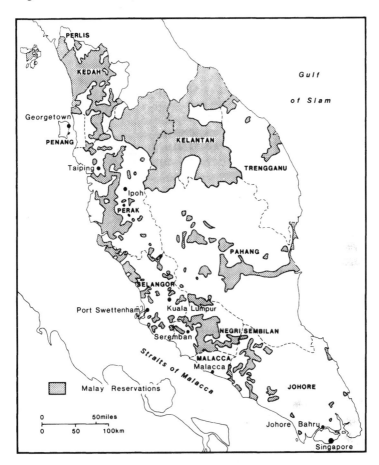

preserve social stability. The process was taken further in Kenya where the 'White Highlands' policy was pursued to protect European interests against what was viewed by the settlers as a threat from Indian land purchases. The Highlands thus become a white reservation (Great Britain, 1934). Similarly agreements with Nigerian rulers prevented European or more particularly Asian ownership of land in the protectorates. An exception to the protection of indigenous land rights was the establishment of mission stations, notably in non-Moslem parts of the Empire. The stations served as refuges and centres of Europeanisation through conversion to Christianity and the provision of training in skills required by the colonial economy.

Figure 7.3: Settlement patterns on Malay Reservation and European estates, Perak

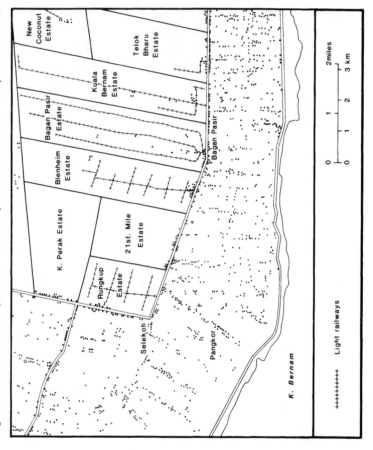

CHANGES IN THE INDIGENOUS AREAS

Areas defined as indigenous fell into two broad categories, directly and indirectly administered. The directly ruled indigenous areas were governed by the colonial or dominion governments through officials responsible to special ministries of 'Native', 'Indian', 'Aboriginal' or 'Maori' Affairs, although for some purposes the reservations were administered as part of the adjacent settler farming areas. Indirect rule applied to tropical and subtropical areas, particularly India and Nigeria where the pre-colonial polities were in effect under a protectorate agreement. British advisers were sometimes extremely influential, but it was the indigenous social system which was maintained and this effectively checked any rapid attempt to anglicise the social structure and economy. Clearly in such a loosely held Empire the range of administrations was immense and only a few aspects can be indicated.

The keys to understanding the development of the indigenous landscape were the extent of the incorporation of the rural economy into the Imperial economy and the degree of its dependence upon a settler community. Dependency might take extreme forms. Thus little attempt at even self-sufficiency was possible on some Canadian reserves where the Ministry of Indian Affairs became a universal provider in the painful transition period from nomadic to sedentary life. Dependence upon government assistance clearly acted as a brake upon economic progress.

Economic viability was maintained for longer in the South African reserves where agricultural expansion accompanied the growth of population and the rise of the sub-continental economy. However, the imposition of taxation in cash upon a basically subsistence economy, and the introduction of new consumer demands, resulted in the emergence of 'Africa of the Labour Reserves' (Crush, 1982). In South Africa a weakening rural reserve economy was maintained by an increasingly significant contribution from migrant labourers working in the settler economy. Increasing pressure of population and the exhaustion of new land for colonisation, as a result of the tight definition of reserve boundaries, resulted in a swelling pool of relatively cheap labour for the mining industry in particular (Crush, 1986). The much discussed proletarianisation of the peasantry was the end product of this process. The degree to which colonial administrations sought this end is disputed, although it was widely held in official circles that civilisation was to be achieved through the work ethic. Other administrations sought to ensure labour forces for settler enterprises through the imposition of taxation on able-bodied men not working for European employers.

Clearly such a dramatic change in the economy of the indigenous areas was dependent upon the overwhelming strength of the settler economy. Processes similar to those examined in South Africa were evident in settler colonies in Southern Rhodesia and Kenya. However, the indigenous economy proved to be more robust in these states and through internal colonisation and agriculture development it maintained greater independence of the weaker settler economies.

In colonies without a significant settler community, change occurred within the indigenous agricultural regions as a result of the improvement of communication systems and the exploitation of new markets consequent upon incorporation into the Imperial economy. The success of African peasant cultivation of cocoa in the Gold Coast is a case in point. The colonial authorities placed their confidence in gold mining and did little to assist the peasantry in its adoption of cocoa cultivation and the consequent colonisation of new areas in Ashanti suited to the crop. Similarly official expectations of a cotton cultivation boom in Northern Nigeria following the construction of the railway line to Kano were misplaced as Nigerian cultivators gained greater returns from groundnuts. Improvements in internal communications also resulted in the adoption of crops not destined for the international market. Thus kolanut production in Southern Nigeria, for purely internal consumption, was facilitated by the construction of the colonial road system which ensured efficient distribution (Akinbode, 1974).

Colonial intervention in the indigenous rural areas was often active in the promotion of change through improved agricultural techniques and stock management. Agricultural colleges and extension officers introduced new ideas and practices which enabled farmers to increase yields and stocking densities. Some of the most noticeable advances in indigenous agriculture came through the programmes launched by veterinary officials. Consequently animal diseases, particularly in tropical Africa, were controlled through new serums and restrictions on the movement of livestock. Measures to eradicate tsetse fly resulted in new areas being opened up for agriculture and livestock production. Other measures designed to eliminate disease such as malaria similarly increased the range of human settlement.

COLONISATION

Most of the writings on the colonisation of rural areas within the British Empire have been directed towards the settlement of Europeans, particularly British settlers. Nevertheless, other rural colonisation schemes achieved noteworthy results involving the resettlement of several million people. Intercontinental migrations of rural settlers from the extra-European parts of the Empire and indeed other parts of the world were slight compared with the outflow from Europe, but locally significant. Thus Indian settlement throughout the tropical Empire was associated with indentured plantation labour but not exclusively limited to that group. Chinese settlement in Malaya and North Borneo similarly provided the manpower for major agricultural as well as mining and commercial developments. However, there was a general official resistance to the encouragement of large-scale Indian colonisation outside the Indian Empire. When the Indian settlement of the lowlands of the Transvaal was proposed after the Anglo-Boer War, it was found not to be politically acceptable (Willcocks, 1901). One of the few independent intercontinental movements of non-British settlers was associated with the Jewish settlement of Palestine which proved to be a source of controversy for the British administration.

The majority of state administered colonisation schemes for non-European settlers involved internal colonisation and the construction of irrigation schemes. In addition to India, extensive irrigation schemes were undertaken in Burma, where the provision of land at reasonable terms resulted in a substantial resettlement of the Irrawaddy delta region after 1880 (Fenichel and Huff, 1971). Burma became one of the major rice surplus regions of Asia in consequence of a five-fold expansion of the rice acreage in Lower Burma between 1880 and 1930. Other schemes in Egypt, although nominally not within the Empire, resulted in the regulation of the flow of the Nile through the construction of the Aswan low level dam. After 1918 a start was made on the reopening of the irrigation systems of Iraq. New schemes involved the establishment of the Gezira system between the Blue and White Nile Rivers in the Sudan at one end of the scale and various smaller works on the coastal belt of Malaya at the other end.

India

The most important Imperial irrigation works were undertaken in India in the nineteenth and early twentieth centuries to expand the irrigable area of the sub-continent, particularly in the Punjab and Madras (Kumar and Desai, 1982). Here colonisation schemes were designed by British engineers, not for British settlers, but for Indian settlers in an effort to expand the Indian rural economy and lessen the dangers of famine. By 1926 some 10.8 million hectares of government irrigation works had been constructed at a cost of £74.9 million (Great Britain, 1928). The irrigation schemes in Northern India were based on a series of major canals including the Ganges Canal which was officially described as 'a work which in magnitude and boldness of design has not been surpassed by any irrigation work in India or elsewhere' (India, 1903: 10).

The East India Company had inherited the pre-colonial state irrigation systems of India, which had in the north largely ceased to work by the early nineteenth century. The need to reopen and expand them was evident both to raise revenue to support the administration and as a means of increasing production to overcome the constant spectre of famine in the sub-continent. Restoration work was converted into improvement and expansion programmes. In the south of the country, the Madras Presidency was responsible for the regulation of the major works, the canals, dams, weirs and tanks, but not for the detailed distribution of water (Wallach, 1985). In the north of India the entire system came under government control.

The northern schemes began with the restoration of the Western and Eastern Jumna systems in the 1830s. The programme continued with the construction of the major Ganges Canal, completed in 1854 and capable of irrigating 600,000 hectares (Stone, 1984). The Imperial nature of the design and magnitude was emphasised by the British masonry lions erected along its banks. Until the 1890s the major schemes aimed at the improvement of existing, often dryland, areas of cultivation, by providing irrigation water in drought periods or sufficient water for more limited areas of profitable commercial crops such as wheat or sugar cane in normal years. The twin aims of increased revenue and famine relief were not always compatible, as irrigation schemes tended to be underutilised in years of normal rainfall when only cash crops grown near the headwaters were irrigated. In drought and potential famine years conflict between the continued cultivation of commercial crops and the need for subsistence crops often resulted in an unsatisfactory outcome for the schemes.

Figure 7.4: Barrage on the Sutlej Valley Irrigation Project

Figure 7.5: Irrigation colony, Lyallpur District, Punjab

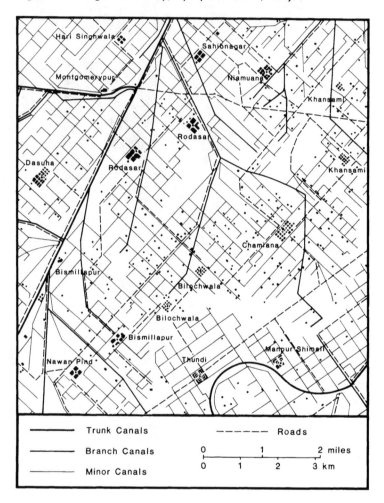

However new areas of cultivation, particularly in the Punjab, were opened for colonisation as a result of the irrigation projects undertaken in the semi-arid lands of India. The first major scheme, based on the Lower Chenab Canal, made some 400,000 hectares available for agricultural settlement in the period 1892–1905. This was followed by the Lower Bari Doab Canal, completed in 1917 and colonised in the period between 1912 and 1922. Other ambitious projects followed, harnessing the Jhelum and Sutlej Rivers, which resulted in over 2.5 million hectares being brought under irrigation by the 1930s (Figure 7.4). Whereas irrigation schemes in the better watered areas had often been unprofitable, the major projects in the Punjab and North West Frontier Province were in the main extremely profitable to operate. Cultivators were totally dependent upon the water supplied by the government and hence the water budget could be anticipated from one year to another. In these regions the entire scheme was planned in advance with attention not only directed towards the construction of the barrages, canals and distributory works, but also to the detailed layout of the settlement pattern and land holdings as part of a comprehensive colonisation programme. Furthermore the new settlers tended to be more innovative and adaptable than those in established agricultural zones, where the provision of irrigation water was but an adjunct to the existing system of cultivation. A measure of the transformation of the landscape and economy may be gauged from the Lyallpur District in the Punjab which in 1891 supported some 60,000 people, whereas by 1931 the population had risen to 1.2 million (Figure 7.5).

Palestine

The contradictory position into which colonial administrations were placed with regard to land affairs is most clearly exhibited in the mandatory regulation of Palestine after the First World War. The Balfour Declaration of 1917 offered the prospect of a Jewish national home in Palestine. Subsequently the terms of the League of Nations mandate imposed two mutually conflicting objectives upon the British government, namely the promotion of close settlement by Jewish immigrants upon the land, and the safeguarding of the rights and position of other sections of the population (Great Britain, 1937). The Jewish settlement which ensued was unlike most other European colonisation programmes in the Empire as it was almost entirely conducted by independent organisations, notably the Jewish National Fund, which purchased land from Arab landowners, and the Settlement Department of the Zionist Organization which laid out and initiated the settlements. Thus the British administration played no role in the planning of colonisation schemes, although it was expected on the one hand to facilitate the transfer of land from Arab to Jew and on the other to protect the rights of Arab cultivators.

Jewish settlement was spread across Palestine according to the availability of land on the market, yet also with strategic concentrations to provide a measure of security in periods of increasing Arab hostility, notably after the 1929 riots. In the main, purchases were concentrated in the coastal plain, the plain of Jesreel and around Lake Hula. Jewish funds were available to develop land for intensive agriculture which previously had been either uncultivated due to a lack of water, or waste land requiring extensive drainage works. Jewish settlement planners abandoned the concept of individual freehold farms, in favour of co-operative and communal farming villages occupying approximately 500–1,000 hectares apiece and inhabited by over a 100 families. The communal kibbutz and the co-operative moshav forms of settlement were designed and developed during the early mandate period and largely superseded the earlier individualistic moshava settlement. The moshav village of Nahalal, founded in 1921 on the plain of Jesreel, illustrates the plan of the new forms of settlement (Figure 7.6). Some 48 villages were established between 1918 and 1930 and the pace of settlement appeared to be increasing as experience was gained in agricultural practices and integrating urban immigrants from eastern and central Europe into the rural environment (Gvati, 1985). Approximately 100,000 hectares had passed into Jewish hands by 1930.

The very success of Jewish agricultural settlement raised problems for the British administration as the perception was developed of a growing pressure upon available Arab lands (Stein, 1984). Following the communal riots in 1929, Sir John Hope Simpson was appointed commissioner to examine the question of the land resources of Palestine in view of the clash of interests. He concluded that with existing technological usage there was no land available for Jewish settlement which would not result in Arab displacement (Great Britain, 1930). The result was the gradual restriction of transfer of land to Jewish purchasers to specific regions of Palestine, essentially creating the territorial base for the eventual establishment of the State of Israel in 1948. Thus two Palestinian rural landscapes, one Jewish and capital intensive and one Arab and labour intensive, developed in the mandate period.

PLANTATIONS

The plantation system was a particularly significant part of the colonial economy (Britton, 1980). It brought together the three

Figure 7.6: Aerial view of Nahalal, Palestine

elements of land, labour and capital in a manner and in a classical economic efficiency which was achieved by few other rural enterprises. The availability of land within the British Empire and the ease with which it could be acquired by capitalists in England provided the first impetus to the system. The second concerned the need for substantial inputs of capital to establish a plantation with its prepared fields, workshops and processing plants. Investors needed patience, as several years of heavy expenditure were necessary before the first returns materialised. The third aspect involved the employment of a controlled and regular labour force to undertake the basic hard work on the plantation. The organisational system proved to be suitable for only a few crops, requiring a certain degree of skill and capital expenditure. These crops proved to be virtually all tropical or subtropical in nature as temperate crops were not successfully subjected to the plantation system (Earle, 1978).

It was often the third aspect of labour which presented the major problems for plantation development and called for solutions with the most longlasting repercussions. The early British overseas settlements all suffered from chronic labour shortages. Plans for commercial crop production, whether in Virginia or the West Indies, experienced problems caused both by a limited number of free settlers and a not surprising unwillingness on the part of the indigenous population to work for the immigrants. Free settlers preferred to work for their own account or supervise the labour of others. In order to supply this labour, experiments with English indentured labour were tried but the numbers were limited and the results not successful. The labour problems of the Spanish and Portuguese Empires in the Americas had been partially alleviated in the sixteenth century by the introduction of slaves from Africa. The same iniquitous solution was adopted by the British colonial authorities. The transatlantic slave trade became one of the largest colonial enterprises and indeed in the eighteenth century was dominated by British vessels (Rawley, 1981). However, under pressure, the British slave trade was abolished in 1809 and slavery itself was finally abolished in 1834. During the period of the trade approximately 2.4 million African slaves were sent to the British West Indian islands.

The main plantation crop in the West Indies was sugar cane and its production dominated many of the island economies until well after the emancipation of the slaves. It was a demanding crop in terms of the physical exhaustion of the labour force, with the result that there was a constant demand for new labourers. Attempts were even made to establish slave-raising islands, notably Barbuda, to reduce the colonial plantations' dependence upon importation from Africa, but the results were not regarded as conducive to the extension of the experiment. Plantation agriculture was also wasteful in its use of the physical resources of the islands. Excessive forest clearance and environmental degradation were noted as early as the late seventeenth century on Montserrat, less than 50 years after settlement (Pulsipher, 1986).

The various West Indian islands together with British Guiana and Mauritius suffered an economic setback at emancipation, as the newly freed slaves generally and not unnaturally, had little desire to continue to work for their former masters, albeit on a different basis. In some cases plantations were divided and sold as smallholdings to the freed slaves, in others they moved on to Crown Lands and squatted on or leased them establishing semi-subsistence smallholdings. The result was the demise of the centralised sugar plantations on some islands and the introduction of new crops and products demanding less labour, such as citrus and tropical fruits. The success of lime growing on Grenada and bananas on Jamaica are two examples of this adaptation.

However, on a number of islands and in British Guiana, the planters sought new sources of controlled labour. India provided such a source. Indentured labourers from India were introduced to several colonies from the 1830s onwards. The most important were Trinidad, British Guiana and Mauritius, followed by the new plantation colonies of Natal, Fiji and Malaya later in the century. Although the terms of indenture included a return passage to India, many workers chose to remain in the colonies rather than return home at the end of their service. Consequently by the 1920s there were approximately 2.3 million Indians living in these countries (Great Britain, 1928).

The plantation system thus survived and was introduced to new regions in its classic form. Indicative of this was the emergence in 1900 of the combine, Bookers Brothers, McConnell Limited, which through the purchase of estates controlled half the sugar trade of British Guiana (Mandle, 1973). As a result of technical innovation and scientific research in the colony, sugar remained the major agricultural export commodity, valued at some £1.1 million in 1930. The plantations were reorganised around centralised milling facilities and integrated through a complex network of roads, light railways and tramways linking the fields to the mill. (The refinery was usually situated at the point of importation not of production.)

Plantations were measured usually in hundreds and occasionally in thousands of hectares, divided into smaller management units. Linked to them were the smallholdings measured in single or tens of hectares producing for sale to the estate mills. The smallholders included the descendants of freed slaves, descendants of indentured Indians who had been promised small plots of land if they remained in the colony for an extended period of indenture, and others who purchased small plots subsequently (Moohr, 1972). The plantation landscape thus became progressively more complex in terms of the holding and cultivation pattern. However, in terms of land usage it became simplified. Land previously set aside for fuel and sub-sistence crops declined as new machinery and improved communi-cations allowed such areas to be devoted to more profitable commercial cropping. Thus monocultural regions came into being where sugar occupied as much as 80 per cent of the total surface area.

Government intervention to promote peasant settlement schemes in the plantation colonies only came some time after emancipation. In Jamaica the authorities began the subdivision of Crown Lands into smallholdings in 1895. The subdivision of privately owned plantations as an official policy only began in 1929, although private subdivision had begun in the 1830s (Beckford, 1972). A measure of subdivisional activity may be gained from the 1930 enumeration of 171,683 peasant holdings under 4 hectares in extent covering some 207,000 hectares. In British Guiana the government reduced the price of Crown Lands in the 1890s to facilitate peasant settlement. The measures were so successful that by the 1920s over half the total population of the colony lived in non-estate villages surrounded by their own lands. This colonisation movement prompted the descrip-tion of British Guiana as 'the underdeveloped southern frontier of the British Caribbean' (Mandle, 1973: 5).

In the course of the nineteenth and early twentieth centuries several new plantation crops were developed, initially with the introduction of tea, which were planted in other parts of the Empire. Tea had been imported from China by the East India Company as one of the components of its trade monopoly (Awasthi, 1975). However, the ending of the monopoly in 1833 spurred the Company to seek control of its own supplies through production in India. Tea plants were acquired illegally from China and planted under the supervision of Chinese gardeners in Assam in the 1830s, where they thrived. Thus with careful breeding and planting the Indian tea industry was established. The land chosen for cultivation varied

from the upland regions of the foothills of the Himalayas at Darjeeling for quality teas, to the Assamese flood plains for bulk
production (Figures 7.7, 7.8) (Antrobus, 1957). Later planting was
extended to the Nilgiri Hills in southern India. In all these regions
the local population was sparse and not attracted to the work conditions of the plantations. Once more workers were imported, this
time from other parts of India, a movement which was regularised
under the Inland Emigration Act of 1863. Thus the labour indenture
system was applied within India as well as for other colonies. Tea
cultivation was also transferred to Ceylon, which became the leading
exporter of fine teas in the twentieth century. Planters again copied
the system of importing labour from India and using lands outside
the regions of established agricultural settlement.

The transference of tea from China to India and later other parts
of the Empire was but the first in a series of spectacular plant
transfers for plantation production. The cinchona plant of the Andes,
whose bark was used for the manufacture of quinine was removed,
against the laws of Peru, from South America and propagated
through the facilities offered by the Royal Botanical Gardens at
Kew. Its subsequent development in India as a plantation crop
constituted a major breakthrough in the control of malaria, thereby
providing a greater degree of survival for persons living in the
tropics.

A later but more widespread transference was that of the rubber-
tree from the Amazon basin to Kew and thence to the various Royal
Botanical Gardens in Asia, more especially to Calcutta, Peradeniya
and Singapore. The acclimatisation and development of a suitable
high-yielding tree and tapping process took several decades, lasting
until the end of the nineteenth century, by which time experimentation had shown the adaptability of the trees to a variety of
conditions, particularly in Ceylon and Malaya. Increasing world
demand and the subsequent overcropping of the Brazilian and Congo
wild rubber regions early in the twentieth century provided the
impetus for investment. The remaining problems of tapping techniques and the mass propagation of seedlings were overcome as the
opportunities to expand production became apparent (Petch,
1914).

The pre-First World War rubber boom affected a large number
of tropical colonies. Rubber companies were floated and schemes
projected widely, often in areas unsuited to the plant. Schemes, even
plantations, were initiated in Africa in states ranging from Natal to
the Gold Coast but with little lasting success. It was Malaya,

Figure 7.7: Tea plantation, Darjeeling

Figure 7.8: Plan of tea estates, Assam

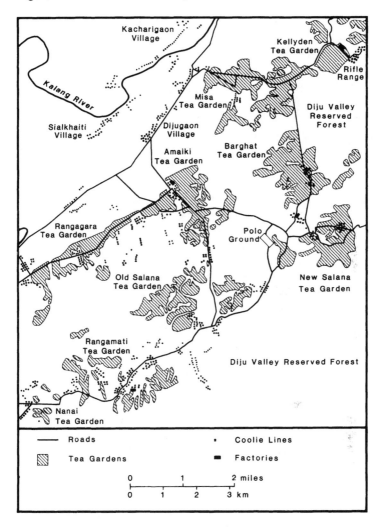

followed by Ceylon and North Borneo, which proved to have the most favourable conditions. The organisation both at production and marketing levels, together with the employment of skilled workforces, enabled the planters in these colonies to capture the main share of the market. Once again the plantation companies varied greatly in size with some no more than 40 hectares in extent, while others measured their estates in thousands of hectares. The land disposal policies of the Straits Settlements and the various Malay state governments encouraged rubber planters to acquire estates in the late 1890s and early 1900s with offers of cheap land and tax holidays (Drabble, 1973). The area under rubber trees in Malaya thus increased from 2,500 hectares in 1900 to 174,000 hectares in 1910, reaching 931,000 hectares by 1922. This coincided with dramatic increases in demand as the motor car industry introduced mass production methods in the first decade of the century. Smallholding production, particularly in Indian and Chinese lands, was significant in Malaya. The resultant plantation landscape represented a marked intrusion into the pre-existing agricultural economy and measures were taken in most Malay states to segregate Malay from immigrant farming regions. Thus the production of export crops was prohibited in the Malay Reservations which were established from 1913 onwards, resulting in the cultivation of subsistence crops in one part of the country and export crops in the other (Tan, 1981).

The plantation mode of production was important in a great many tropical and subtropical colonies, providing an export income for economies which offered little other form of support. Thus coffee in Kenya, sisal in Tanganyika and coconuts in the Solomon Islands represented specific attempts to introduce commercial cropping, not into the indigenous economy, but through new forms of management dependent upon metropolitan capital investment (Middleton, 1952). Some introductions, such as cotton in Uganda, proved to be more successful in the hands of indigenous cultivators than under the planned settler management. Others including jute in Bengal were introduced as crops for contracting out to indigenous cultivators. Only the mills were directly controlled by urban financiers in Calcutta. The means of obtaining commercial crops in the tropical and subtropical colonies thus varied substantially. However, the plantation because of its organisation and dependence upon metropolitan finance, has often been taken as the epitome of colonial relationships and indeed impress upon the landscape. In this sector, the organisation and high capital investment of the plantation contrasted with the apparent lack of organisation and capital in indigenous agriculture. Although regarded with suspicion in many independent states, plantations through their access to investment capital and technical expertise have survived as profitable supports to the national economy.

The plantation economy was susceptible to external pressures even in the colonial period. Thus trade agreements, pressure groups and planters' associations played a vital role in the development of the late nineteenth century and early twentieth century plantations. The link to the London capital market in particular produced a greater degree of direct pressure upon the Imperial government through stockholders and directors than that exerted by colonial based industries lacking London representation. Furthermore the system through its efficiency was chronically liable to overproduction. The rapid growth of production areas which characterised the pre-First World War era gave way to a more stable pattern thereafter as a result of government intervention aimed at achieving order in the production of plantation crops. The international commodity agreements of the post-1929 depression era sought to restrict production and hence maintain prices, most noticeably through the 1933 tea and rubber agreements. Within the colonies planters' associations wielded considerable influence in the formulation of state policies. The Assam Tea Planters Association controlled the recruitment and distribution of labour in the province, while the United Planters Association in Malaya was instrumental in the establishment of the Malay Reservations and subsequent elimination of Malay holdings among their own.

WASTELANDS

Although British administrators and settlers viewed colonial lands and their resources as exploitable, the late nineteenth century witnessed a reappraisal and aesthetic appreciation of the variety of fauna, flora and landscapes of the remoter parts of the Empire. The reappraisal took a practical form in the attempt to preserve the more spectacular physical features and rare wild animals. The first impetus derived its origin from American experience in its western lands (Gates, 1968). Spectacular physical features such as the assemblage at Yellowstone Park and the Yosemite Valley were declared national parks to preserve their unique scenic character from the depredations of settlers and timber exploitation. The second impetus came from an awareness that big game animals, notably in Africa, were faced with extinction. Public attention was initially mainly directed towards elephant and lion, and international conventions were signed covering tropical Africa in an attempt to preserve some vestiges of the indigenous fauna. Usually such projects were only undertaken when wildlife was seen to be nearing extinction as settlement and exploitation removed the natural habitat.

185

In a somewhat different vein, it was noted that in India much of the early environmental protection, notably the government reservation of the right to prevent deforestation of hills, was inspired by the desire to maintain the 'British' character of the hill tracts concerned. Thus in the Nilgiri Hills nature protection was placed ahead of profits from the commercial exploitation of the wood (Brockway, 1979). However, plantings with Australian acacia and eucalyptus species were undertaken to enhance the forested appearance of the region (Noble, 1980).

The national parks movement in the colonies of settlement in the nineteenth century was fragmentary, with little overall thought or planning in the provision of rural amenity areas akin to the formal planning of urban parks and public places. Undoubtedly the United States provided a model which was emulated elsewhere. However, one of the earliest of the rural reservations was proclaimed in New South Wales in 1866. It incorporated the Jenolan Caves in the Blue Mountains and preserved some 2,000 hectares of land as 'a source of delight and instruction to succeeding generations and to excite the admiration of tourists from all parts of the world' (Powell, 1976: 114). In 1879 the more accessible Royal Park at Port Hacking, covering 7,000 hectares, was set aside for the enjoyment of the inhabitants of Sydney. Other parks were proclaimed in the following two decades. Nearly all were directed towards the provision of public amenities, thereby effectively permitting the long-term modification of the natural environment, more especially the flora and fauna.

Canada followed the American experience of preserving the physical environment more closely. In 1885 the Banff National Park with an area of some 660,000 hectares in the Rocky Mountains was created. By 1930 some 7,000,000 hectares of National Parks had been proclaimed, mostly in the more spectacular mountainous regions of the country. The desire to preserve the most imposing examples of natural scenery applied equally to countries such as New Zealand where the first National Park at Tongawiro was established in 1894. In Victoria proposals for parks in a wide variety of regions were accepted, covering some 70,000 hectares by 1911.

The 1890s also witnessed the beginning of official recognition of the need to protect fauna and flora, rather than to preserve open spaces *per se* or the main physical features of the landscape. The conservation movement had diverse origins ranging from Tasmanian concern for the survival of its unique animal life to recognition of the extent to which the African elephant had been decimated in the second half of the nineteenth century. Although relatively little progress was made in the period before the First World War, a number of game reserves were established in Africa in the 1890s. The first Cape of Good Hope reserve in Bushmanland proved to be ephemeral as poachers were too effective and destroyed the animals despite official attempts to prevent the slaughter. This experience illustrated the fact that it could only be in particularly remote areas that game animals stood any chance of survival, even with government protection. The Sabi Reserve in the Transvaal proved to be more long lasting, although it was only in the 1920s that farmers' grazing animals were removed and the entire area of the park was acquired by the state, and became the basis of the modern Kruger National Park. The major game parks in Africa followed, including the Wankie Reserve in Southern Rhodesia and the extensive complex of parks in Kenya and Tanganyika. Successful attempts were made to exclude indigenous graziers and to create attractions for European tourists, even if the numbers were limited and hunting the preserved animals was initially the main attraction.

However, most of the wastelands of the dominions and colonies remained unused and unmanaged. Accordingly in 1930 some 311.2 million hectares, a third of the entire area of Australia, was classified as unoccupied, and with little prospect of occupation or use. The boundary between extensive grazing areas and unused lands fluctuated according to climatic cycles, but there remained a large permanent core of wasteland.

FORESTS

The forested lands presented an equally grave problem of preservation and conservation as well as exploitation. The wholesale destruction of forests in New Zealand and parts of Canada for lumber reduced such areas to a wasteland (Wynn, 1979). Logging continued throughout the colonial period with little thought of reafforestation. In the tropics the forests were similarly exploited for export rather than local consumption. Hardwood supplies from India and Burma entered the British market for construction, industrial use and furniture. Additional supplies were sought and concessions granted in colonies such as British Honduras, North Borneo, Southern Nigeria and Lagos. Problems of exploitation were serious. Usually forests were 'creamed' of the largest trees, leaving most uncut and as a result often unprofitable to work (Adeyoju, 1969). Problems of transport were constant owing to the size and weight of logs to be taken to the mills. In Southern Nigeria light railways were constructed, supplemented by wagon-way networks to transport the logs; but again costs were high restricting the area which could be exploited, as manual haulage of 30–40 tonne logs was limited to 5 kilometres and light railways cost £250 per kilometre. The softwood lumber industries of Canada, Newfoundland and New Zealand presented fewer problems as overland transport was developed with ice roads and wagons in winter and flotation in the river in summer, to reach strategically placed sawmills.

Government control sought no more than to regulate exploitation on a more scientific basis, as the appointment of a conservator in British Honduras in 1921 illustrated (Metzen and Cain, 1925). Forestry services were established in a number of colonies, emulating the Indian Forestry Service. Essentially the services were concerned with conservation and the attempt to create forestry reserves, for protection from the depredations of graziers and wood cutters. Active planting of forests was also part of the state's function with the attempt to designate areas suitable for timber growth and the management of state forests. In Cyprus, for example, the Forestry Service was set up immediately after the establishment of a British administration on the island (Dunbar, 1983). The new service turned first to India for advice. However, Indian observation overlooked the depredations of goats in the Mediterranean, as in India they presented few problems. The later service after 1880 was more intent on keeping goats out of forests and increasing the area of designated forests for conservation purposes. Conservation and scientific plantings prompted the comment: 'the forests of Cyprus . . . would not have reached their present comparatively healthy state if it had not been for the stewardship of the British for more than eighty years' (Dunbar, 1983: 117).

8

European Farmlands

Extensive regions of the temperate Empire, together with more restricted areas of the tropical colonies, were appropriated for European-style or European-managed agriculture. These ranged from the 'plantations' of the seventeenth century in the West Indies to the extensive prairie settlement of the early twentieth century in terms of temporal origin; and from the closer-settlement irrigation schemes to the multimillion hectare cattle ranching stations of the Australian outback in terms of size. With the exception of a brief period in the mid-nineteenth century there was no overall colonial philosophy of colonisation and settlement, with the result that a great diversity of settlement forms eventuated. However, preconceived ideas on the part of settlement scheme promoters, both official and private in England, resulted in many unsuccessful ventures which had to be drastically modified in the light of colonial experience. The climatic and disease environments of the colonies, in particular, were rarely anticipated and the limitations which they placed upon European-style farming regimes were only evaluated through an extended process of trial and error.

The attempt to recreate England in many overseas guises is a constant theme of colonial settlement. Only a small number of individual emigrants sought radically different forms of settlement in extensive ranching or tropical plantations, which were usually the preserve of corporate investment. However, few imagined the complete reproduction of English institutions and society, including landlord-tenant relationships in the temperate colonies. Emigration to the rural areas of the colonies was more egalitarian in concept than the rural England of the nineteenth or early twentieth centuries, and it was the United States of America which provided many of the models of settlement (Powell, 1977). This is not to suggest that the

Imperial frontier replicated the American frontier. Government control was more pervasive in British territories with a resultant greater degree of orderliness in the process of settlement. Also the imprint of government intervention was more complex than on the American frontier and consequently the range of settlement patterns which ensued more variable.

SETTLEMENT SCHEMES

The basic building block of British overseas rural settlement schemes was the family farm, held on freehold or other inheritable tenure (Figure 8.1). In size it had to be capable of supporting a family and its dependent workers, and provide sufficient production to meet domestic consumption as well as surpluses for sale on the colonial and international markets. Variants on this theme included the essentially commercial enterprises of the plantation and ranch at one end of the scale and the semi-rural smallholding at the other. Few settlements aimed at no more than mere subsistence; commercial gain was the underlying objective throughout the history of British settlement.

Settlers from the British Isles and other countries in Europe emigrated to the lands of the temperate Empire in the first instance for the opportunities afforded in agricultural enterprise. In an era when land was readily available to colonial governments and the object of official policy was to attract settlers, free grants were offered. The headrights of North America, military bounties payable in land, and the homesteads of the nineteenth and early twentieth century, were all variations on the theme. Free land, extensive enough to develop a self-sufficient farm was an undoubted element in the inter-colonial competition for settlers. Some colonies offered excessive tracts with the consequent rapid depletion of the Crown Land as in Western Australia in the 1820s and 1830s. While others permitted squatting on Crown Lands, most noticeably in New South Wales, but emulated by the other Australian colonies (Roberts, 1924). In virtually all cases the areas offered by colonial governments and the promoters of colonial settlement schemes were well beyond the sizes of farms available to the potential emigrant in the United Kingdom. Indeed the seemingly limitless land areas and the prospects of rising from labourer in England or Scotland to gentleman in the colonies were powerful advertisements for colonial emigration.

Figure 8.1: Pioneer family, New South Wales

If a free land policy was pursued in the early stages of colonial development, the wholesale alienation of Crown Lands was regarded as anathema to an early nineteenth century group of 'Colonial Reformers', led by Edward Gibbon Wakefield, who sought to establish and implement general colonisation theories. They held that colonial development was dependent upon a proper balance between land, labour and capital. Systematic colonisation, creating such a balance, was linked to the sale of land at a sufficient price to prevent the rapid spread of settlement and the retention of a labour force upon the farms. Control through price and prior survey led to more ordered settlement and the utilisation of the land sold to settlers. Predetermined farm prices and sizes restricted access to land and helped to foster a more noticeable rural class system. The size for such a system was debated particularly in South Australia and New Zealand, where the principles of systematic colonisation were most stringently applied. Areas from a few hectares up to 64 hectares were selected with marked changes in the resultant settlement patterns. Prices of £1 per acre (£2.50 per hectare) were introduced for most Australian colonies, but differed over time and place. Certainly the poor in Australia or New Zealand who earned a few pence per day had little prospect of becoming landed proprietors under such schemes, although the possibility was theoretically placed before them after the collapse of the initial gold rush. Indeed back-to-the-land movements had a major attraction for a society undergoing industrialisation (Hadfield, 1970).

Such thinking was, however, rejected by the authorities responsible for the largest of the British overseas colonisation schemes — the Prairie Provinces of Canada. The Canadian government recognised that it was in direct competition for settlers with the United States. In 1872 it adopted the Dominions Lands Act, based on the American Homestead Act of 1862, because 'it was known all over the world' (Morton, 1938). Homesteads of 64 hectares (160 acres) were offered to *bona fide* settlers, with blocks offered on a *pro rata* basis to groups who wished to settle as a unit. This allied to the disposal of railway and other lands endowed to the Hudson's Bay Company, gave rise to a massive immigration drive which resulted in the population of the Prairie Provinces increasing from 100,000 in 1901 to 2,400,000 30 years later (Mackintosh, 1934). By 1931 some 44.5 million hectares in the three provinces had been occupied and 24.3 million hectares cultivated (Table 8.1). The former area was almost as large as the entire alienated freehold area of Australia at that date.

Table 8.1: Progress of settlement in the Prairie Provinces, 1881–1931

	Area occupied (million hectares)	Area improved (million hectares)	Area of wheat (million hectares)	Population (millions)	No. of farms (000s)
1881	1.1	0.1	—	0.12	—
1891	3.3	0.6	—	0.25	—
1901	6.3	2.3	1.0	0.42	55
1911	23.3	9.3	3.2	1.32	199
1921	35.6	18.2	6.8	1.96	256
1931	44.5	24.3	10.3	2.35	288

The other colonies with extensive Crown Lands pursued their own policies of free grants and sales, but large tracts fell into the hands of speculators and pastoralists, neither of whom were viewed with favour by the colonial legislatures of the late nineteenth and early twentieth centuries. As a result the Australian and South African colonies embarked upon policies of closer-settlement in the 1880s and 1890s in an attempt to break up estates and pursue the objectives of denser rural settlements and a more egalitarian distribution of land resources. One prong of the programme encouraged private division of estates through land taxation policies. The other involved a more active government role in the management of land. Government schemes provided for the subdivision of farms and the construction of irrigation works, often at considerable cost (Rutherford, 1968). The main areas in Australia were on the Murray River in Victoria and New South Wales where a series of schemes established small (20 hectares) irrigated farms (Langford-Smith, 1968). Irrigation possibilities were limited and the majority of schemes involved the subdivision of farms for dryland agriculture (Williams, 1976). After the First World War small farms were offered under the Empire soldier settlement schemes in a range of countries from Canada to Swaziland (Powell, 1981). Possibly the most successful were those offered lands for tobacco cultivation in Southern Rhodesia, but in general good soldiers did not necessarily make good farmers. Unlike the urban and industrial sectors of the economy, colonial and dominion governments were willing to spend considerable sums to promote crop farming, through costly irrigation works. The results were often disappointingly meagre but few politicians were willing to admit that their country faced environmental limitations (Davidson, 1969). As in so many ways

Australian agricultural planners borrowed heavily from American experience in irrigating drylands (Rutherford, 1964).

Closer settlements and soldier settlements were but an extension of group colonies planned in many parts of the Empire to create compact blocks of population. The village, with the assumption of community organisation, was a significant element in the colonisation of many parts of the temperate Empire. The Canterbury settlement in New Zealand in the 1840s, that of Natal in the 1850s, or indeed the poor white colonies in South Africa in the present century, were all planned on the assumption of close settlement by groups with common ideals. In general the communal organisation of medieval England could not be re-created in the colonies. Thus the villages were abandoned by settlers who erected farmsteads on their own plots while the commanges were divided among them.

Even more cohesive were the group settlements attracted to the Canadian prairies. Ethnic or religious groups were encouraged to settle in clusters. For example the Doukhobors were exiled from Russia in 1899 and by 1901 some 47 villages had been planned in Canada, spaced at intervals of 3–6 kilometres (Dawson, 1936). Similarly the Menonites, seeking religious exclusivity sought isolation in the Prairies where land could be arranged in traditional style around small villages with arable strips and common pasturage. Under the dominion regulations a group of 16 families could acquire a block of land some 1,024 hectares in extent, providing space for a model village plan (Dawson, 1936). Although villages were planned, even occupied for a while, individualism proved to be a dominant force in the rural areas and the majority of settlers moved on to their own lands within a couple of generations, usually leaving only the Menonites in group settlements. One of the largest groupings on the Prairies were the Ukrainians from Austria-Hungary, who in the period 1880–1919 established themselves in extensive blocks on the margins of settlement. Although not organised in villages, but homesteading individual quarter sections, the Ukrainians sought to group themselves together in a strange cultural and linguistic environment, often choosing land poor in productive terms in order to be close to the group (Lehr, 1985).

SURVEY SYSTEMS

Colonial surveyors exercised a profound influence upon the landscape. In many temperate colonies the land was assumed to be a *tabula rasa*, with indigenous settlement either erased or confined to compact blocks. Thus the land surveyor was charged with the definition of a new landscape upon the ground. This was inevitably an ordered one, reflecting government policies and, literally, the impress of central authority upon the landscape. Four Canadian landscapes, representing four differing theories of colonisation, illustrate the point (Figure 8.2). The French introduced French concepts of land tenure based on the seigneurial system with a hierarchical legal concept of land holdings. In practice each seigneur's block of land was divided into a series of long lots for tenant farmers, stretching for a specified distance from the river frontage (Harris and Warkentin, 1974). The resultant settlement pattern was one of an incipient street village, based on long narrow plots. At a later date a second range was established, creating a second line of farmsteads. In contrast early English settlement in the Maritime Provinces was based on the grant of irregular sized and shaped blocks of land, dependent upon the resources and social or military rank of the colonist. The consequent irregular pattern of farms resembled the western part of England. However, the introduction of theories of systematic colonisation in the early nineteenth century resulted in the ordered county and township system of Ontario, with regularly laid out roads and farms. Finally the adoption of a modified form of the American rectangular survey system for the colonisation of the Prairie Provinces resulted in the highly ordered grid of roads and regularly spaced farmsteads, which express a degree of governmental control which is one of the most impressive examples of central authority impress upon the landscape to be found anywhere in the world.

The Canadian example illustrates the range of systems available to the authorities in the laying out of a new landscape. Variations of all four are to be found throughout the British Empire. It is noticeable that each settlement system was based upon a certain set size of farm and the landscape was duly ordered to create such units. Accordingly in South Australia the first farms were only 16 hectares in extent, while early settler experience resulted in an official doubling of the area for later colonists (Williams, 1974). Thus the initial closely drawn road and settlement pattern was, in effect, expanded to cope with the increase in farm size in later areas of occupation. Survey and settlement were generally locally controlled, with the result that survey systems fitted the topographic features and with the exception of the Canadian prairies and parts of eastern Australia, the complications of the American rectangular survey system were

Figure 8.2: Patterns of Canadian rural settlement

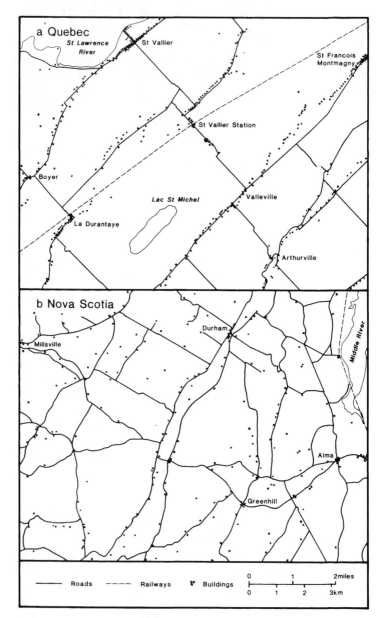

Figure 8.2: *contd.*

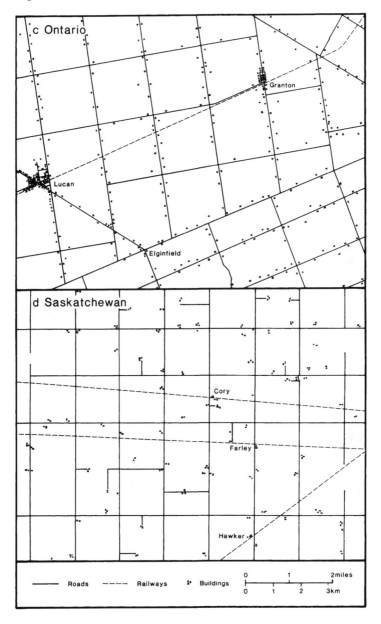

avoided. However, colonies as far removed as the Falkland Islands were influenced by the rectangular survey system (Royle, 1985).

The survey systems adopted throughout the Empire provided the framework within which later settlers and systems had to operate. Thus the surveys devised for one form of settlement have had to be adopted to the requirements of later forms. Survey lines once placed on a map, and particularly when transferred to the ground, have shown remarkable persistence. Accordingly survey lines for pastoral farms in South Africa provided the framework within which later agricultural settlers have had to work, and the land ownership system has consequently also had to be adapted. Agricultural survey systems have been incorporated into town plans as the towns have sprawled in the twentieth century. Hence the initial decisions on farm sizes, survey layout and property rights determined for the first colonial settlements, are often of significance for all subsequent settlement forms. The ground plan and property register have been among the most enduring aspects of colonial settlement, where free enterprise and individual rights have been respected. Attempts in the colonial era to expropriate properties in order to force changes in the economic system were regarded as 'communistic' and generally resisted. Even in the Australian colonies and New Zealand where such expropriation was possible, the prohibitive costs of replanning were such as to limit its effectiveness.

AGRICULTURAL REGIONS

European farmers who settled in the colonies attempted almost universally to recreate the rural landscapes and economies of Europe. Thus throughout the British Empire it was the rural economies of England and Scotland which were most widely reproduced. The imitation ranged from names to building styles and from cattle breeds to farm implements. Thus the agricultural systems of the United Kingdom, evolving from the agricultural revolution and enclosure movement, were viewed as the starting points for colonial enterprises. Only a few settlements looked back further to an often rose-tinted spectacle of medieval communalism and co-operative farming, which proved to be impossible to transplant to the colonies where different social and economic conditions prevailed.

In all colonies the first essentials had been to establish farms and achieve agricultural self-sufficiency. Thus in most colonies settled prior to the twentieth century this had meant the adoption of mixed subsistence farming with livestock for motive and transport power, meat and often clothing, and crops for bread and vegetables. Surpluses, in the way of livestock breeding and if close to towns additional crop production, were sold locally. Due to high transportation costs only a few favoured regions could engage in long-distance trade. Semi-sufficiency was thus a first stage of virtually all agricultural settlements. Prosperity could only be achieved through the production and marketing of surpluses. In this respect family farms lacked access to capital so characteristic of plantations and many pastoral enterprises. Hence the process of attaining prosperity was slow and it was only with the development of the railway and steamship systems in the second half of the nineteenth century that the large-scale development of many middle-latitude regions became possible.

One of the characteristics of land grants in most colonies was size. Grants in excess of 20 hectares were general and few smallholdings under 5 hectares were laid out, except for market gardens within township boundaries. The most usual grants were in the range of 50–200 hectares. The amount of land which a family received was thus in excess of the ability of the family to cultivate and therefore included substantial areas which could be devoted to grazing purposes. In the wooded zones of Canada, Australia and New Zealand the process of land clearance provided the basic materials for the construction of houses, barns and fences (Figure 8.3). Whereas in the grasslands of the prairies, lumber from British Columbia was railed in once the credit was available. The clearance of the land was thus a long-drawn-out process, and the semi-self-sufficient stage was retained for a considerable time in some of the more remote areas. Only on the grasslands could large-scale cropping begin almost immediately after occupation, resulting in often spectacular advances in settlement, but equally disastrous retreats (Meinig, 1962). Relics of early, overhasty agricultural expansion and practices are to be found in the landscapes of numerous colonies, as for example the strip field patterns of South Australia (Twidale and Bourne, 1978).

Mixed farming, often with a livestock emphasis, remained significant in most temperate colonies and dominions in the 1930s. However, improved cultivation practices, particularly the adoption of American machinery and extensive methods, new transport links and increased demand from the growing towns, enabled surplus production to be sold and increased rural prosperity to be achieved.

Figure 8.3: Pastoral station, New South Wales

Specialised farming regions were developed through the planting of new crops and the development of new strains. The major regions of specialisation were linked to the international markets, more specially to Great Britain. Hence the fruit regions of British Columbia and the western Cape were planted in response to demands exerted elsewhere, using imported finance and expertise (Koroscil, 1986). The fruit farms, either in the form of estates or small farms, represented a new variant on the response to international demand in the twentieth century.

The most spectacular landscape transformations took place in the grassland regions of Canada, South Africa and Australia, where initial pastoral development was displaced by extensive cereal cropping. This is best illustrated in the Canadian Prairie Provinces which experienced a tenfold increase in both cultivated area and wheat acreage in the first 30 years of the twentieth century. By 1931 half the 44.5 million hectares of occupied land was cropped in one of the most remarkable planned landscape transformations of the present century (Figure 8.4). The rapid change was wrought by the immigration of large numbers of settlers. In the peak year of 1913 some 135,000 immigrants settled on the Prairies. Indeed between 1901 and 1916 the population of the three Prairie Provinces quadrupled to some 1.7 million inhabitants. In addition there was a major improvement of transport facilities as a result of a massive railway construction programme, with the provision of bulk grain storage facilities at regular intervals along the lines to facilitate the export of the commercial crops upon which the settlers depended for their livelihood (Figure 8.5). Subsistence farming had no place in this massive settlement programme geared to the demands of an overseas market.

By the time the remaining Crown Lands were transferred to the Provincial governments in 1930 the colonisation of the Prairie Provinces had essentially been completed. Homesteaders had directly appropriated a total of 56.4 million hectares. There had been losses in the process as nearly twice as many had attempted to create a farm in the region but had lacked the ability or means to sustain the effort. The railways had been granted a further 12.9 million hectares, school endowments 3.8 million hectares and the Hudson's Bay Company compensatory lands to the extent of 2.8 million hectares. Each of these proprietors shared the government's interest in settling families on the land as rapidly as possible and actively promoted settlement schemes. Under the 1908 Dominion Land Act homesteaders were allowed to pre-empt a further quarter section (64

Figure 8.4: Pioneer farms, Alberta

Figure 8.5: Grain elevators, Prairies

hectares) adjoining their land for a fixed price, providing certain minimum cultivation quotas were introduced (Martin, 1938). As a result by 1931 the average size of farm in the prairie provinces (135 hectares) was twice the basic homestead area.

A problematic aspect of the process of homesteading was eased in the early years of the twentieth century. The lack of wood or building stone presented a major constructional problem which was solved initially through the temporary expedient of building sod houses. However, the introduction of prefabricated housing influenced both urban and rural areas. In 1904 British Columbia Mills offered a new weatherproof house which satisfied legal homestead requirements and removed the physical burden of house construction from the settler. The basic pattern for a 3 metres by 3 metres cabin cost only £20. Variations fancifully named 'Canterbury Cathedrals' and 'Lambeth Palaces' were railed to Canadian Pacific Railway settlements in Saskatchewan (Mills and Holdsworth, 1975).

The study of colonial agricultural regions suggests a steady expansion of cultivation and of rural population until the Great Depression. Indeed this is what colonial propagandists projected in their writings until the 1920s. However, by the late nineteenth century early settled regions were already in decline paralleling the experience of the British Isles. For example, Prince Edward Island in Canada lost rural population steadily between 1881 and 1931, partly to the western colonial regions of Canada, but also the United States. The exploitable land on the island had been fully occupied by the mid-nineteenth century and the process of adjustment to changing commercial conditions had resulted in a virtually stable farm pattern from the 1860s, but at a time when other provinces still offered the opportunities of the initial colonisation boom. Prince Edward Island with its mixed farming economy based on relatively small farms averaging only 35 hectares in the first third of the twentieth century, represented a very different image to the prairies (Clark, 1959).

Although the building styles adopted by pioneers in the various agricultural regions of the British Empire reflected their countries of origin, and notably those of the British Isles with its marked regional variations; profound modifications ensued with reference to other models and the test of practicability. Thus in one of the most mixed ethnic areas in the British Empire, the Canadian prairies, the variety of styles evident in the initial stages of colonisation gave way to prairie-style farm houses with designs common to large tracts of the American midwest and Great Plains (Proudfoot, 1973).

PASTORAL REGIONS

A significant departure from the colonial pattern was the evolution of the extensive grazing farm. Warnings against the spread of settlement, particularly in Australia, were noticeable in the early nineteenth century. Fears for the loss of civilisation by people beyond the areas of regular settlement were expressed. However, possibly more than the arable agriculturalist, the pastoral farmer within the Empire was by the mid-nineteenth century producing for the international market. When this was apparent the authorities proceeded to regularise the status of the pastoralist and sought to tax him for his use of the Crown Lands, in marked contrast to the policy of the United States government which sought to ignore both the pastoralist and the possibility of barrenness within the Republic's boundaries until the early twentieth century (Kollmorgen, 1969).

There were few colonists who emigrated to raise livestock or engage in extensive pastoralism. Livestock formed an essential part of virtually all agricultural enterprises prior to the introduction of motor transport and tractors. However, the differing man:land relationships existing in many mid-latitude colonies was such that European conceptions of mixed farming proved to be inappropriate. The apparent availability of inexhaustible land resources induced men with little capital and often little additional manpower to seek new solutions to surviving and prospering in a strange environment. Pastoralism offered a degree of self-sufficiency and independence in regions of poor communications and low levels of population occupation. Other European groups had pioneered the approach before British settlers were faced with the problem. The Spanish in the frontierlands of Argentina and Mexico and the Dutch in the Cape of Good Hope had evolved viable pastoral economies geared to livestock production in isolated regions. Their experiences benefited the American and British colonial heritages with the incorporation of these two groups into their states.

Pastoral activity was developed independently in Australia, although the flow of information and livestock between the various colonial regions and Europe was such as to link them closely with innovations transferred readily by the nineteenth century. As in the Cape of Good Hope, the expansion of the New South Wales pastoral frontier was accomplished through the quest for seasonal grazing lands, beyond the settled agricultural areas. Temporary occupation gave way to permanent settlements and large areas were appropriated rapidly as pastoral farmers entered the interior grasslands and semi-arid scrublands. Until the 1830s leases and licences, even free grants, were readily available for such activity, and after a brief official attempt to halt the expansion of the settled area in the 1830s and 1840s, the frontier continued to be extended under a system of leases. The Australian leasehold systems as developed in the six colonies differed according to the relative strengths of the farming and pastoral communities. The governmental aim was to regulate the use of Crown Lands and to derive some revenue from lands which remained unsold. In this respect the Australian experience diverged from that of the United States in recognising the permanence of pastoralism and therefore seeking to regulate its progress and to tax the pastoralist's use of the Crown Lands. In all cases the government retained the option of dispossessing the pastoralist if conditions for agricultural settlement improved. Pastoralism was officially considered to be but a stage in the evolution of the rural economy, and indeed the agricultural frontier steadily dispossessed pastoral farmers throughout the nineteenth century.

The areas taken for pastoral farming were thus substantial, although by 1930 they represented a decline on the area occupied half a century earlier. In 1930 some 384.3 million hectares were occupied under pastoral lease in Australia. Working units ranged substantially in size, as two processes had been at work. First, governments had been concerned to establish as many families on the land as possible. This policy applied as equally to the pastoral as to the agricultural regions. Constant Crown revisions of the terms of contract and the termination of leases had resulted in a significant reduction in the size of pastoral units in the late nineteenth century. The reassessment of land holdings has been well illustrated in the dry Warrego lands of New South Wales and Queensland, where attempts were made to halve the size of holdings between 1880 and 1900 (Heathcote, 1965). The inevitable result was environmental deterioration and the reassessment of closer settlement in the semi-arid lands. However, at the other end of the scale large commercial companies were associated with the pastoral industry virtually from its inception. Vast tracts were offered by the colonial and dominion governments to concerns with substantial sums to invest in sheep and cattle stations (Figure 8.6) (Australia, 1937). In these cases the relative strengths in bargaining ran against the government, which was willing to allow large tracts to be acquired on favourable terms by companies for multiple farm station use. In this category smaller concerns in the early nineteenth century, such as the Clyde Company

Figure 8.6: Pastoral leases, Northern Territory, Australia, 1935

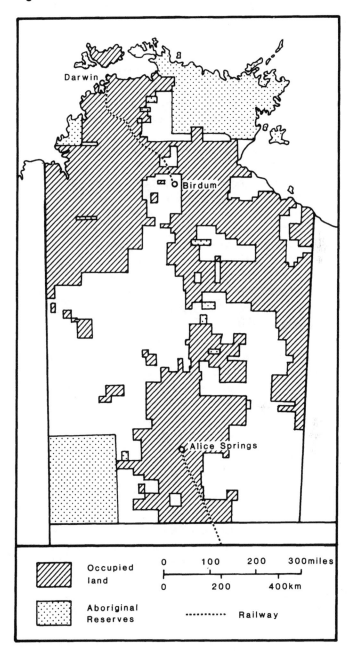

in Victoria, gave way to the multinationals of the twentieth century, notably Liebigs and Bovril, concerned with the Northern Territory (Powell, 1970).

Pastoral farming by its very nature is precarious in its economic returns. Accordingly the cycles of droughts took their tolls on the Australian enterprise. Substantial fluctuations in animal numbers together with variations in produce prices resulted in marked instability in the economy and settlement patterns of the arid and semi-arid regions. The remarkable initial expansion of activity and the virtual destruction of the best edible pastures and bushes resulted in environmental degradation and overstocking on an enormous scale. Added to this, the advent of the introduced rabbit wreaked havoc with natural rangelands throughout Australia. The delicate balance of the natural environment in the semi-arid lands was not understood by pioneers who in many cases effectively mined the land and moved on when profits declined (Bailey, 1966; Butlin, 1962). Thus Australian sheep numbers totalled 106.4 million in 1891 but had declined to 53.7 million by 1902 as the impact of drought, environmental degradation and poor financial management took their toll. A slow recovery simply resulted in the restocking of the lands at previous levels by 1930. Conservation and rehabilitation only came into consideration in the twentieth century when the option of moving on no longer existed.

The main objectives of Australian, and indeed most commercial pastoral farmers, were the raising of cattle and sheep for the meat trade and the production of wool, mohair and other by-products for the textile trade. Initially the first objective was to satisfy local markets, provisioning the towns and cities and the fleets and vessels which passed through the colonial ports. Livestock was raised close to the cities and ports, but with agricultural development the livestock regions were displaced to become more and more extensive. Stock thus had to be driven long distances on the hoof to the markets, often with a period of fattening on farms close to the port cities to recover from the long journey. Travelling stock routes were surveyed and maintained with waterholes to facilitate this movement. However, the development of chilling and freezing processes in the late nineteenth century resulted in a major change in the international trade in meat. Exports of beef, mutton and lamb to the United Kingdom became feasible from the overseas dominions, and a new wave of pastoral expansion began. However, chilled beef, which commanded higher prices than frozen beef, could only be kept for approximately 35 days after slaughter. Thus transport times were vital to the success of commercial ranching enterprises. Australia was consequently too distant to supply the British chilled meat market, whereas Canada could do so. The southern African, notably Rhodesian, ranches proved to be marginal in this respect and were unable to compete with Great Britain's main suppliers, Argentina and Uruguay (Phimister, 1978). Such handicaps did not deter the major corporations from investing heavily in ranching in Australia and Southern Rhodesia. Cattle raising in the Northern Territory of Australia was pursued fitfully on an extensive scale. In 1917 the holdings of the ten major pastoral companies in the Northern Territory averaged 800,000 hectares apiece. Vesty Brothers erected an abattoir and meat packing plant in 1914 but closed in 1920 after an expenditure of over £1,000,000 (Rose, 1954). In a highly competitive market the major international corporations tended to concentrate upon their more profitable South American enterprises.

The earlier and most spectacular pastoral development was associated with the supply of wool for the British and foreign markets. The expansion of woollen manufacture in the United Kingdom and other industrial countries in the nineteenth century was made possible by the development of new sources of supply. The unused or lightly occupied semi-arid lands of the world presented opportunities for the establishment of extensive grazing practices, which were evolved in the late eighteenth and nineteenth centuries. Various parts of the British Empire, more especially Australia, and to a lesser extent South Africa and New Zealand, were well suited to this development. Wool became the staple export of all the Australian colonies and indeed the basis of their wealth, with the exception of Victoria, in the nineteenth century. The breeding of the Australian flocks again illustrates the flow of information and breeding stock between several parts of the world. The merino sheep, which formed the basis of the industry, was imported in the first instance from various European countries, more particularly Spain and Germany, but also from other colonies of experimentation, notably the Cape of Good Hope.

Australia was the largest and most productive of the British Empire's pastoral regions. However, other areas, more especially Southern Africa, New Zealand and Canada, were of importance. New Zealand initially followed the pattern established in Australia, except in its smaller scale and concentration upon sheep. The New Zealand experience is however most noticeable for the radical changes which pastoralism wrought in the landscape. The most significant was the virtual elimination of indigenous grasses and reseeding with European species. Thus unlike most colonial pastoral regions the pasturelands have been resown, permitting increased stock-carrying capacities. Furthermore, because the climate was not as arid as most other pastoral regions of the Empire, pastoralism became more intensive and geared to the meat market rather than dependent upon wool sales. With intensification went a concentration on dairying for the export of cheese and butter. It was the highland zone of Great Britain, not the Australian outback, which provided the model for twentieth-century New Zealand development.

Canada offered only limited opportunities for commercial pastoralism. The agricultural systems of the eastern provinces followed the more traditional non-specialised practices of pioneer times, and later commercial mixed farming became the dominant means of livelihood. Only in the Prairie Provinces did opportunities for extensive pastoral farming arise. The Canadian government recognised that the southern triangle region, surveyed by Captain John Palliser in 1857–60, was unsuited to crop farming. Ranching under lease was therefore permitted when colonisation began in 1872 — in marked contrast to the situation across the border in the United States, where the authorities refused to recognise or profit from pastoralists' holdings. The cattle ranches were smaller than those in the contemporary United States as official attempts were made to settle as many people upon the land as possible, and they were also constrained by the rectangular survey system (Jameson, 1970). Initially 40,000 hectares had been permitted, but this was progressively reduced to 5,000 hectares. In 1913 the formal recognition of the permanence of ranching came with the abolition of the two-year notice period for lessees of land required for agriculture, while regulations were introduced for the removal of failed homesteaders in the pastoral zone. The cowman and the farmer were thus effectively separated according to the environmental capabilities of their zones (Martin, 1938).

The most noticeable deviation from the patterns noted in other mid-latitude regions occurred in southern Africa. Here the British government inherited the settlement pattern and practices of an established group of European settlers, the Dutch, who had evolved a system of semi-subsistence farming based on extensive pastoralism in the course of the eighteenth century (Christopher, 1976a). Subsequent British administrations had sought to control this movement with varying degrees of success as groups of pastoralists migrated

Figure 8.7: Farm patterns in southern Africa

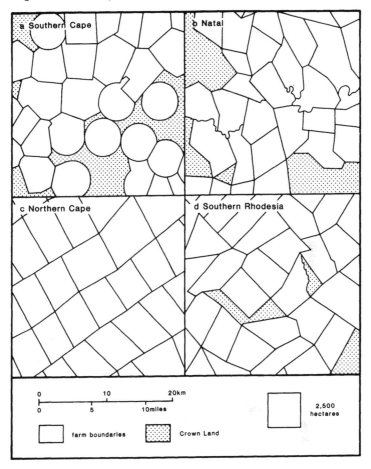

ever further into the interior of the African continent. The process had been prompted by the need for seasonal grazing grounds beyond the zone of established settlements, but had been increasingly powered by a rapidly expanding European frontier population. The system had revolved around the established right of a pioneer to a farm of approximately 2,500 hectares. This right became fixed in the cultural background of the colonists and was quickly adopted by other immigrants. The result was the laying out of a series of farm patterns of remarkable uniformity, ranging from the south-western Cape of Good Hope in the early eighteenth century to Northern and

Southern Rhodesia in the early twentieth century (Christopher, 1976b) (Figure 8.7).

Southern African frontier farmers retained only tenuous links with the colonial economy, and limited trade, owing to the distances and difficulties in communication. Commercialisation came with the extension of the wool trade in the Cape of Good Hope and neighbouring territories in the mid-nineteenth century and the development of the internal meat market dependent upon mining and industrialisation after 1870. Distance, however, defeated any attempt to break into the international meat trade, even when undertaken by London-based companies on extensive ranches. Commercialisation on most farms in the wetter eastern regions revolved around the conversion to crop production, rather than new forms of pastoralism. The Cape of Good Hope did, however, develop two other specialised products, namely mohair from angora goats and feathers from domesticated ostriches, both of which successfully diversified the pastoral economy.

The twin features of local subsistence and overseas exports dominated the pastoral industries of the various mid-latitude colonies. Commercialisation as a result was brought about both by enterprises financed directly by British companies, which in organisational methods resembled the tropical crop plantations, and local farmers employing local finance. Wool entered the intercontinental trade in the nineteenth century as the pioneering commercial product and a major staple to several colonial economies. Meat exports from the end of the nineteenth century were technically more problematical and only a few states were able to compete in the ensuing trade (Perren, 1971). New Zealand became most highly geared to the British meat market while Australia remained the bulk wool exporter.

THE IMPERIAL FRONTIER

The frontier concept has attracted much attention since Frederick Jackson Turner (1894) put forward his well-known thesis. Walter Prescott Webb (1953) extended the scope of Turner's writings as part of a universal framework of economic development, while Isiah Bowman (1931) examined the frontier as a settlement process. Frontiers have now been distinguished in a wide variety of places and periods (Savage and Thompson, 1979). The concept of a British Imperial frontier has been well exercised both as a pioneering enterprise and as a political and military organisation. The epic stories from the North-West Frontier of India were among the most widely disseminated and effective Imperial propaganda of the era. However, not all colonial frontiers were of this direct confrontational nature. The settlement frontiers within the various regions of both European colonisation and indigenous commercialisation may be distinguished as nominal colonial space was incorporated into the world economy. Political boundaries and settlement frontiers were only rarely made coincident and large tracts of the British Empire, even in 1930, were still regarded as being in the pioneering stage.

Turner in his thesis suggested a series of groups who progressively transformed the landscape from wilderness to civilisation. Other actors have been ushered in, while the impact of the indigenous population has assumed greater significance in recent writings. On the British frontiers of settlement it may be asked whether further factors need to be introduced and whether they developed on different lines to the United States model or the Latin American variant. The greater influence of state authority and official supervision are immediately apparent. The Imperial forces of law and order were an omnipresent part of society in all colonies and initially often the largest government spenders (Jorgensen, 1981). Army manpower was directed not only to the development of a network of forts and cantonments, but also towards road construction and town foundation, therefore providing an infrastructure lacking on many contemporary frontiers. Law and order were regarded as essentials of the British civilising process and this was visibly impressed upon the landscape through the posts of such forces as the Royal Canadian Mounted Police and the British South Africa Police. In some colonies the law court and the prison became the first symbols of power and authority and were placed in prominent positions in town plans, and it was from this urban focus that control was spread outwards.

Authority was of significance for the order which was exercised over rural settlement processes. Illegal, and therefore officially unprofitable, squatting on Crown Lands was rarely tolerated and licensing and enumeration were carried out as a matter of course. Thus authority was present at every stage of pioneering endeavour, whether determining grazing licences in Australia, organising and supervising settlements on the Canadian prairies or building and regulating irrigation schemes in South Africa. The government imprint was substantial in the rural areas of European settlement and no less so in the regions of indigenous settlement organised by the British authorities. In much of northern India the authorities inherited the Moghul Empire's administrative and taxation system, while the irrigation systems involved as much planning and supervision as regions of European settlement. Authority therefore was at the forefront of Imperial expansion and the policeman was a prominent character in the frontier process, a marked variation from the United States or Latin American frontiers.

The pastoralist in British colonies in the temperate world similarly was a recognised and permanent part of the frontier settlement process. It was early recognised in all the relevant colonies that the cattle and sheep farmer was not going to be removed and that such elimination would not be desirable from an economic point of view. Thus the systems of settlement provided some measure of security in most colonies. In southern Africa the pastoralist was afforded total security by 1813 with holdings subject merely to a modest quitrent.

The pastoralist with his extensive areas and export product thus became the equivalent of a colonial aristocracy. Indeed in the original negotiations for responsible government in New South Wales in the 1850s an upper house of parliament for a colonial nobility was seriously suggested. This was but one case of the maintenance of a class system in the colonies. No attempt was made to assume all men were equal, with equal rights to land or other resources, or to power in the form of universal franchise. The theory of Systematic Colonisation included the assumption that all men were not equal but should have equal opportunities to achieve prosperity. Thus land prices were set to ensure that only a few could purchase property and in consequence would be assured of a steady supply of labourers who were aspiring to obtain their own land. Land was available for the moderately wealthy. Indeed proposed budgets for emigrants suggest that sums of several hundred pounds were necessary to establish a farmer in the colonies. Only in the late nineteenth and early twentieth centuries was land available for the poor on the Canadian prairies or settlement schemes in Australia and South Africa. However, colonial rural societies tended to be more egalitarian than in England. Few members of the aristocracy settled in the colonies. The Duke of Westminster might initiate settlement schemes in Canada and South Africa, and even build himself a manor house at Westminster in the Orange Free State, but he still lived permanently in England (Figure 8.8). Some younger sons of eminent families together with remittance men emigrated

Figure 8.8: Duke of Westminster's House, Westminster, Orange Free State

permanently, but failed to establish an English rural nobility. Only in tropical colonies, and then in reference to the indigenous population, did feudal conditions reassert themselves.

A further variant on the American frontier theme was the plantation. Turner had looked to the experience of the northern States as the source of frontier expansion for his model. The American South presented a very different image with the commercial plantation and small farm akin to the West Indies (Meinig, 1986). The commercial plantation of sub-tropical and tropical colonies was an integral part of frontier expansion, but in areas usually separate from the other characteristics of frontier settlement. Thus the plantation frontier gave way after the emancipation of the slaves and the expiry of indenture contracts to smallholding settlement and colonisation by people previously working upon the plantation. Owing to the non-European nature of such settlement it received less attention and encouragement than an equivalent British colonisation process would have done and hence lacked many of the frontier's expansive characteristics, owing to the often official policies restricting its progress.

Thus the Imperial frontier introduced characteristics of law and order through the presence of the army and police at an early stage of development. It also was not conducive to, nor did its administrators wish to produce, an egalitarian society. Rather the British authorities sought to re-create an idealised image of English rural settlement from the rich man in his castle to the poor man at his gate. However, frequently it was the American frontier with its society and landscape which was reproduced as a result of the changed colonial relationships between land, labour and capital. Consequently in New Zealand comparisons must be made with the United States, not England (Grey, 1984). In the rural areas it was the villageless settlement pattern of the Trans-Appalachian United States, not the English village system, which was established in most colonies of settlement. However, in Australia the frontier must be viewed in urban, not the rural, terms propounded by Turner, as frontier farmers were most closely tied to the ports and to the international markets for their products (Winks, 1981). Here the financier was vital to the opening of the frontier. Accordingly on the Imperial frontier the official, policeman, planter and financier must be placed alongside the settler and trader.

9

Imperial Landscapes

An attempt has been made in previous chapters to derive some order from the varied landscapes created under a system of Imperialism. The comprehensive nature of British Imperial intervention through a variety of physical and cultural environments around the world makes it a particularly important agent of landscape transformation. The British Empire is now largely a matter of history, yet that history is indelibly stamped into the landscape of a substantial portion of the globe.

Over large parts of the world the British established the first effective occupation, operating on what was perceived to be a virtual *tabula rasa* upon which they determined the main lineaments of communication and the urban and rural settlement patterns. In other regions they had to share the colonial state with an indigenous population and adapt a pre-colonial system to a greater or lesser extent to their own needs. In all cases the results were British colonial landscapes impressed upon various parts of the globe, which owed much to the concepts and enterprise of British officials, merchants and settlers. Unlike certain other European empires with which it was contemporary, the British developed no overriding Imperial theory to be put into practice worldwide, but adopted an often highly pragmatic approach to colonisation.

A wide variety of themes emerge from the investigation of the relationship between Imperialism and landscape which are worthy of future consideration. They include, among others, the impact of colonial policies upon the various settler states, the impact of colonialism upon other societies, the impress of central authority upon the landscape, and the adaptation of official and settler perceptions to strange environments. Finally some preliminary assessment of the heritage of the Imperial era is required, and recognition of the degree to which the current move towards conservation has been applied to the British colonial structures. In each of these cases comparative examination of the imprint and its heritage in one area may heighten awareness of the same heritage in others, as well as an appreciation of the significance of the unity of the whole endeavour. The Imperial system provides an integrative approach to the problem of landscape formation in the last few centuries in many parts of the world.

COLONIES OF SETTLEMENT

The colonies of settlement which developed into the dominions of Canada, Australia and New Zealand present the clearest example of the Imperial transfer of British society *in toto* from one part of the world to another. Several other states, including South Africa, Jamaica and Barbados, exhibit a strong impact of the settlement programme, but without the numerical dominance of British settlers. In these it was often non-British settlers from other continents who occupied British planned landscapes and worked under British supervision. Only late in the colonial period did the weak British demographic position make itself evident in political terms, after the impress of settlement had been effected.

What do the landscapes of these states have in common? Firstly, the British authorities planned and surveyed much of the rural property and settlement pattern which provided the framework for occupation and colonisation. Secondly, the towns were founded, planned and built in the image of Britain or other parts of the English-speaking world. Thirdly, as part of a common culture region the initial imprint has been modified by similar processes to produce landscapes culturally akin to one another, and differentiated more by features such as architectural styles marking an adaptation to the climate than to national styles. Here it must be emphasised that the new environments which the colonists encountered were evaluated in terms of their own, European, backgrounds. Thus the local, indigenous, past was considered 'largely irrelevant to settlers who impressed on the new lands not only some of the familiar elements from their homeland but also such foreign ones as they thought might help in subduing what they perceived as wilderness' (Grey, 1984: 66).

Rural settlement patterns imprinted upon the landscape were diverse in plan but related to the perceived physical environment and official concepts of the nature of the future colonial society (Cameron, 1974). Environmental perception was often erroneous and governments tended to learn about the capabilities of the land through a process of trial and error. Settlements were laid out within a number of constraints imposed by the system of land holdings designed to establish colonial society within fairly narrow confines. Secure freehold tenure for family farmers, the desired end product of colonisation, was the standard throughout much of the colonial era. The myth of the 'yeoman farmer' was a constant element in settlement schemes, paralleling the nineteenth century American agrarian ideal. Thus relatively small farms of under 100 hectares, surrounded by ring fences, dominated cadastral plans. Communal tenures, of the Medieval period, although periodically introduced, particularly early in the colonial period, were rejected in favour of individual tenure. Settlement dispersion was thus the dominant colonial pattern despite a frequent return to a village-based organisation of government, but usually without the element of a landed aristocracy. Dispersion was even more in evidence in the pastoral regions, where arid and semi-arid lands were encountered and new forms of tenure and settlement were adopted after many painful experiments. Crown leases, quitrents and other forms of non-freehold tenure were devised to retain a government interest and hence partial control over land usage where capabilities were virtually unknown. Colonial solutions have been retained to the present. The resulting rural settlement patterns reflect a range of colonial philosophies propagated by colonial governors and legislatures, often borrowing from one another.

In terms of urban settlement, the British Empire lacked the town planning patterns of the Spanish colonial Empire in the Americas and the Philippines. The range of layouts was thus considerable, but the basic range of town economies was fairly limited until late in the colonial era. In general, settler colonial towns were characterised by an abundance of space, allowing the design of low-density settlements with extensive open places and generous private gardens. In addition a degree of uniformity of style was imported from England, but modified under local circumstances. Simplicity was enforced through the small size of settlements and the lack of conspicuous spending in the colonies. Thus the settler colonial cities were more closely related to one another than to the British cities upon which they were originally modelled. Once again the availability of space, noticeably lacking in most cities in the British Isles, enabled colonial town planners to provide for generously proportioned public and

private buildings. Garden cities were built in the colonies before
Ebenezer Howard wrote on the subject. Nevertheless, British town
planners did not consider the colonies had much to offer them and
tended to ignore the colonial experience until late in the era. It is also
noticeable that apart from mining settlements, few colonial foundations were designed to be industrial towns. High-density industrial
designs thus only featured in the southern African Black single-sex
mining compounds where totally different solutions to the housing
of industrial workers were adopted. Mine owners employing British
overseas workers adopted a more generous approach to company
housing and settlement layout. The North of England back-to-back
house and the society which went with it had few parallels in the
colonies.

COLONIES OF EXPLOITATION

The extensive tracts of the world where the British came to trade,
exploit and ultimately to govern, have retained another heritage.
Here the Empire as the home of a nation of builders may be most
forcefully remembered. The classic mercantilist network of
communications based on the ports and extending along the lines of
roads and railways, provided a lasting monument to the Imperial
system with the reorientation of trade and industrial patterns which
this implied. The systems evolved in the nineteenth and early twentieth centuries have remained virtually intact and have profoundly
influenced the economic and political structures which replaced
colonialism, ensuring the continuing link to the world economic
system.

The major transport systems, of which the Indian railway
network is one of the foremost examples, reorientated trade towards
the ports, indeed towards colonial cities specially built for the
purpose. These systems have acted as unifying forces in the post-
colonial era in the process of integrating the population through the
encouragement of long-distance travel, as the passenger complement
of any Indian express train testifies. The reorientation of trade,
industry and population to new centres was a permanent legacy of
the colonial era. Thus Calcutta and Bombay, the major seventeenth-
century city foundations in India, remain today as the two largest
cities on the subcontinent 40 years after independence. The cities
therefore pose as monuments to the colonial era not only in their
siting and functions but also in their appearance (Figure 9.1). Often

Figure 9.1: Calcutta townscape

colonial cities erected fine examples of British architecture which have been maintained in more complete order than those in the British Isles. Indeed it has been suggested that India possesses a finer assemblage of Victorian government and private buildings than remain in the United Kingdom and that some British assistance should be offered to the Indian authorities for the preservation of a part of the British cultural heritage (Davies, 1985). The introduced European-style colonial city remains as a significant element in the landscape of many countries betraying the nationality of that power, and the changed economic relationships wrought by the colonial era.

If direct colonial influence in the tropics was predominantly urban, the rural areas were not entirely neglected. At one extreme colonial administrations often sought radically to change the rural economy through the introduction of a plantation economy. The opportunities for such change were limited by the availability of colonial land, suitable plantation crops and metropolitan capital. As a result only restricted areas throughout the tropical Empire were designated plantation lands. Consequently two economies, plantation and indigenous, separated by partition lines were major heritages for the post-independence governments, which were almost universally suspicious of the social aspects of plantations, but for whom the enterprise represented a major source of foreign exchange earnings. Hence plantations, often in modified form, have remained as a distinctive survival from the colonial era, and frequently acted as innovators for the indigenous rural economy. Smallholding production of staple plantation crops began after the colonial era, where restrictions on cultivation were imposed, and even earlier where no restrictions were introduced. Accordingly plantation and smallholder production often developed in symbiosis. However, not all rural export production was initiated by the colonial planter. The cultivation of cocoa in the Gold Coast and groundnuts in Nigeria were two significant examples of indigenous enterprise transforming the local economy as a result of the opportunities offered by colonial economic relations.

The reinterpretation of the African colonial era in Africanist terms has viewed the period as one of underdevelopment. The opinions of Rodney (1972) have been expanded by later writers who have discerned a systematic exploitation and despoilation of the continent by the colonial powers, wielding through means of coercion the ability to transfer the material resources of the continent to Europe at minimal cost through a system of unequal exchange. The theme of underdevelopment through the destruction of indigenous polities and their reduction to client status has been widespread. However, it was in the southern part of the continent that the process was taken to its most complete form (Palmer and Parsons, 1977). The establishment of a capitalist form of enterprise, notably through the development of the mining sector in the late nineteenth century, and the commercial farming sector in the twentieth century, profoundly changed class relationships. These relationships to a large extent coincided with racial divisions, or were made to do so by subsequent legislation and practice.

Underdevelopment was pursued through the systematic exploitation of the labour supplies of the subcontinent, created through the impoverishment of the indigenous rural reservation areas. The causes of impoverishment have been variously ascribed to increased pressure on agricultural resources brought about by a rapidly expanding population, the systematic exclusion of the reserves from the commercial farming sector and the imposition of new forms of taxation upon the indigenous society. The subsequent impoverishment led to a rising number of workers entering the colonial labour market, who because of the security of the land they possessed in the rural areas could be paid single men's wages lower than those required to support a family. The indigenous reserves thus acted as an insurance policy for the urban working class, who were housed in single quarters, and forced to leave their families behind in the reserves. Wage rates thus fell in real terms between the 1890s and the 1950s, leading to an increasing level of crisis in the African rural areas of southern Africa. The same process afflicted the poor rural White population, which was reduced to poverty, but without the land resources to support a family. The result was also destitution, but concomitantly a flow of migrants, with their families, to the towns. Hence through political action the poor White population was able to alleviate their situation. In the colonies of exploitation the indigenous population was without recourse to such action and the crisis was only tackled after the Second World War.

The mining industry, particularly that on the Witwatersrand, has been subjected to increased scrutiny to demonstrate the influence of the mining magnates through their manipulation of labour supplies, and even colonial governments, to provide the political environment most conducive for maximum profitability (Van Onselen, 1982). The results of the new labour relationships were imprinted upon the landscape. Urban class segregation within European society as well as race segregation ensued. The colonial city took on a new industrial form distinguishing it from the earlier mercantile model.

In the second half of the present century it was transformed yet again into the Apartheid city (Christopher, 1983b). The latter was viewed entirely in racial terms, although class differentiation existed within each of the racially defined sectors.

The economic relationships established in the colonial era have proved to be remarkably resistant to change in the post-colonial era. Colonial boundaries, colonial trade patterns, colonial cities and frequently colonial class relations have survived long after the political *raison d'être* for their establishment has been removed. Thus the land division enacted in Southern Rhodesia survives in modern Zimbabwe despite the rhetoric of socialism. The railway lines constructed to aid the exploitation of resources in central Africa in the 1890s and 1900s have effectively tied the Zambian and Zimbabwean economies to that of South Africa in the 1980s, and changes are remarkably expensive to effect, as the Southern African Development Coordinating Council has discovered.

THE IMPRESS OF CENTRAL AUTHORITY

It is perhaps one of the paradoxes of colonialism that a system built on free trade, *laissez-faire* and minimal government intervention in Great Britain depended upon a high degree of regulation and control in the colonies. The supreme position of the government in the colonies, often endowed with dictatorial powers vested in the governor, was reflected in the landscape through the decisions taken and the structures erected for the maintenance of administration. Government control was exercised over land ownership and usage, and frequently over the movement of population and residential rights. The means of communication were usually government owned and the economy closely regulated through taxation and legal prescription. Colonial bureaucracy was powerful and often all pervading in its influence, although laws may not always have been carried out as intended.

The administration influenced colonial development through the drawing of boundaries, building of towns and the detailed planning of urban and rural areas. Capital cities of the Empire, as the places of residence of the most important officials, exhibit these influences most clearly. The layout of government precincts, with the assemblage of government houses, secretariats, offices and parliamentary buildings, together with public parks and accumulated statues and monuments to sovereigns, governors and other notables, provide distinctive, Imperial elements in the landscape. In a large degree government districts have survived as preserved areas of the capital. Certain of the details have been removed, but the main structures retain the colonial image, even if dwarfed by later accretions of ministries and new and larger parliamentary complexes. It is noticeable that the government enclaves represent a marked departure in British planning and are a far more prominent feature of colonial cities than London or English provincial cities. This is due to the vast area appropriated for government use, and the resultant spacious nature of colonial plans. Only the late nineteenth and twentieth century additions to Whitehall emulated colonial planning, but on a very cramped site.

Central authority was impressed upon the colonial city far beyond the bounds of the government precinct. The formal plans of most cities and towns were produced by government officials. The grid pattern of straight streets intersecting at right angles dominated the majority of colonial layouts. The width of roads, size of plots, and provision of space for public parks and future expansion also indicated a spaciousness in design more akin to Renaissance or later garden city concepts and were indicative of an official liberality with the land resources of the colonies. Private developers had to work within a governmental framework in the colonial city.

Again, in contrast to contemporary England, the military imprint was an important and often continuing feature of colonial urban development. Forts were built to a variety of designs depending upon the era of construction. They emphasised the military role of the state in the protection of British interests both against direct attack by other European powers and in the control of indigenous populations. In trading establishments the fort initially housed the entire European population, while in settlement and plantation colonies the military and police contingents were quartered in the fort. Walled forts were replaced by more expansive facilities in the late nineteenth and early twentieth centuries as the influence of the Indian military cantonment penetrated other parts of the Empire. The military and police posts were linked to the worldwide system of naval bases upon which British power depended. It was these which have had particularly serious problems of adjustment as a result of the termination of the British global political role. Conversion to commercial shipyards, industrial zones and yacht basins has ensued where the post-colonial state did not develop an independent naval capability. Depressingly forts have also continued to be used as prisons in a number of post-colonial states, or have retained their original functions as army and police bases. However, a number have been converted to tourist attractions, while many others have been demolished or simply allowed to decay.

State control often extended from the mere provision of an administrative and communication infrastructure to an active role in the running of the economy through the redistribution of resources within the colonial state and occasionally the direct management of those resources. Government farms, the Royal Botanical Gardens, and their supply garden predecessors, were instrumental in the diffusion of crops to new environments where the Crown undertook the developmental costs. Forests were generally regarded as Crown preserves and harvested under contract. Similarly minerals were regarded as part of the Crown's eminent domain in many colonies, which then controlled the licensing of concessionaires. Land was one of the major resources which the government had to offer and the systems and schemes through which it was taken from the indigenous people and distributed to immigrant communities played a major role in the layout of the rural areas. Official attempts at social engineering in the settler colonies were usually directed towards the establishment of an independent yeoman farmer class upon the land, rather than the reproduction of the English tenant farming system. Concepts such as the living area, upon which a family could make a living, akin to the living wage, and the deliberate breakup of large holdings suggest a degree of colonial socialism at variance with contemporary British political principles.

It is one of the most significant aspects of colonialism that the state intervened directly through conquest and economic reorientation to create a new economic and political dispensation. Rarely was this imposed upon a *tabula rasa*, but was most often planned as though it was so organised. Because of the importance of the colonial era many of the political and administrative decisions made at that time have survived until the present, as post-independence governments have operated within the colonial state framework which gave them initial legitimacy.

THE IMPRESS OF RELIGION

The impress of the state was paralleled by the impress of the Church. The place of religion in the Imperial system was always of importance as the British Empire was a nominally Christian society. Because of their size and the expense of replacement, church buildings have proved to be even more resistant to change than government buildings. Neo-classical and particularly neo-gothic structures are the legacy of the bursts of religious enthusiasm which accompanied certain periods of the colonial era. Cathedrals in particular survive on prime sites in ex-colonial capitals, often dwarfed by later commercial and administrative structures. They remain as English refuges where the banners of colonial regiments and monuments to colonial personages may still be found — a very tangible link with the past (Figure 9.2).

If considerable community expense was directed towards church building, private money was directed towards cemeteries. The commemoration of the dead was an important part of human activity and the burial grounds of colonial cities played a particular role in the society which developed. Cemeteries were laid out adjacent to new towns from their inception, usually in English style as a church-yard adjacent to the church, although large peripheral cemeteries were necessary at a later stage. High death rates in many colonies resulted in rapid filling of churchyards and the appropriation of more land for burials. Segregation between various denominations and between races became general, hence the creation of a multiplicity of graveyards, either adjacent to one another or in different parts of the town. The picture was further complicated by the presence of Moslems and Chinese in many tropical colonies, with their own separate burial grounds.

Graveyards were embellished with gravestones of varying elaboration. The unmarked graves of early cemeteries or poor communities were paralleled by the major tombs erected for people of wealth and status. The size and design of tombs frequently followed English fashion, indeed many were imported directly from England. Thus the variety of designs included reproductions of Absalom's Tomb, Greek coffins, pyramids and colonnaded temples, with a range of obelisks, angels and urns on less grandiose graves. The major cemeteries in India, notably the presidency cities and larger cantonments, provide fine examples of funereal art, which were reproduced in all the main towns of the country. A reminder of Imperial linkages is presented by the tomb of Elizabeth, Lady Donkin, who died in 1818 in Meerut (Figure 9.3). Two years later her husband, as Acting Governor of the Cape of Good Hope, named the settlement of Port Elizabeth in her honour, and erected a more substantial monument to her memory which still dominates the town.

Military graveyards present a distinct group of cemeteries. These

227

Figure 9.2: St George's Cathedral, Jerusalem

Figure 9.3: St John's churchyard, Meerut

were laid out on the battlefields of the Empire, and indeed beyond it as a result of the numerous campaigns fought by British armies throughout the world. Notably, little attempt was made to repatriate coffins to the United Kingdom and the cemeteries were often laid out where the soldiers fell. The rows of crosses and headstones, all regularly organised, provide a noticeable contrast to the more chaotic and flamboyant characteristics of the civilian graveyards. Many military graveyards were reorganised later, to group soldiers, while those attached to the military bases also gave rise to the extensive fields of graves. The Imperial War Graves Commission, after the First World War, planned and erected many of the impressive monuments to the dead, providing a measure of uniformity throughout the Empire.

Commemoration of the dead was a major part of communal effort in the Empire prior to 1930. Settlers died in substantial numbers, particularly in tropical colonies, and the wars constantly fought throughout the era contributed to the toll. Thus colonial society lived with death and commemorated its victims. War memorials are consequently the most numerous type of monument erected by the colonial authorities. Many are general memorials, notably the All India War Memorial Arch in New Delhi, erected to commemorate the dead of the First World War and campaigns on India's borders. Cenotaphs, modelled on the one in Whitehall, were reproduced with suitable adaptations on a worldwide basis. Monuments to earlier wars, including the Anglo-Boer Wars, the Crimean War, the Napoleonic Wars, as well as individual campaigns, particularly from the 1850s onwards, were erected in considerable numbers. Whereas the statues and monuments to the individual generals and field-marshals who commanded the armies have been removed in some states since independence, the general war memorials survive, providing a historic link with the landscapes of Empire.

PLACE NAMES

One of the lasting legacies of British settlement has been the place names given by explorers, officials, settlers and others in the course of the last 500 years, over large parts of the ex-British Empire. The British influence, however, was not as great as the Spanish and Portuguese, who as the first European explorers throughout much of the world left a universal imprint upon the names of coastlines and islands as well as the more localised regions they settled. The British explorers and officials merely anglicised many names of Iberian origin in the New World. Further, large parts of the world were occupied by literate societies which resisted the renaming of their countries' towns, rivers and mountains, although again anglicised versions went into general usage. In other countries European and indigenous names were intermingled as their societies were intermingled, or where European inventiveness became exhausted. Even within colonies, marked variations occur in the survival of indigenous names. In New Zealand, Maori names were retained where Maori numbers were sufficient to impress them upon European consciousness (Yoon, 1980). In contrast on the Avalon Peninsula of Newfoundland, Indian names were virtually erased from the map (Seary, 1971).

Europeans encountering new lands were faced with the problem of nomenclature. A place, a mountain or a river had to be given a name for identification and mapping, as did the farms granted in the course of settlement. Many names were chosen to be purely descriptive, noting the colour or nature of the feature such as Blue Mountains or Rocky River. Others recorded incidents in the experience of the explorers such as Shipwreck Point or Mount Misery. Some were given personal names connected with the explorer or people he met such as Turners Beach or Anna Creek. Occasionally names were manufactured such as the Northern Territory of Australia settlements of Humpty Doo and Rum Jungle. Promotional names including Paradise and Heart's Delight were widely used. Clearly surveyors and explorers needed to be men of some ingenuity.

However, the British overseas borrowed heavily upon their own geographical backgrounds. It was only natural that the place names of the British Isles should have dominated the minds of many of the explorers and parties of settlers. Thus New Englands, New Scotlands together with the counties, towns and villages were used and reused, as were the names of the rivers and hills of the United Kingdom. At the official level, administrators frequently chose the names of the main towns and of administrative units, which until the early nineteenth century relied heavily upon the English and to a lesser extent the Scottish county system. In this respect the largest area of British name reproduction was the United States. At a more local level areas of British colonisation reflected the counties from which the settlers were drawn. Hence the north coast of Tasmania reflects the West Country origin of many of the settlers with the appearance of such situations as Launceston on the Tamar River (Figure 9.4). However, the geographical anomaly of Devonport at the mouth of the Mersey River suggests other influences as does the

Figure 9.4: Place names in northern Tasmania

proximity of Breadalbane to Perth not only in Scotland but also in Tasmania. Elsewhere specific groups of settlers, including Cornish and Welsh miners, left their mark in the names chosen for the mines and villages established.

A further source of names was provided by the royal family. Variations on the basic Kingston or Queenstown sufficed in many cases for major settlements ranging from Jamaica to Ontario. Personal names, James and Charles in the seventeenth century, George in the eighteenth and early nineteenth centuries and ultimately Victoria in the heyday of Empire, were universally employed. Queen Victoria was commemorated in mountains, lakes and waterfalls as well as colonies and towns. Four colonial capitals (those of British Columbia, Hong Kong, Seychelles and Labuan) were named after her: an indication of the major expansion of British territory during her reign. Royal consorts, notably Queen Charlotte wife of King George III, and Prince Albert husband of Queen Victoria, were similarly honoured in a wide range of settlements and physical features. Royal princes and princesses expanded the range of personal and jurisdictional names, which again found favour with officials seeking those of a non-controversial nature.

Officers and ministers of the Crown presented another source for nomenclature. Military leaders, government ministers, colonial governors and administrators all lent their names to new lands. War heroes, such as Wellington and Kitchener, were honoured in the Empire at the time of and for a while after their exploits. Prime ministers, particularly in the nineteenth century, were frequently 'placed upon the map' often with political connotations, as Conservative prime ministers tended to be regarded more favourably in the colonies in the latter part of the century than the Liberals. Accordingly Beaconsfield and Salisbury have a more Imperial connotation than Gladstone. Colonial secretaries fared particularly well in having settlements named after them. Thus the foundation of the several Stanleys, Bathursts and Kimberleys may be pinpointed to the period of those ministers' incumbency of the Colonial Office. Colonial governors similarly were commemorated, often in several colonies following the territorial movements of their careers. Hence Dundas may be located in Canada and Australia and Darling in four Australian provinces and South Africa. Colonial officials were similarly commemorated in the nature of their work. Thus Mount Everest was named after the Surveyor-General of India, during whose period of office the triangulation was completed to positively identify the mountain as the highest in the world.

Certain names were chosen specifically to identify political, social or religious programmes. Consequently the founders of the New Zealand mining towns of Cromwell, Hampden and Naseby stated their political affiliations as clearly as the founders of Orangeville, Ontario, stated their persuasions. Few names of a utopian nature were adopted in the British colonies, neither were the classical analogies popularised in the United States after independence. Religion was rarely a source of inspiration in the place naming process. The Saints' names, used widely by the

Spanish, Portuguese and French and inherited by the British, were only rarely adopted by the British after the late seventeenth century. Later settlements very occasionally used religious or biblical names. Christchurch, New Zealand, is the most notable example of a large nineteenth-century settlement based specifically upon Church of England foundations. There are few Salems or Bethels within the British Empire, again in noticeable contrast to the other major state of the English-speaking world.

Not all settlers within the British Empire came from the British Isles. German and Scandinavian names were used widely in the eighteenth and nineteenth centuries reflecting an immigration of groups from those regions of Europe. The Empire also incorporated other European groups settled prior to conquest and annexation. Thus the expansion of French-Canadian or Afrikaner-Dutch settlement was expressed through distinctive place names maintaining a separate identity from the politically and often numerically dominant British settlers. The appearance of names such as Ste Rose de Lac (Manitoba) or Enkeldoorn (Southern Rhodesia) marked French-Canadian and Afrikaner settlement, respectively, beyond their initial heartlands. There appears to have been an aversion to Indian and Chinese names on the part of European officials in colonies of Asian immigration and with the exception of a few isolated names in Malaya (Singapore and Taiping), no new Indias or new Chinas emerged.

Within towns and cities the names of streets and suburbs similarly give an indication of the origins and periods of expansion. Thus King George V Avenue, whether in Durban or Jerusalem, clearly dates the thoroughfare and the sections of the cities through which it passes. Similarly Waterloo and Balaclava were commemorated in streets throughout the Empire. The First World War elicited little such desire and the costly victories of 1914-18 were not the inspiration of street names. By contrast, technical innovation, notably the railway, the commemoration of commerce and industry or the corporation, provided a standard set of names for many streets, both in the British Isles and in the colonies. There is therefore much to be learnt from Imperial place names, and also much that is familiar to the inhabitants of the late Empire in this shared heritage.

THE IMPERIAL HERITAGE

As has been shown the British Empire had a profound effect upon the lands which were colonised. The establishment of colonial rule resulted in the imposition of British administration and a distinct national image upon the landscape. British-style towns and country-side as well as distinctive British colonial towns and modifications to indigenous rural landscapes were planned, built, laid out and imposed. Decolonisation in turn led to some symbolic attempts to decolonise the landscape in certain countries. General Gordon no longer looks out over Khartoum nor Cecil Rhodes over Bulawayo. However, the main lineaments of the colonial landscapes could not be changed as readily, even if the political will to do so was there. Political boundaries, cadastral lines, road patterns as well as structures, have outlived the people who placed them in the landscape, along with a host of more subtle reminders. The Imperial heritage remains firmly in place in tangible and intangible form.

The current revival of interest in the past, more particularly through the conservation movement and the search for roots, has resulted in an added appreciation of the colonial heritage. Even eighteenth-century architecture in Dublin, decried earlier in the present century as of alien culture by Irish nationalists, has been accepted as a part of the history of the city and indeed of the Irish historical experience. However, at independence the desire for indigenisation in non-British nations resulted in the move to foster indigenous styles and erase colonial styles. Often this was difficult and was limited to the construction of new areas of cities. Thus Lusaka's 1930s British garden city image on the one hand and the southern African Black location township image on the other were supplemented by an indigenous administrative and legislative quarter after independence (Davies, 1972). There was, however, another alternative, the construction of new cities rejecting the image of colonialism. Hence Pakistan abandoned the provisional capital at the colonial port city of Karachi in favour of the new city appropriately named Islamabad. Tanzania is similarly in the process of moving the captial to Dodoma built in the image of African socialism as opposed to colonial Dar es Salaam with its British and German connotations. Considerations of expense limit such flamboyant gestures of decolonisation.

The urban colonial heritage has been more imperilled by urban redevelopment than deliberate political policies. Urban renewal schemes and the process of Central Business District redevelopment have taken their toll on the stock of private and corporate colonial structures. Government buildings have proved to be more immune to demolition to make way for new offices. Comprehensive redevelopment schemes such as the one in Singapore have obliterated much of the colonial landscape in an effort to modernise the urban fabric and eliminate slums (Teo and Savage, 1985). In general such modernisation has been limited in tropical countries for lack of capital for redevelopment and different priorities in urban planning. In the settler dominions major Central Business District redevelopment in the main centres, particularly in the 1950s and 1960s, severely depleted the colonial building stock as Central Business Districts have tended to remain where they were originally designed. In the smaller centres the colonial heritage has survived far more completely through a lack of profitable opportunity to redevelopers. Governments have generally adopted a more conservative attitude to rebuilding their own structures, resulting in an often incongruous proximity of nineteenth-century government buildings and twentieth-century corporate structures.

Preservation and conservation have assured greater significance in the 1970s and 1980s as alternatives to expensive new buildings were sought in a period of financial restraint (Latreille *et al.*, 1982). The question of urban preservation is a vexed one as the example of Georgian Dublin illustrates (Kearns, 1982). Conservation is the product of the politically dominant group, consequently the cultural landscapes of other groups have tended to show less chance of survival (Turnbridge, 1984). In the colonial era it was the settler society which decided what to preserve and what to commemorate. In the post-colonial era it has been the successor elites who have made the decisions on what to preserve. Thus the club in Salisbury (Harare) has a position in Rhodesian history and in Zimbabwean history as the place where the trials of Africans taken prisoner during the rising of 1896–7 were held. Accordingly events of significance for both societies may ensure the survival of colonial relics. Where settler societies achieved independence the sensitivity of colonial reminders is less and continuity of interest is evident, including preservation of early forts and townscapes. Significant areas may be restored as urban parks such as Ballarat or rebuilt such as the Hudson's Bay Company fort at Edmonton. In an era when few new monuments are erected those from the colonial period continue to fulfil a vital function, while in countries with few buildings earlier in date than 1900, all such buildings assume a significance absent in more established countries with longer histories in the built environment. The commercialisation of colonial history has also assumed some importance with the introduction of reproduction colonial towns for visitors to 'experience' the Victorian heritage. Gold Reef City in Johannesburg is but one example of the profitable exploitation of an idealised version of the colonial past.

The colonial conservation movement has had wider geographical implications. Concern for the preservation of the architectural heritage of the West Indies, the scene of some of the earliest stages of Great Britain's overseas enterprise, was first expressed in the 1920s on the island of St Christopher at the time of the tercentenary of British settlement. However little was done to maintain the surviving structures as a result of 'popular indifference wedded to official neglect' (Acworth, 1951: 10). It has been domestic and international tourism which has influenced the preservation of many tangible parts of the colonial heritage. This is particularly noticeable in the West Indies, where American tourists have promoted an appreciation of the colonial impress of the half dozen colonial powers who held sway in the islands during the peak of plantation prosperity in the eighteenth century. As a result the restoration and refurbishment of some fine examples of colonial Georgian public and private architecture, military and naval installations and rural landscapes, has ensued to balance the Imperial legacy.

POSTSCRIPT

The British colonial enterprise has left a lasting imprint upon the landscapes of vast portions of the world. There was no overall system or model for the establishment and planning of colonies, although many blueprints were devised. Pragmatism tempered most colonial enterprises with the result that although general themes may be discerned, the regional variations are marked. Imperialism contributed much to the areas under British colonial control through the incorporation of large tracts into the world economy and the organisation of those tracts with their populations, whether indigenous or settler, for profitable development and exploitation. Organisation involved the radical transformation of the landscapes of large parts of the Empire, with few areas remaining untouched either as wildscape or in the hands of an unregulated indigenous economy.

Transformation of the landscape through the application of new technologies involved the establishment of new cities, extensions to old cities, new lines of communications, new farm patterns and major migrations of people from one part of the world to another. Although the major act of decolonisation took place 40 years ago, there is still much to be seen in tangible form of the impact of the

Empire which reached its apogee half a century beforehand, and whose servants were the first to apply the technology of the Industrial Revolution on a worldwide basis. The British during their colonial and imperial venture devoted much attention to innovation, engineering, architecture and construction. Sir Philip Mitchell was remarkably prophetic in his statement cited at the beginning of this work, that the British would be remembered as builders. Indeed to appreciate the monuments of Empire, no better advice could be tendered than that offered to those who read Sir Christopher Wren's epitaph in St Paul's Cathedral: 'Si monumentum requiris, circumspice'.

Bibliography

Acworth, A.W. (1951) *Buildings of Architectural and Historic Interest in the British West Indies*, London: HMSO

Addison, G.H.M. (1910) 'The possibility of developing an Australian style of architecture', *Report of the Australasian Association for the Advancement of Science*, 12, 678–81

Adeyoju, S.K. (1969) 'The Benin timber industry before 1939', *Nigerian Geographical Journal*, 12, 99–111

Akinbode, A. (1974) 'The spatial diffusion of kolanut production in southwestern Nigeria', *Nigerian Geographical Journal*, 17, 111-25

Allen, C. (1975) *Plain Tales from the Raj*, London: André Deutsch

———— (1979) *Tales from the Dark Continent*, London: André Deutsch

Andrews, K.R. (1984) *Trade, plunder and settlement: maritime enterprise and the genesis of the British Empire, 1480–1630*, Cambridge: Cambridge University Press

———— Canny, N.P. and Hair, P.E.H. (1979) *The Westward Enterprise: English activities in Ireland, the Atlantic and America, 1480–1650*, Detroit: Wayne State University Press

Antrobus, H.A. (1957) *A History of the Assam Company, 1839–1953*, Edinburgh: Constable

Aplin, G. (1982) 'Models of urban change: Sydney, 1820–1870', *Australian Geographical Studies*, 20, 144–58.

Ashton, S.R. (1982) *British policy towards the Indian States, 1905–1939*, London: Curzon Press

Australia (1937) *Report of the Board of Inquiry appointed to inquire into the land and land industries of the Northern Territory of Australia*, Canberra: Government Printer

Awasthi, R.C. (1975) *Economics of tea industry in India, with special reference to Assam*, Gauhati: United Publishers

Bailey, J.D. (1966) *A hundred years of pastoral banking: a history of the Australian Mercantile Land and Finance Company, 1863–1963*, Oxford: Clarendon Press

Bannerjee, B. and Roy, D. (1967) *Industrial profile of the Calcutta Metropolitan Area*, Calcutta: Indian Publications

Barrett, B. (1971) *The Inner Suburbs: the evolution of an industrial area*, Melbourne: Melbourne University Press

Barrier, N.G. (1981) *The Census in British India: New Perspectives*, New Delhi: Manohav Publishers

Barty-King, H. (1979) *Girdle Round the Earth: the story of Cable and Wireless and its predecessors to mark the group's jubilee, 1929–1979*, London: Heinemann

Beckford, G.L. (1972) 'Aspects of the present conflict between the plantation and peasantry in the West Indies', *Caribbean Quarterly*, 18, 47–58

Biger, G. (1979) *The role of the British administration in changing the geography of Palestine, 1918–1929*, London: Department of Geography, University College London

Blakeley, B.L. (1972) *The Colonial Office, 1868–1892*, Durham, N.C.: Duke University Press

Blixen, K. (1937) *Out of Africa*, London: Putnam

Bloomfield, G.T. (1975) 'Urban Tramways in New Zealand, 1862–1964', *New Zealand Geographer*, 31, 99–123.

Blouet, B. (1984) *The Story of Malta*, Valetta: Progress Press

Bowman, I. (1931) *The Pioneer Fringe*, New York: American Geographical Society

Briggs, A. (1968) *Victorian Cities*, Harmondsworth: Penguin

British North Borneo Company (1929) *Handbook of the State of North Borneo*, London: British North Borneo Company

Britton, S.G. (1980) 'The evolution of a colonial space economy: the case of Fiji', *Journal of Historical Geography*, 6, 251–74

Brockway, L. (1979) *Science and Colonial Expansion: the role of the British Royal Botanic Gardens*, London: Academic Press

Burghardt, A.F. (1969) 'The origin and development of the road network of the Niagara Peninsula, Ontario, 1770–1851', *Annals of the Association of American Geographers*, 59, 417–40

Butlin, N.G. (1950) 'Company ownership of New South Wales pastoral stations, 1865–1900', *Historical Studies, Australia and New Zealand*, 4, 89–111

———— (1962) 'Distribution of the sheep population: preliminary statistical picture, 1860–1957', in Barnard, A. (ed.), *The Simple Fleece: Studies in the Australian Wool Industry*, Melbourne: Melbourne University Press, pp. 281–307

Cameron, J.M.R. (1974) 'Information distortion in colonial promotion: the case of Swan River Colony', *Australian Geographical Studies*, 12, 57–76

Camm, J.C.R. (1985) 'The origins of assisted British migrants to Queensland, 1871–1892', *Australian Geographical Studies*, 23, 87–104

Cape of Good Hope (1893) *Selection from Correspondence relating to the Settlement of Loeriesfontein*, G.10–'93, Cape Town: Government Printer

Chapman, S. (1984) *The Rise of Merchant Banking*, London: George Allen & Unwin

Chaudhuri, N.C. (1959) *A Passage to England*, London: Macmillan

Christopher, A.J. (1971) 'Land Tenure in Rhodesia', *South African Geographical Journal*, 53, 39–52.

———— (1976a) *Southern Africa: Studies in Historical Geography*, Folkestone: Dawson

———— (1976b) 'The variability of the southern African standard farm', *South African Geographical Journal*, 58, 107–17

———— (1982) *South Africa*, London: Longman

———— (1983a) 'From Flint to Soweto: reflections on the colonial origins of the Apartheid city', *Area*, 15, 145–9

———— (1983b) 'Official land disposal policies and European settlement in Southern Africa, 1860–1960', *Journal of Historical Geography*, 9, 369–83

———— (1984a) *The Crown Lands of British South Africa, 1853–1914*, Kingston, Ontario: Limestone Press

———— (1984b) *Colonial Africa*, London: Croom Helm

———— (1985) 'Patterns of British overseas investment in land, 1885–1913', *Transactions of the Institute of British Geographers*, New Series, 10, 452–66

———— (1987) 'Race and residence in colonial Port Elizabeth', *South African Geographical Journal*, 69

Chubb, H.J. and Duckworth, C.L.D. (1973) *The Irrawaddy Flotilla Company Limited, 1865–1950*, London: National Maritime Museum

Church of England (1662) *The Book of Common Prayer*, Oxford: Oxford University Press

Churchill, W.S. (1908) *My African Journey*, London: Macmillan

Clark, A.H. (1959) *Three Centuries and the Island: a historical geography of settlement and agriculture in Prince Edward Island, Canada*, Toronto: University of Toronto Press

Clarke, C.G. (1975) *Kingston, Jamaica: Urban development and social change, 1692–1962*, Berkeley: University of California Press

———— (1984) 'Pluralism and plural societies: Caribbean perspectives', in Clarke, C.G., Ley, D. and Peach, C. (eds), *Geography and Ethnic Pluralism*, London: Allen & Unwin, 51–86

———— (1985) 'A Caribbean Creole Capital: Kingston, Jamaica, 1692–1938', in Ross, R.J. and Telkamp, G.J. (eds), *Colonial Cities: essays on urbanism in a colonial context*, Dordrecht: Martinus Nijhoff, 152–70

Clemenson, H.A. (1982) *English Country Houses and Landed Estates*, London: Croom Helm

Collins, J. (1980) 'Lusaka: urban planning in a British colony', in Cherry, G.E. (ed.), *Shaping an Urban World*, London: Mansell, 227–41

Crush, J.S. (1980) 'The colonial division of space: the significance of the Swaziland land partition', *International Journal of African Historical Studies*, 13, 71–86

———— (1982) 'The Southern African regional formation: a geographical perspective', *Tijdschrift voor Economische en Sociale Geografie*, 73, 200–12

———— (1986) 'Swazi migrant workers and the Witwatersrand gold mines, 1886–1920', *Journal of Historical Geography*, 12, 27–40

Cunningham, C. (1981) *Victorian and Edwardian Town Halls*, London: Routledge & Kegan Paul

Curzon, Lord (1984) *A Viceroy's India: Leaves from Lord Curzon's Note-Book*, London: Sidgwick & Jackson

Davidson, B.R. (1969) *Australia Wet or Dry? The physical and economic limits to the expansion of irrigation*, Melbourne: Melbourne University Press

Davies, D.H. (1972) 'Lusaka: from colonial to independent capital', *Proceedings of the Geographical Association of Rhodesia*, 5, 14–21

Davies, P. (1985) *Splendours of the Raj: British architecture in India, 1660–1947*, London: John Murray

Davies, W.J. (1971) *Patterns of non-White population distribution in Port Elizabeth, with special reference to the application of the Group Areas Act*, Port Elizabeth: University of Port Elizabeth, Institute for Planning Research

Davies, L.E. and Huttenback, R.A. (1982) 'The Political Economy of British Imperialism: measures of benefit and support', *Journal of Economic History*, 42, 119–32

Dawson, C.A. (1936) *Group Settlement: Ethnic Communities in Western Canada*, Toronto: Macmillan

Demangeon, A. (1925) *The British Empire: A Study in Colonial Geography*, London: George Harrap

Dennis, R. (1984) *English industrial cities of the nineteenth century*, Cambridge: Cambridge University Press

Drabble, J.H. (1973) *Rubber in Malaya, 1876–1922: the genesis of the industry*, Kuala Lumpur: Oxford University Press

Dunbar, G.S. (1983) 'The forests of Cyprus under British stewardship', *Scottish Geographical Magazine*, 99, 111–20

Dunstan, D. (1984) *Governing the Metropolis: Politics, Technology and Social Change in a Victorian City: Melbourne, 1850–1891*, Melbourne: Melbourne University Press

Earle, C.V. (1978) 'A Staple interpretation of slavery and free labour', *Geographical Review*, 68, 52–65

——— (1979) 'Environment, disease and mortality in early Virginia', *Journal of Historical Geography*, 5, 365–90

Edelstein, M. (1982) *Overseas investment in the Age of High Imperialism: The United Kingdom, 1850–1914*, New York: Columbia University Press

Edwards, N. (1981) 'The Sydney business frontier, 1856–92: a building stock approach', *Australian Geographical Studies*, 19, 78–98

Ehrlich, C. (1973) 'Building and Caretaking: Economic Policy in British Tropical Africa, 1890–1960', *Economic History Review*, Second Series, 26, 649–67

Eisner, G. (1961) *Jamaica, 1830–1930: A Study in Economic Growth*, Manchester: Manchester University Press

Emery, F.V. (1984) 'Geography and Imperialism: the role of Sir Bartle Frere (1815–84)', *Geographical Journal*, 342–50

——— (1986) *'Marching Over Africa' — Letters from Victorian Soldiers*, London: Hodder & Stoughton

Fawcett, C.B. (1933) *A political geography of the British Empire*, London: University of London Press

Fenichel, A.H. and Huff, W.G. (1971) *The Impact of Colonialism on Burmese economic development*, Montreal: Centre for Developing Area Studies, McGill University

Ferenczi, I. (1969) *International Migrations, Vol. 1 — Statistics*, New York: Gordon & Breach Science Publishers

Fieldhouse, D.K. (1978) *Unilever Overseas: the anatomy of a multinational*, London: Croom Helm

——— (1984) *Economics and Empire, 1830–1914*, London: Macmillan

Fletcher, W.E.L. (1961) 'The Barbados Railway', *Journal of the Barbados Museum and Historical Society*, 28, 86–98

Freeland, J.M. (1968) *Architecture in Australia: a history*, Melbourne: Cheshire

Fuller, H.A. (1976) 'Landownership and the Lindsey Landscape', *Annals of the Association of American Geographers*, 66, 14–24

Gann, L.H. and Duignan, P. (1978) *The Rulers of British Africa, 1870–1914*, Stanford: Stanford University Press

Gates, P.W. (1968) *History of Public Land Law Development*, Washington: United States Government Printing Office

Gentilli, J. (1979) *Western Landscapes*, Nedlands: University of Western Australia Press

Ghosh, M., Dutta, A.K. and Ray, B. (1972) *Calcutta: a study in urban growth dynamics*, Calcutta: Mukhopadhyay

Goheen, P.G. (1970) *Victorian Toronto 1850 to 1900: Pattern and Process of Growth*, Chicago: University of Chicago Department of Geography

Goudie, A.S. (1980) 'George Nathaniel Curzon — Superior Geographer', *Geographical Journal*, 146, 203–9

Gowans, A. (1966) *Building Canada: An architectural history of Canadian life*, Toronto: Oxford University Press

—— (1968) 'The Canadian National Style', in Morton, W.L. (ed.), *The Shield of Achilles: Aspects of Canada in the Victorian Age*, Toronto: McClelland and Stewart, 208–19

Great Britain (1899) *Report on the Finances of Jamaica*, C9412, London: HMSO

—— (1928) *Report of the Royal Commission on Agriculture in India*, Cmd 3132, London: HMSO

—— (1930) *Palestine: Report on Immigration, Land Settlement and Development*, Cmd 3686, London: HMSO

—— (1933) *Statistical Abstract for the British Empire for each of the seven years, 1925 to 1931*, Cmd 4393, London: HMSO

—— (1934) *Report of the Kenya Land Commission*, Cmd 4556, London: HMSO

—— (1937) *Palestine Royal Commission Report*, Cmd 5479, London: HMSO

Grey, A.H. (1984) 'North American influences in the development of New Zealand's landscapes, 1800 to 1935', *New Zealand Geographer*, 40, 66–77

Griffiths, P. (1974) *A Licence to trade: the history of English Chartered Companies*, London: Macmillan

Gvati, C. (1985) *A hundred years of settlement: the story of Jewish settlement in the Land of Israel*, Jerusalem: Keter

Hadfield, A.M. (1970) *The Chartist Land Company*, Newton Abbot: David & Charles

Harris, R. (1984) 'Residential segregation and class formation in Canadian cities: a critical review', *Canadian Geographer*, 28, 186–96

—— Levine, G. and Osborne, B.S. (1981) 'Housing tenure and social classes in Kingston, Ontario, 1881–1901', *Journal of Historical Geography*, 7, 271–89

Harris, R.C. (1966) *The Seigneurial system in early Canada: a geographical study*, Madison: University of Wisconsin Press

—— (1977) 'The simplification of Europe overseas', *Annals of the Association of American Geographers*, 67, 469–83

—— and Warkentin, J. (1974) *Canada before Confederation: a study in historical geography*, New York: Oxford University Press

Harrison-Church, R.J. (1948) 'The case for colonial geography',

Transactions of the Institute of British Geographers, 14, 17–25

Headrick, D.R. (1981) *The Tools of Empire: Technology and European Imperialism in the Nineteenth Century*, New York: Oxford University Press

Heathcote, R.L. (1965) *Back of Bourke: A Study of Land Appraisal and Settlement in Semi-arid Australia*, Melbourne: Melbourne University Press

—— (1975) *Australia*, London: Longman

Herman, M. (1970) *The early Australian architects and their work*, Sydney: Angus & Robertson

Higgins, B. (1951) 'Canberra: a garden without a city', *Community Planning Review*, 1, 88–102

Hobsbawn, E.J. (1968) *Industry and Empire, From 1750 to the Present Day*, London: Weidenfeld & Nicholson

Houston, C. and Smyth, W.J. (1978) 'The Orange Order and the expansion of the frontier in Ontario, 1830–1900', *Journal of Historical Geography*, 4, 251–64

Hoyle, B.S. and Hilling, D. (1970) *Seaports and Development in Tropical Africa*, London: Macmillan

Huttenback, R.A. (1976) *Racism and Empire: White Settlers and Colored Immigrants in the British Self-Governing Colonies, 1830–1910*, Ithaca: Cornell University Press

Hyam, R. (1976) *Britain's Imperial Century, 1815–1914: A Study of Empire and Expansion*, London: Batsford

Ijere, M.O. (1973) 'The impact of Nigerian Railways on agricultural development', *Nigerian Geographical Journal*, 16, 137–43

India (1903) *Report of the Indian Irrigation Commission, 1901–03*, Calcutta: Office of the Superintendent of Government Printing, India

—— (1912) *Report of the Delhi Town Planning Committee on the choice of a site for the new Imperial Capital at Delhi*, Simla: Government Central Branch Press

—— (1945) *History of Indian Railways*, Simla: Government of India Press

Ironside, R.G. and Hamilton, S.A. (1972) 'Historical Geography of Coal Mining in the Edmonton District', *Alberta Historical Review*, 20 (3), 6–16

Irving, R.G. (1981) *Indian Summer: Lutyens, Baker and Imperial Delhi*, New Haven: Yale University Press

Jameson, S.S. (1970) 'Era of the Big Ranches', *Alberta Historical Review*, 18, 1–9

Jeans, D.N. (1972) *An Historical Geography of New South Wales to 1901*, Sydney: Reed Education

—— (1975) 'The Impress of Central Authority upon the Landscape: south-eastern Australia, 1788–1850', in Powell, J.M. and Williams, M. (eds), *Australian Space: Australian Time: Geographical Perspectives*, Melbourne: Oxford University Press, 1–17

Johnson, H.B. (1967) 'The location of Christian Missions in Africa', *Geographical Review*, 57, 168–202

Johnston, R.J. (1968) 'An outline of the development of Melbourne's street pattern', *Australian Geographer*, 10, 453–65

Jorgensen, J.J. (1981) *Uganda: A Modern History*, London: Croom Helm

Kearns, K.C. (1982) 'Preservation and transformation of Georgian Dublin', *Geographical Review*, 72, 270–90

Keswick, M. (1982) *The Thistle and the Jade: a celebration of 150 years of Jardine, Matheson and Company*, London: Octopus

Kindersley, R. (1932) 'British foreign investments in 1930', *Economic Journal*, 42, 177–95

King, A.D. (1976) *Colonial Urban Development: Culture, Social Power and Environment*, London: Routledge & Kegan Paul

—— (1980) 'Export planning: the colonial and neo-colonial experience', in Cherry, G.E. (ed.), *Shaping an Urban World*, London: Mansell, 203–26

—— (1984) *The Bungalow: the production of a global culture*, London: Routledge & Kegan Paul

Knight, D.B. (1977) *A Capital for Canada: Conflict and Compromise in nineteenth century Canada*, Chicago: University of Chicago, Department of Geography

Kollmorgen, W.M. (1969) 'The Woodsman's assaults on the domain of the Cattlemen', *Annals of the Association of American Geographers*, 59, 215–39

Koroscil, P.M. (1986) 'The transformation of the Okanagan valley landscape, British Columbia, Canada: 1890–1914', in Peltre, J. (ed.), *Transformations historiques du parcellaire et de l'habitat rural*, Nancy: Presses Universitaires de Nancy, 515–46

Kumar, D. and Desai, M. (eds) (1982) *The Cambridge Economic History of India, Vol. 2, c1757–c1970*, Hyderabad: Orient Longman

Lamb, W.K. (1977) *History of the Canadian Pacific Railway*, New York: Macmillan

Langford-Smith, T. (1968) 'Murrumbridgee Land Settlement 1817 to 1912', in Dury, G.H. and Logan, M.I. (eds), *Studies in Australian Geography*, London: Heinemann, 99–136

Latreille, A., Latreille, P. and Lovell, P. (1982) *New uses for old buildings in Australia*, Melbourne: Oxford University Press

Lehr, J.C. (1985) 'Kinship and society in the Ukrainian pioneer settlement of the Canadian West', *Canadian Geographer*, 29, 207–19

Lemon, A. (1983) *The Northcote side of the River*, Melbourne: Hargreen Publishing Company

Lewcock, R. (1963) *Early nineteenth century architecture in South Africa. A study of the Interaction of two cultures, 1795–1837*, Cape Town: A.A. Balkema

Lim, H.K. (1978) *The evolution of the urban system in Malaya*, Kuala Lumpur: Penerbit Universiti Malaya

Linge, G.J.R. (1975) 'The forging of an industrial nation: manufacturing in Australia, 1788–1913', in Powell, J.M. and Williams, M. (eds), *Australian Space: Australian Time: Geographical perspectives*, Melbourne: Oxford University Press, 150–81

Lock, M. and Theis, M. (1967) *Kaduna, 1917–1967–2017*, London: Faber & Faber

Lucas, C.P. (1887) *Introduction to a historical geography of the British Colonies*, Oxford: Clarendon Press

Mabin, A. (1985) 'Concentration and dispersion in the banking system of the Cape Colony, 1837–1900', *South African Geographical Journal*, 67, 141–59

——— (1986) 'Labour, capital, class struggle and the origins of residential segregation in Kimberley, 1880–1920', *Journal of Historical Geography*, 12, 4–26

Mackenzie, J.M. (1984) *Propaganda and Empire: the manipulation of British public opinion, 1880–1960*, Manchester: Manchester University Press

Mackintosh, W.A. (1934) *Prairie Settlement: the Geographical Setting*, Toronto: Macmillan

McMichael, P. (1984) *Settlers and the agrarian question: foundations of capitalism in colonial Australia*, Cambridge: Cambridge University Press

McQuillan, D.A. (1980) 'Creation of Indian Reserves on the Canadian Prairies, 1870–1885', *Geographical Review*, 70, 379–98

Mandle, J.R. (1973) *The Plantation Economy: population and economic change in Guyana, 1838–1960*, Philadelphia: Temple University Press

Martin, C. (1938) *'Dominion Lands' Policy*, Toronto: Macmillan

Meinig, D.W. (1962) *On the Margins of the Good Earth: The South Australian Wheat Frontier, 1869–1884*, Chicago: Rand McNally

——— (1982) 'Geographical analysis of imperial expansion', in Baker, A.R.H. and Billinge, M. (eds), *Period and Place: Research Methods in Historical Geography*, Cambridge: Cambridge University Press, 71–8

——— (1986) *The Shaping of America: geographical perspectives on 500 years of history, Volume I — Atlantic America*, New Haven: Yale University Press

Metzen, M.S. and Cain, H.E.C. (1925) *Handbook of British Honduras*, London: West India Committee

Middleton, J.H. (1952) *Lever's Pacific Plantations Proprietory Limited: A History, 1902–1941*, London: Unilever

Mills, G.E. and Holdsworth, D.W. (1975) 'The B.C. Mills prefabricated system: the emergence of ready-made buildings in western Canada', *Canadian Historic Sites*, 14, 127–69

Moodie, D.W. and Lehr, J.C. (1981) 'Macro-Historical Geography and the Great Chartered Companies: The case of the Hudson's Bay Company', *Canadian Geographer*, 25, 267–71

Moohr, M. (1972) 'The economic impact of slave emancipation in British Guiana, 1832–1852', *Economic History Review*, Second Series, 25, 588–607

Moorhouse, G. (1983) *Calcutta*, Harmondsworth: Penguin

Morgan, W.T.W. (1963) 'The White Highlands of Kenya', *Geographical Journal*, 129, 140–55

Morison, M.P. and White, J. (1979) *Western Towns and Buildings*, Nedlands: University of Western Australia Press

Morris, J. (1982) *The Spectacle of Empire: Style, Effect and the Pax Britannica*, London: Faber & Faber

——— and Winchester, S. (1983) *Stones of Empire: the buildings of the Raj*, Oxford: Oxford University Press

Morton, A.S. (1938) *History of Prairies Settlement*, Toronto: Macmillan

Mutibwa, P.M. (1976) 'White settlers in Uganda: the era of hopes and disillusionment, 1905–1923', *Transafrican Journal of History*, 5, 112–22

Neidpath, J. (1981) *The Singapore Naval Base and the Defence of Britain's Eastern Empire, 1919–1941*, Oxford: Clarendon Press

Newbury, C. (1984) 'The march of Everyman: mobility and the Imperial Census of 1901', *Journal of Imperial and Commonwealth History*, 12, 80–101

Noble, W.A. (1980) 'The Upper Nilgiris, South India habitat change and the Todas', in Singh, R.L. and Singh, Rana P.B. (eds), *Rural Habitat Transformation in World Frontiers*, New Delhi: National Geographical Society of India, 137–51

Ogundana, B. (1972) 'Oscillating seaport location in Nigeria', *Annals of the Association of American Geographers*, 62, 110–21

Osborne, B. and Pike, R. (1981) 'Lowering "the Walls of Oblivion": The revolution in postal communications in Central Canada, 1851–1911', in Akenson, D.H. (ed.), *Canadian papers in rural history, Vol. 4*, Gananoque, Ontario: Langdale Press, 200–25

Packenham, V. (1985) *The Noonday Sun: Edwardians in the Tropics*, London: Methuen

Palmer, R. (1977) *Land and Racial Domination in Rhodesia*, London: Heinemann

—— and Parsons, N. (1977) *The Roots of Rural Poverty in Central and Southern Africa*, London: Heinemann

Parker, W.H. (1982) *Mackinder: Geography as an aid to Statecraft*, Oxford: Clarendon Press

Pearn, B.R. (1939) *A history of Rangoon*, Rangoon: American Baptist Mission Press

Perren, R. (1971) 'The North American Beef and Cattle Trade with Great Britain, 1870–1914', *Economic History Review* (2nd Series), 24, 430–44

Perry, P.J. (1974) *British farming in the Great Depression, 1870–1914: An historical geography*, Newton Abbot: David & Charles

Petch, T. (1914) 'Notes on the History of the Plantation Rubber Industry of the East', *Annals of the Royal Botanic Gardens, Peradeniya (Ceylon)*, 5, 433–520

Phimister, I.R. (1978) 'Meat and Monopolies: Beef Cattle in Southern Rhodesia, 1890–1938', *Journal of African History*, 19, 391–414

Picton-Seymour, D. (1977) *Victorian Buildings in South Africa*, Cape Town: A.A. Balkema

Pirie, G.H. (1982) 'The Decivilizing Rails: Railways and Underdevelopment in Southern Africa', *Tijdschrift voor Economische en Sociale Geografie*, 73, 221–28

Platt, D.C.M. (1986) *Britain's Investment Overseas on the Eve of the First World War: The Use and Abuse of Numbers*, London: Macmillan

—— and Di Tella, G. (eds) (1985) *Argentina, Australia and Canada: Studies in comparative development, 1870–1965*, London: Macmillan

Powell, J.M. (1970) *The Public Lands of Australia Felix*, Melbourne: Melbourne University Press

—— (1974) *Yeomen and Bureaucrats: The Victorian Crown Lands*

Commission, 1878–79, Melbourne: Oxford University Press

—— (1976) *Environmental management in Australia, 1788–1914: Guardians, improvers and profit: an introductory survey*, Melbourne: Oxford University Press

—— (1977) *Mirrors of the New World: Images and Image-Makers in the Settlement Process*, Folkestone: Dawson

—— (1981) 'The debt of honour: soldier settlement in the Dominions, 1915–1940', *Journal of Australian Studies*, 8, 64–87

Preston, B.T. (1985) 'Rich town, poor town: the distribution of rate-borne spending levels in the Edwardian city system', *Transactions of the Institute of British Geographers*, New Series, 10, 77-94

Proudfoot, B. (1973) 'Agricultural settlement in Alberta, North of Edmonton', in Rasporich, A.W. and Klassen, H.C. (eds), *Prairie Perspectives*, Toronto: Holt, Rinehart & Winston, 142–53

Pulsipher, L.M. (1986) *Seventeenth century Montserrat: an environmental impact statement*, Norwich: Geobooks

Purcell, V.W.W.S. (1928) *Early Penang*, Penang: Pinang Gazette Press

Puthucheary, J.J. (1960) *Ownership and control in the Malayan economy*, Singapore: Eastern Universities Press

Ramaswami, N.S. (1979) *Indian Monuments*, New Delhi: Abhinav Publications

Ransford, O. (1983) *'Bid the Sickness Cease'*, disease in the history of Black Africa, London: John Murray

Rawley, J.A. (1981) *The Transatlantic Slave Trade: a history*, New York: W.W. Norton

Reps, J.W. (1965) *The Making of Urban America: a history of city planning in the United States*, Princeton: Princeton University Press

—— (1972) *Tidewater Towns: City Planning in Colonial Virginia and Maryland*, Williamsburg: Colonial Williamsburg Foundation

Richardson, H.W. (1972) 'British emigration and overseas investment, 1870–1914', *Economic History Review*, Second Series, 25, 99–113

Rimmer, P.J. (1967) 'The search for spatial regularities in the development of Australian seaports, 1861–1961/2', *Geografiska Annaler*, 49B, 42–54

—— (1975) 'Politicians, public servants and petitioners: aspects of transport in Australia, 1851–1901', in Powell, J.M. and Williams, M. (eds), *Australian Space: Australian Time: Geographical Perspectives*, Melbourne: Oxford University Press, 182–225

Roberts, S.H. (1924) *History of Australian Land Settlement, 1788–1920*, Melbourne: Oxford University Press

Robinson, W.S. (1957) *Mother Earth: Land Grants in Virginia, 1607–1699*, Williamsburg: Virginia 350th Anniversary Celebration Corporation

Rodney, W. (1972) *How Europe Underdeveloped Africa*, London: Bogle L'Ouverture Publications

Rose, F.G.C. (1954) 'The pastoral industry in the Northern Territory during the period of Commonwealth administration', *Historical Studies, Australia and New Zealand*, 6, 150–72

Ross, R. (1982) *Racism and Colonialism: Essays on Ideology and Social Structure*, The Hague: Martinus Nijhoff

Roth, L.M. (1979) *A concise history of American architecture*, New York:

Harper and Row

Royle, S.A. (1985) 'The Falkland Islands, 1833–1876: the establishment of a colony', *Geographical Journal*, 151, 204–14

Rutherford, J. (1964) 'Interplay of American and Australian Ideas for development of Water Projects in Northern Victoria', *Annals of the Association of American Geographers*, 54, 88–106

—— (1968) 'Government irrigation and its physical environment', in Dury, G.H. and Logan, M.I. (eds), *Studies in Australian Geography*, London: Heinemann, 137–94

Sahni, J.N. (1953) *Indian Railways: One Hundred Years, 1853 to 1953*, New Delhi: Ministry of Railways

Salmon, J.H.M. (1963) *A History of Goldmining in New Zealand*, Wellington: Government Printer

Savage, W.W. and Thompson, S.I. (1979) *The Frontier: Comparative Studies, Volume Two*, Norman: University of Oklahoma Press

Scott, P. (1951) 'The Witwatersrand Goldfield', *Geographical Review*, 41, 561–89

Seary, E.R. (1971) *Place names of the Avalon Peninsula of the Island of Newfoundland*, Toronto: University of Toronto Press

Shapiro, S. (1973) 'Planning Jerusalem: the first generation, 1917–1968', in Amiran, D.H.K. *et al.* (eds), *Urban Geography of Jerusalem*, Jerusalem: Massada Press, 139–53

Simon, D. (1984) 'Third world colonial cities in context: conceptual and theoretical approaches with particular reference to Africa', *Progress in Human Geography*, 8, 493–514

Solomon, V.E. (1982) *The South African Shipping Question, 1886–1914*, Cape Town: Historical Publications Society

Sorrenson, M.P.K. (1968) *Origins of European Settlement in Kenya*, Nairobi: Oxford University Press

Southern Rhodesia (1926) *Report of the Land Commission, 1925*, C.S.R. 3–1926, Salisbury: Government Printer

Srivastava, R.P. (1979) 'Politico-territorial structure during British period', *National Geographer*, 14, 175–91

Stacpoole, J. (1976) *Colonial Architecture in New Zealand*, Wellington: Reed

Stamp, G. (1981) 'British architecture in India, 1857–1947', *Journal of the Royal Society of Arts*, 129, 357–79

Stein, K.W. (1984) *The Land Question in Palestine, 1917–1939*, Chapel Hill: University of North Carolina Press

Stone, I. (1984) *Canal Irrigation in British India*, Cambridge: Cambridge University Press

Taaffe, E.J., Morrill, R.L. and Gould, P.R. (1963) 'Transport expansion in underdeveloped countries: a comparative analysis', *Geographical Review*, 53, 503–29

Tan, Y.K. (1981) *The Land and Agricultural Organisation of Peninsular Malaysia: a historical interpretation*, Swansea: University College of Swansea, Centre for Development Studies

Taylor, P.J. (1985) *Political Geography: World-economy, nation-state and locality*, London: Longman

Teo, S.E. and Savage, V.R. (1985) 'Historical overview of housing change,

Singapore', *Singapore Journal of Tropical Geography*, 6, 48–63

Tindall, G. (1982) *City of Gold: The Biography of Bombay*, London: Temple Smith

Tomlinson, B.R. (1979) *The Political Economy of the Raj, 1914–1947: the economics of decolonization in India*, London: Macmillan

Transvaal (1908) *Report of the Transvaal Indigency Commission, 1908*, T.G. 13–'08, Pretoria: Government Printer

Tregonning, K.G. (1967) *Home Port Singapore: A History of the Straits Steamship Company Limited, 1890–1965*, Singapore: Straits Steamship Company

Tunbridge, J.E. (1984) 'Whose heritage to conserve? Cross-cultural reflections on political dominance and urban heritage conservation', *Canadian Geographer*, 28, 171–80

Turner, F.J. (1894) 'The significance of the frontier in American history', *American Historical Association Report for 1893*, 199–227

Twidale, C.R. and Bourne, J.A. (1978) 'Distribution of Relic "lands" or strip fields in South Australia', *Australian Geographer*, 14, 22–9

Tyrwhitt, J. (1947) *Patrick Geddes in India*, London: Lund Humphries

Urlich Cloher, D. (1979) 'Urban settlement process in lands of "recent settlement" — an Australian example', *Journal of Historical Geography*, 5, 297–314

Vail, L. (1975) 'The Making of an Imperial slum: Nyasaland and its railways, 1895–1935', *Journal of African History*, 16, 89–112

Van Onselen, C. (1982) *Studies in the Social and Economic History of the Witwatersrand, 1886–1914*, London: Longman

Vance, J.E. (1970) *The Merchant's World: the geography of wholesaling*, Engelwood Cliffs: Prentice Hall

Von Dantzig, A. (1980) *Forts and Castles of Ghana*, Accra: Sedco Publications

Wallach, B. (1985) 'British irrigation works in India's Krisha Basin', *Journal of Historical Geography*, 11, 155–73

Wallerstein, I. (1974) *The Modern World-System I — Capitalist Agriculture and the origins of the European world-economy in the sixteenth century*, New York: Academic Press

—— (1980) *The Modern World System II — Mercantilism and the consolidation of the European world-economy, 1600–1750*, New York: Academic Press

Ward, D. and Radford, J.P. (1983) *North American Cities in the Victorian Age*, Norwich: Geobooks

Webb, W.P. (1952) *The Great Frontier*, Boston: Houghton Mifflin

Western, J. (1985) 'Undoing the colonial city?' *Geographical Review*, 75, 335–57

White, H.L. (1954) *Canberra: A Nation's Capital*, Sydney: Angus and Robertson

White, L.W.T., Silberman, L. and Anderson P.R. (1948) *Nairobi: Master Plan for a Colonial Capital*, London: HMSO

Willcocks, W. (1901) *Report on Irrigation in South Africa*, Johannesburg: Transvaal Government

Williams, M. (1966) 'The Parkland Towns of Australia and New Zealand', *Geographical Review*, 56, 67–89

—————— (1974) *The Making of the South Australian Landscape*, London: Academic Press

—————— (1976) 'More and smaller is better: Australian rural settlement, 1788–1914', in Powell, J.M. and Williams, M. (eds), *Australian space: Australian time: Geographical perspectives*, Melbourne: Oxford University Press, 61–103

Wilson, G. and Sands, P. (1981) *Building a city: 100 years of Melbourne architecture*, Melbourne: Oxford University Press

Wilson, M.G.A. (1968) 'Changing pattern of pit location on the New South Wales coalfield', *Annal of the Association of American Geographers*, 58, 78–90

Winks, R.W. (1981) 'Australia, the Frontier, and the Tyranny of Distance', in Wolfskill, G. and Palmer, S. (eds), *Essays on Frontiers in World History*, Austin: University of Texas Press, 121–46

Wood, J.D. (1982) 'Grand design on the fringes of Empire: new towns for British North America', *Canadian Geographer*, 26, 243–55

Wynn, G. (1979) 'Pioneers, politicians and the conservation of forests in early New Zealand', *Journal of Historical Geography*, 5, 171–88

Yoon, H.K. (1980) 'An analysis of place names of cultural features in New Zealand', *New Zealand Geographer*, 36, 30–34

Zelinsky, W. (1973) *The Cultural Geography of the United States*, Engelwood Cliffs: Prentice Hall

Index

Printed in the United States
by Baker & Taylor Publisher Services